AE

Andrew Martin is a psychologist specialising in student motivation. He is regularly invited to conduct parent nights on student motivation as well as teacher professional development days at schools, aimed at enhancing motivation in the classroom.

Over the past ten years Dr Martin has taught child psychology and educational psychology at the University of Sydney and the University of Western Sydney and conducted research in education and student motivation for Commonwealth, state and territory governments. He regularly presents keynote papers on student motivation and writes practical articles in parent-oriented publications. His work on student motivation is featured on television and radio and in major newspapers and magazines.

Dr Martin has published his research in many of the world's top academic journals, and in 2002 the American Psychological Association judged his PhD the most outstanding doctorate in educational psychology.

Dr Martin is Research Fellow at the Self-concept Enhancement and Learning Facilitation (SELF) Research Centre at the University of Western Sydney. He lives in Sydney with his wife and children.

How to Motivate Your Child

for
School and Beyond

Andrew Martin

Motivation Matters!

Best Wishes

Andrew Martin

BANTAM BOOKS
SYDNEY • AUCKLAND • TORONTO • NEW YORK • LONDON

How to Motivate Your Child for School and Beyond
A BANTAM BOOK

First published in Australia and New Zealand in 2003
by Bantam

Copyright © Andrew Martin, 2003

All rights reserved. No part of this publication
may be reproduced, stored in a retrieval system,
transmitted in any form or by any means, electronic,
mechanical, photocopying, recording or otherwise,
without the prior written permission of the publisher.

National Library of Australia
Cataloguing-in-Publication Entry

Martin, Andrew J. (Andrew James).
How to motivate your child for school and beyond

Bibliography.
Includes index.
ISBN 1 86325 391 2

1. Motivation in education. 2. Education - Parent
participation. I. Title.

370.154

Transworld Publishers,
a division of Random House Australia Pty Ltd
20 Alfred Street, Milsons Point, NSW 2061
http://www.randhouse.com.au

Random House New Zealand Limited
18 Poland Road, Glenfield, Auckland

Transworld Publishers,
a division of The Random House Group Ltd
61-63 Uxbridge Road, London W5 5SA

Random House Inc
1540 Broadway, New York, New York 10036

Typeset by Midland Typesetters, Maryborough, Victoria
Printed and bound by Griffin Press, Netley, South Australia

10 9 8 7 6 5 4 3 2

Internal cartoons by John Shakespeare
Cover and internal design, and illustrations by Darian Causby, Highway 51

To my wife and children

with love and gratitude

Contents

PART THREE

SPECIAL ISSUES IN MOTIVATION

Part One

INTRODUCING MOTIVATION

CHAPTER 1

RAISING HAPPY LEARNERS

Three parents sat on a park bench. One sighed. Another groaned. The third muttered, 'I thought we agreed we wouldn't talk about the kids today.'

This was how a speaker began his presentation at a recent conference for psychologists, school counsellors and teachers. It got a good laugh. But deep down all the participants, me included, recognised the truth behind the humour: parenting presents challenges that can outweigh any we experience in other parts of our lives. It seems as soon as we've dealt with one challenge, two others are quick on its heels. Just as we've got our son or daughter worked out, they go and change on us again. These challenges arise in all aspects of our children's life: in their personal life, in their social life, in their part-time job, on the sporting field, in their club, in relation to us as parents, with their brothers and sisters and, of course, in their school and study life.

Many parents have difficulty dealing with the challenges that arise in their child's school and study life. One issue that parents feel they need a lot of guidance with is their child's motivation. Some of the more frequent comments I hear when people discover I am an educational psychologist go along the lines of:

- My son's not motivated.
- My daughter isn't interested in her schoolwork.
- My son is always wasting time.
- My son did well last year, but this year he's not doing very well.
- My daughter's got a bad attitude.
- My daughter is terrified of tests and exams.
- None of my children are doing as well as they could.
- My son is okay in most subjects but just won't do any work in maths.
- My daughter thinks she's hopeless and won't try.
- My son thinks school is a waste of time.
- My daughter is terrified of failing.
- My daughter wants to drop out of school.
- My son is the class clown and isn't getting very good marks.

Of course, there are also more positive responses which go something along the lines of:

- I'm pretty happy with how my son is going at school and want to keep that up.
- My daughter is doing okay, but I want to make sure I'm bringing out her best.
- My son's finals are at the end of the year and I want to get him ready early.

Both sets of comments show two things. First, motivation is a hot topic for many parents. Second, motivation is relevant to all students – good students as well as students who aren't travelling so well.

This book is aimed at helping you boost your child's motivation if you believe he or she isn't as motivated as a student should be. If your child is already motivated, this book shows you how to maintain his or her motivation – and perhaps even build on it.

But first, I want to outline my approach. When it comes to student motivation I am an optimist and I believe in students' ability to change. I also firmly believe in parents' ability to help them do this. Every student has the potential to improve, reach personal bests, become more interested in schoolwork and deal more effectively with setbacks and study pressure.

Why can I be so optimistic about students' ability to improve? First, I can draw on decades of high-quality educational research to prove it. Secondly, I can point to the many students I have personally dealt with over the last ten years who have had the courage – and the necessary support – to change the way they go about their studies. Thirdly, I need to look no further than my own experience as a student to know that change for the better is possible.

My story

In primary school and early high school I was a pretty good student. Not the best, but probably in the top 15 per cent. Then I hit what I call the 'motivation wilderness' of the middle years of high school, and I just couldn't get it together. I wasn't really interested in my schoolwork, my marks were falling, I talked a lot in class and didn't pay attention, and I wasn't doing much homework. The finishing line seemed a long way away, yet it was an eternity since I'd started high school.

At a parent–teacher night in my last year of middle high, the teacher told my parents that I might not be up to the hard work required for the final two years of high school. It wasn't that I lacked ability; I lacked application. I wasn't putting in the effort or using the effective study strategies needed to get through senior high. As any teacher will tell you, these years are in many ways more about personal application than ability.

Because I had always planned on doing the final two years of school, the teacher's comments horrified me. Just like most kids, I hadn't really thought through the consequences of what I was doing. It was one of those wake-up calls that turn your life around. But this was only the start of a long climb back, a climb that was greatly assisted by support from my parents and teachers. I did turn my academic life around and I am still struck by the important role my parents and teachers played in this.

To cut a long story short, I went on to university to do honours in child psychology and later completed a PhD in educational psychology, focusing on student motivation. Over the last ten years I have been researching and testing student motivation, working closely with students and schools, conducting workshops for teachers showing them how to increase their students' motivation, and also giving presentation nights for parents interested in increasing their child's motivation. Student motivation is my passion – and I am delighted to be able to share some of my thoughts, experiences and research findings with you in this book.

What is motivation and what can you do about it?

Motivation is your child's energy and drive to try hard, study effectively, improve and work to his or her potential.

I separate motivation into the thoughts and behaviours that are helpful to your child's motivation – motivation boosters – and those that are not helpful to his or her motivation – motivation mufflers and guzzlers. Boosters include things like self-belief, persistence and planning. Mufflers and guzzlers include things like anxiety and fear of failure. The next chapter describes all the boosters, mufflers and guzzlers in detail. This book is essentially about how to increase the boosters in your child's life and reduce the mufflers and guzzlers in his or her life.

What can you do about your child's motivation? Lots! You increase your child's motivation by:

- enhancing your child's self-belief and building more success into his or her life
- increasing your child's belief in the value of school
- developing your child's learning focus and helping your child to reach personal bests
- assisting your child to study more effectively
- helping your child plan and monitor schoolwork and study
- enhancing your child's persistence
- building your child's personal control over success
- reducing your child's anxiety leading up to tests and exams
- reducing your child's fear of failure and increasing his or her focus on success

- reducing your child's self-sabotage
- building a good relationship with your child.

Just as your child may have developed unhelpful thoughts and behaviours, he or she can turn that around with guidance and support from you. It is not at all uncommon for students to hit a bad patch in their school and study life, and to learn better ways of thinking about and approaching their studies. In fact, working through tough times can build very valuable skills in your child to help him or her next time school and study present challenges that need to be dealt with in order to move forward.

Why is motivation important?

We often tell our children that they need to be more motivated. Many children would probably agree that they need to be more motivated. Indeed, when teachers reach for reasons why a child does not do well at school, lack of motivation is usually one of the first factors identified.

Research shows – and any teacher would tell you – that motivation not only leads to better results in schoolwork, better behaviour and higher quality study, it also makes the journey through school a happy, satisfying and fulfilling one. Parents will tell you that when their child is motivated, the home is a happier and more harmonious place, their child is more responsible and associates with other students who are motivated. Even the child will tell you that he or she is more confident, optimistic and enjoys school more.

The diagram on page 7 illustrates some of the effects of motivation.

Parents' effect on their child's motivation

Many things influence your child's motivation, including his or her friends, his or her teachers and school life in general. In addition to these influences, what goes on in the home has an enormous impact on your child's motivation.

Your influence on your child's motivation comes through in a number of ways. Some include:

- the extent to which you affirm your child
- your own belief in the value of education

SOME EFFECTS OF MOTIVATION

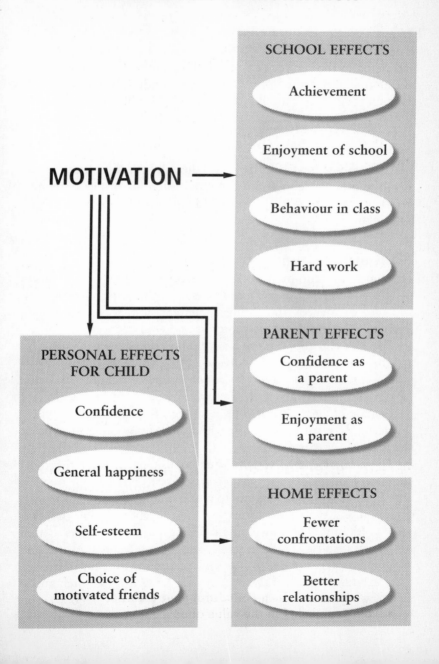

- the home conditions in which your child studies
- the amount and type of pressure you place on your child to succeed
- the messages you give your child about success and what it means to be successful
- the extent to which you focus on your child's shortcomings or strengths
- whether or not you compare your child with other children
- the goals you have for your child
- the expectations you have for your child.

Each of these factors influences your child's confidence, optimism, interest in school and desire to reach his or her potential. As such, they are also the keys to help you unlock your child's potential.

What are we aiming for?

There are three common student categories. Our aim as parents is to help our children move out of categories that aren't very helpful and into a category that brings out their best, focuses them on learning and stimulates their interest and enjoyment in school.

The first category, *failure acceptance*, comprises students who are the least motivated. Failure-accepting students do not try at school, are often at risk of dropping out of school (or being kicked out), have given up on schoolwork and study, do not participate in class and behave as though they are quite helpless. We certainly want to move our child out of this category if he or she is in it.

The second category, *failure avoidance*, is perhaps the most common student category. These students fear failure. If they do any work at school it's mainly to avoid failing, getting bad marks, disappointing their parents, letting their teachers down, or being seen as 'dumb'. The down side of being a failure avoider is that the journey isn't a very happy one. School, study, tests, exams and assignments evoke anxiety, fear and pessimism for these students. They are filled with self-doubt and their hard work is often aimed at trying to make sure that all the doubts they have about themselves don't come true.

Some parents suggest to me that a bit of anxiety and fear is a small price to pay for good results. What I tell them is that although the failure avoider may achieve good results, they can be very unsettled by setback and pressure. A poor mark, negative feedback or excessive pressure can fuel their self-doubt, and if they experience another setback they are at risk of moving closer to the failure-accepting category and giving up trying altogether.

The third category, *success striving*, is the one this book is aimed at promoting. A success striver is a student who succeeds by focusing on success. This is in contrast to the failure avoider who can also succeed – but only to avoid failure. The difference may seem subtle, but in practice it is dramatic. It is the difference between students who set a positive goal and always reach forwards, striving with optimism and energy and students who are terrified of failing, are pessimistic, anxious and constantly looking over their shoulder at the wolves snapping at their heels. It is the difference between a student who enjoys the journey and responds to a challenge with energy and enthusiasm and a student who has a tough time along the way, always wishing the challenges would ease up. I must make the very important point that success strivers are found at all levels of ability. For example, your child might be ranked in the middle of the class but if he or she is performing to potential and looking to improve as much as possible, then he or she can be considered a success striver.

The diagram on page 10 summarises each of these categories.

Success strivers do exist and a good part of their success focus is learnt at home. I will show you how to support your child's move from failure-accepting or failure-avoiding approaches to school and study into a success-striving way of going about things. It is possible. I am constantly struck by students' and parents' capacity to change and for this reason I am optimistic that you and your child can do this also. For some parents and students it may take a commitment over the medium to longer term, but the commitment will be well worth it.

Academic resilience – a vital ingredient

Before moving to the next chapter to look at motivation more closely, I want to briefly introduce another important ingredient in

STUDENT MOTIVATION CATEGORIES

Motivation Category	Characteristics
Success striver	• High self-esteem • Confident • Succeeds by focusing on success • Not overcome by setbacks • Enjoys challenge • Enjoys hard work
Failure avoider	• High self-doubt • Anxious • Can succeed, but mainly to avoide failure • Can be overcome by setbacks • Is frightened of challenge • Does not enjoy hard work
Failure accepter	• Low self-esteem • Uninterested and disengaged • Pessimistic • Accepts failure • Accepts setbacks • Does not accept challenges • Does not try

a child's school life – academic resilience. Resilience is a word that refers to how a person deals with pressure, tough times, setbacks and challenges. There is a lot of research at the moment looking into why some children rise above their difficult upbringings, poverty, poor education or abuse and go on to lead happy and healthy lives. Researchers call these children resilient.

In my work, I have seen students effectively deal with failure, poor grades, study stress and pressure. They are not beaten by this adversity. They respond with confidence, control and energy. These students are what I call 'academically resilient'.

I have seen many students who are smart and motivated come unstuck when the going gets tough. They have trouble coping with a poor grade, negative feedback from a teacher, stress or study pressure. At first I had trouble understanding what the problem was. I thought if a child was smart and motivated, he or she would have no problems dealing with challenge or adversity. But it became clear to me that there is another factor that a child needs to become a well-rounded and effective student. This factor is academic resilience – the ability to effectively deal with setbacks, pressure, poor grades, negative feedback and study stress in the school setting.

The student who is motivated and academically resilient is a well-rounded student. This student has the energy and drive to try hard and study effectively, and also copes when the going gets tough.

Motivation + Academic resilience = The well-rounded student

Ideally then, we not only want our child to be motivated but also to be able to cope when the chips are down. Parents have a big part to play in developing and nurturing their child's academic resilience, and as this book shows there are some straightforward ways to increase it.

When reading this book

There are some general principles, discussed below, I want you to remember as you read this book.

Different children respond in different ways

For some children, the impact of their parent reading this book will be dramatic. For other children, the effect may be more subtle and you may not think that your child has changed much. Don't underestimate the subtle changes. Children can tuck an idea away and draw on it at the most unexpected times. A small change now can mean significant changes later. Mark Twain got it right when he said, 'Habit is habit and is not to be flung out the window, but to be coaxed downstairs a step at a time.'

If your child is not very motivated, this does not mean he or she is a bad person

Don't fall into the trap of connecting your child's behaviour to his or her worth as a person. I will later show that this can be very de-motivating. It is important to send positive messages to your child about their worth as a person even though they may not be making you very happy from a motivation perspective.

Every child has motivation strengths

I have yet to find a child who scores absolute rock bottom on each measurement of motivation. Every child has some glimmers of strength and these are the windows through which to increase other aspects of your child's motivation. Never lose sight of your child's strengths – they are the launch pad for success.

Good students need to be sustained

When we focus on the unmotivated students it is very easy to forget that our good students also need to be sustained and encouraged. This means identifying strong students' strengths, the reasons they are strengths and the ways to maintain these strengths – or even build them further.

Not everything in this book will be suited to you or your child

Many ideas and strategies are presented in this book. I'd be dreaming if I thought all of them were suitable for every child or every home. Different children and homes are suited to different messages and strategies. You know your child best and what is realistic and achievable when aiming to boost his or her motivation. The aim of this book is to present lots of ideas and strategies so that you have a good range to select from, or if something doesn't work you have some fallback strategies. This also means that you can adapt or change some of the strategies to better suit you and your child.

Focus on doing fewer things well rather than many things not so well

There are many ideas and strategies in this book, but it is not realistic to expect to use every one of them. When I talk to parents at schools they get very excited when I present ten or fifteen strategies they can use to build their child's motivation. Before they leave to test their new-found knowledge, I tell them to try fewer strategies rather than more, and to apply them effectively and consistently. It is important to have a solid and successful start to your work with your child. This is done by being very focused and doing a good job on a small and manageable number of strategies.

If your child is not motivated it does not mean you are a bad parent

Most parents want to do the best for their child. However, in my research into parenting I have found that parents can lack the knowledge and confidence to do what's best for their child. My aim in this book is to give you the knowledge and confidence to do the best for your child from a motivation perspective.

There's no magic pill

I can't deceive you. There is no magic pill. More often than not, increasing your child's motivation takes time, energy, flexibility and a commitment from you over the medium to longer term.

Salt the oats to make the horse thirsty

You can't study for your child and by now many of you have probably found that you can't force your child to do something if they really don't want to do it. But you can certainly lay the foundation for your child to be more interested in learning and more willing to put in some hard work. So even though you can't make the horse that you've led to water drink, you can certainly salt its oats to make it thirsty.

Life is often different from how the experts describe it in books
Along the way, to keep things simple and clear-cut I've had to generalise a bit and present strategies in ways that look really easy on paper but which are much harder to apply in practice. For this reason, I finish each chapter with a section called 'Living in the real world'. This section tries to blend the real world with what I've discussed in that chapter.

You have not failed if you don't motivate your child as much as you would like
It is often the case that a parent can say something to a child five or ten times and it seems to not sink in. Another person can then say it once and it clicks. It could well be the case that this book plants an idea in your child's mind that simply needs the right stimulus or condition to bring it to life.

Chapter summary
This chapter introduced motivation, what it means and why it is important. Motivation has an effect on many important educational outcomes but is also an important goal in itself. Importantly, motivation can be increased through some straightforward and commonsense strategies. This book describes these strategies and how they can be used in your child's life. Because motivation is learnable and changeable I encourage you to be optimistic for your child and to remember that even subtle changes now can make a big difference later in your child's life.

CHAPTER ONE TOP 5

1. Motivation is your child's energy and drive to try hard, study effectively, improve, and work to his or her potential.

2. Motivation leads to better results in schoolwork and also makes the journey through school a happy, satisfying, and fulfilling one.

3. Motivation can be learnt and changed. Every student can improve, work more effectively, become more interested in schoolwork, and achieve to his or her potential.

4. Your child's ability to effectively deal with setback, poor performance, negative feedback, and study pressure – academic resilience – is also important to develop.

5. Parents can make a big difference to a child's motivation and academic resilience.

CHAPTER 2

BOOSTERS, MUFFLERS AND GUZZLERS

In this chapter I describe the key components of motivation. You also get an opportunity to test your own child's motivation. The scores you give your child will be a good way of identifying his or her strengths and also some areas of motivation that can be improved.

Introducing boosters, mufflers and guzzlers

I mentioned earlier that motivation consists of a number of components. These are divided into those that improve your child's motivation and achievement, those that restrict your child's motivation and achievement, and those that reduce your child's motivation and achievement. The parts that improve your child's motivation I call *boosters*. The parts that restrict motivation I call *mufflers*. The parts that reduce motivation I call *guzzlers*. We want our children to be high in boosters and low in mufflers and guzzlers.

Booster thoughts are the helpful thoughts, attitudes and behaviours of students that increase their motivation and achievement.

Mufflers and guzzlers are the unhelpful thoughts, attitudes and behaviours of students that restrict or reduce their motivation and achievement.

The ten boosters, mufflers and guzzlers that affect students' motivation

My research and work with students have identified ten key boosters, mufflers and guzzlers. The diagram below shows these boosters, mufflers and guzzlers.

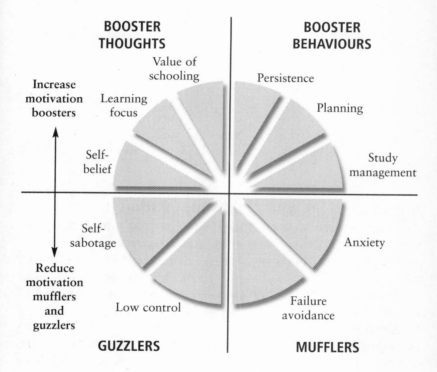

Booster thoughts include:

- self-belief (belief in one's ability to do well)
- belief in the value of schooling (belief that school is useful and important)
- learning focus (focus on doing a good job, improving and developing new knowledge and skills).

Booster behaviours include:

- planning (planning assignments and study and monitoring progress)
- study management (organising study so as to work under the most ideal conditions)
- persistence (persisting in the face of challenging or difficult schoolwork).

Mufflers include:

- anxiety (worry and nervousness leading up to and during assignments, tests, and exams)
- failure avoidance (fearing failure and mainly focusing on avoiding failure)

Guzzler behaviours include:

- low control (belief that one has little control over maintaining success or avoiding failure).
- self-sabotage (reducing chances to succeed through behaviours such as procrastination, time-wasting, lack of study, etc).

A quick test of your child's motivation

Before reading about the ideas and strategies you can use to boost student motivation, it is important to understand a bit more about your own child's motivation. This means knowing more about your child's strengths as well as the parts of your child's motivation that can be improved. The best way to do this is to do a quick test of your child's motivation.

The test on page 19 provides an opportunity for you to rate your child on each booster, muffler and guzzler. You need to circle just one number for each statement. The numbers range from 1 (disagree strongly) to 5 (agree strongly). Read each statement carefully and then circle the response that best fits with what you honestly think about your child. Try not to let your emotions get in the way of your responses when thinking about your child. Be as objective and fair as possible. Your child may vary from day to day and school subject to school subject, so give more of an overall rating if this is the case.

TEST YOUR CHILD'S MOTIVATION

BOOSTERS	Disagree strongly	Disagree	Neither agree nor disagree	Agree	Agree strongly	Booster
My child believes he/she can do a good job on his/her schoolwork	1	2	3	4	5	Self-belief
My child believes that what he/she is taught at school is important and useful	1	2	3	4	5	Valuing school
My child is focused on learning and improving more than beating others and being the best	1	2	3	4	5	Learning focus
My child plans how to do his/her schoolwork and checks how he/she is going as it is done	1	2	3	4	5	Planning
My child uses his/her study time well and tries to study under conditions that bring out his/her best	1	2	3	4	5	Study management
My child persists at his/her schoolwork even when it is challenging or difficult	1	2	3	4	5	Persistence

- The higher scores are some of your child's strengths
- The lower scores are areas where your child can improve

MUFFLERS	Disagree strongly	Disagree	Neither agree nor disagree	Agree	Agree strongly	Muffler
My child gets anxious about his/her schoolwork and tests	1	2	3	4	5	Anxiety
My child mainly does his/her schoolwork to avoid failure or disapproval from me or teachers	1	2	3	4	5	Failure avoidance

- The lower scores are some of your child's strengths
- The higher scores are areas where your child can improve

GUZZLERS	Disagree strongly	Disagree	Neither agree nor disagree	Agree	Agree strongly	Guzzler
My child does not think he/she has much control over how well he/she does at school	1	2	3	4	5	Low control
My child seems to reduce his/her chances of doing well (e.g. wastes time, doesn't study, disrupts others, procrastinates etc)	1	2	3	4	5	Self-sabotage

- The lower scores are some of your child's strengths
- The higher scores are areas where your child can improve

How to understand the scores

The first table is a measure of each booster in your child's life. Your aim is to have your child high in these boosters. Boosters for which your child's score is high are your child's strengths. Aim to keep these high. Boosters for which your child's score is low are where your child can improve. Aim to increase these.

The second and third tables are measures of each muffler and guzzler in your child's life. Your aim is to have your child low in these mufflers and guzzlers. Mufflers and guzzlers for which your child's score is low are your child's strengths. Aim to keep these guzzlers low. Mufflers and guzzlers for which your child's score is high are where your child can improve. Aim to reduce these mufflers and guzzlers.

Don't assume your child is aware of his or her strengths. When I test students' motivation and point out their strengths they are often genuinely surprised to learn that they have strengths. As I identify some of the stronger boosters in their lives it is really satisfying to see their chests puff up when they find that there are some areas of their school and study life that aren't so bad. Never lose sight of your child's strengths because it makes them feel better about themselves when you recognise them.

I should also mention that as students move from primary school to high school their motivation can decline. A good deal of research has shown this. There are a few reasons why this happens. First, students increasingly compare themselves with others and more often than not find that there are a number of students ahead of them. This doesn't make them feel too good. Second, there is more 'norm referenced' grading which puts students in a pecking order of marks. This can deflate motivation particularly for those who aren't near the top of the pecking order. Third, there is less teacher attention in high school and some students can fall between the cracks by not getting the attention and help they need. Finally, there is more uncertainty and less clarity in high school compared to primary school and I will later show that this can reduce motivation and in some cases actually lead to helplessness.

Research shows that this low motivation tends to bottom out in middle high school and begins to recover in the early years of senior high. So if you think your child's motivation seems to be dropping now they're in high school, you're probably not imagining things. This book directly addresses the reasons young people's motivation drops (and sometimes plummets) and what you can do about it.

How do the boosters, mufflers and guzzlers work?

Now you have a better idea about which boosters, mufflers and guzzlers need to be sustained or improved, you are probably interested in knowing a little more about each of these facets of motivation. Here, I briefly describe each booster, muffler and guzzler, their effect on your child's schoolwork, and which chapters in this book are particularly important to read to address them.

Self-belief

Self-belief is students' belief and confidence in their ability to understand or to do well in schoolwork, to meet challenges they face and to perform to the best of their ability. If your child has a positive self-belief, he or she tends to do difficult schoolwork confidently, feels optimistic, tries hard and enjoys school. To increase your child's self-belief or to keep it high, you might like to pay particular attention to chapter 3, 'Increasing your child's self-belief'.

Control

Students have a sense of control when they are clear about how to do well or how to avoid doing poorly. If students are low in control, they can feel somewhat helpless when doing their schoolwork, fear failure and have negative thoughts about their ability to do well. To increase your child's control, you might like to pay particular attention to chapter 4, 'Building your child's sense of control'.

Value of schooling

Students who believe in the value of school believe what they learn at school is useful, important and relevant. If your child values school, he or she tends to be interested in what he or she learns, persists when schoolwork gets difficult and enjoys school. To build your child's belief in the value of school or to sustain a high valuing of school, you might like to pay particular attention to chapter 5, 'Increasing your child's belief in the value of school'.

Learning focus

If your child has a strong learning focus, he or she is focused on learning, solving problems and developing skills. The goal of a learning-focused student is to be the best student he or she can be. If your child is learning focused, he or she tends to enjoy learning, does a good job for its own satisfaction and not simply for any rewards involved, and enjoys challenges. To increase your child's learning focus or to keep your child's learning focus high, you might like to pay particular attention to chapter 6, 'Increasing your child's learning focus'.

Planning

Planning is concerned with the extent to which students plan assignments and study and whether they keep track of their progress. If your child plans schoolwork, he or she tends to feel in control of it, persists with challenging tasks and assignments, and makes good use of his or her time and abilities. To develop your child's planning skills or to maintain effective planning, you might like to pay particular attention to chapter 7, 'Assisting your child's schoolwork and study'.

Study management

Study management is the way students use study time, organise a study timetable and choose and arrange where they study. If your child effectively manages study, he or she tends to study in places that maximise concentration, uses study time well and plans and sticks to a study timetable. To help your child manage study better or to keep your child studying effectively, you might like to pay particular attention to chapter 7, 'Assisting your child's school-work and study'.

Persistence

Persistence is concerned with whether students keep trying to work out an answer or understand a problem even when that problem is difficult or challenging. If your child is persistent, he or she tends to set effective goals, achieve what he or she sets out to do, is motivated to succeed and is good at problem solving. To develop your child's persistence or to keep your child persistent, you might like to pay particular attention to chapter 8, 'Enhancing your child's persistence'.

Anxiety

Anxiety has two parts: feeling nervous and worrying. Feeling nervous is the uneasy or sick feeling students get when they think about or do their schoolwork, assignments, and exams. Worrying is their fear of not doing very well in their schoolwork, assignments and exams. If students are too anxious, they tend to have difficulty concentrating, paying attention, remembering things and doing good-quality schoolwork. In terms of school, test anxiety is the most common type of anxiety students experience. To reduce your child's anxiety or to keep your child relaxed and focused, you might like to pay particular attention to chapter 9, 'Reducing your child's test anxiety'.

Failure avoidance

Students are failure avoidant when the main reason they do their schoolwork is to avoid doing poorly or to avoid being seen to do poorly. If students are failure avoidant, they tend to fear failure, feel pessimistic and feel anxious when thinking about or doing schoolwork. To reduce your child's failure avoidance or to maintain his or her success focus, you might like to pay particular attention to chapter 10, 'Reducing your child's fear of failure'.

Self-sabotage

Students self-sabotage when they do things that reduce their chances of success at school. Examples are putting off doing an assignment or wasting time while they are meant to be studying for an exam. If students self-sabotage, they do not feel good about being at school and tend not to achieve as highly as they are able. To reduce your child's self-sabotage or to keep your child studying effectively, you might like to pay particular attention to chapter 10, 'Reducing your child's fear of failure'.

In the final chapters I discuss four other important issues.

The first is about building a good relationship with your child. In my research into parenting and student motivation I am constantly surprised and encouraged by the extent to which good motivation is underpinned or accompanied by a good parent–child relationship. I am not talking about perfect parenting because there is probably no such thing. I am talking about developing a more healthy, supportive, positive and mutually respectful relationship between parent and child. A lot of student motivation – particularly in the home – can follow from this.

The second issue is how to re-engage the disengaged students. These students tend to be stuck in a repetitive cycle of poor performance and for all intents and purposes appear to be quite helpless in the face of challenge and difficulty. This chapter presents some strategies parents can use to help these students back into their studies.

The third issue I discuss is how boys and girls differ in their motivation and which particular strategies are more effective for boys. There is a lot of information available about boys' education and this chapter looks at what really works.

The fourth issue is how to motivate gifted and talented (or highly capable) children. Gifted and talented students can be underachievers too, and this is often the case because they have lost their motivation to work to their potential. This later chapter therefore looks at how to energise them again, present challenges that match their skill and ability, keep them interested in school and provide a learning and study environment that brings out their best.

How do boosters, mufflers and guzzlers operate in students' lives?

It is all well and good to have a model of boosters, mufflers and guzzlers and I'm sure you'd agree that in principle each of the ten boosters, mufflers and guzzlers looks important to a student's motivation. But it is when you look at the details of students' lives that you can really see how boosters, mufflers and guzzlers come to life.

I want to share two students' stories with you that bring these boosters, mufflers and guzzlers to life. To ensure the students' anonymity, the details in these stories have been changed slightly and the names are different. (This also applies to all the student case studies in this book.) The stories are about a high achiever and an underachiever – the two opposite ends of achievement and motivation. I find that most parents recognise at least some aspects of their own child in each story.

Nicole's story

Nicole performs extremely well at school and thoroughly enjoys her time there. She is high in all the motivation boosters and low in most of the mufflers and guzzlers. She is more focused on learning and improving herself than beating or comparing herself with others: 'If I can grasp something by stretching my mind or working really hard then I've made a progression in myself and I'm proud of myself, more so than being able to do something better than someone else.'

Nicole works by a structured study timetable that she organised for herself early in the year. She plans her work carefully, and checks how she is going as she does it: 'I try to be pretty organised. For an essay I'll do all the reading, I'll take notes for the readings, I'll have an essay plan and have a general outline of where I'm going and where the essay's going. I'm always making sure that it's on track by looking back at the question.'

Nicole is persistent in the face of challenge, saying, 'I'll always work until I get it,' and feels in control of success: 'I will put a lot of work in and then I can control how I'll do.' Nicole does not care how others view her results – it's more important for her to meet personal standards. If she doesn't do so well on an assignment or exam she is not afraid to go to her teacher and ask, 'What did I leave out and how can I improve next time?'

Peter's story

Peter does not perform well at school and is not likely to look back on his time there with fondness. School for him is a roller-coaster ride of anxiety, fear, poor performance, stress and pressure.

Whereas Nicole is focused on learning and doing the best work she can, Peter is focused on how he compares with others: 'It doesn't matter that you learn great things – that's not what school's about.' In contrast to Nicole who does not care what others think of her, Peter would never go to the teacher for help because he is frightened of being seen as a 'dummy'.

Whereas Nicole will keep working at difficult schoolwork until she understands it, Peter is quite different, saying, 'I just write the first thing that comes to mind.' Peter is frightened of failing, and to deal with this he is deliberately pessimistic about how he will do at school: 'I try to be pessimistic because that way

I won't be so disappointed. I think if you border on the pessimistic, if you do worse than expected, then it's less of a fall. You just try to minimise those falls.' Interestingly, Peter's pessimism seems to have come from home where his parents have always said, 'Don't set your goals too high because you'll only get disappointed.' According to Peter, 'They're always careful not to raise my hopes so I don't get disappointed.'

In contrast to Nicole, who has a strong sense of control, Peter feels quite helpless, saying, 'I could work my butt off but I still think I'll fail if my teacher wants me to fail. Just because I work hard won't guarantee that I'll get that mark.'

Unlike Nicole who maximises her chances of success, Peter seems to sabotage his chances, admitting, 'If I have an assignment due, I seem to just want to watch TV or go out.' His fear of failure seems to underlie much of this sabotaging behaviour: 'If I leave study to the last minute, then I've got an excuse if I don't do well. Any excuse is better than, "You're just not smart enough." I know that I should be putting effort in all the time, but then I've got the excuse if I don't go well.'

Boosters, mufflers and guzzlers in the lives of Nicole and Peter
These students are examples of two very different motivation patterns. As you can see, Nicole is high in the boosters such as self-belief, learning focus, study management, planning and persistence, whereas Peter is low in these boosters. On the other hand, Peter is high in the mufflers and guzzlers such as failure avoidance, anxiety and self-sabotage, whereas Nicole is low in these mufflers and guzzlers. Did you recognise any aspects of your own child in these two stories? Which ones?

I should emphasise that most students fall between the two extremes of Nicole and Peter. The reality is that most students have particular booster strengths, but also other boosters that can be improved. Most students are quite low on mufflers and guzzlers, but may be high in one or two that need attention to increase their enjoyment, interest in and performance at school.

Our child's strengths are our windows of opportunity

Latest research suggests that we can gain a lot from focusing on our strengths. When we focus on our strengths, there is a positive flow-on effect to other parts of our lives and this can persist over the longer term. For example, recognising a student's persistence and good study management can have the effect of increasing their self-esteem. I therefore want to emphasise that a student's strengths can be a window of opportunity for developing other parts of his or her life.

Can people change?

The reason many of you picked up this book is because you believe (at least in part) that people can change. In particular, you believe (or hope) your child can become more motivated and develop better ways of going about his or her studies. This raises a few questions, to which I provide a few answers:

Q. Can people change?
A. Yes.

Q. Is change easy?
A. No.

Q. Will it happen overnight?
A. Probably not.

Q. Are there particular things you can do to improve the chances of your child changing?
A. Yes.

I want to focus on this last point because it is very important. Research has found that there are some key reasons why people successfully change their behaviour, why others don't do as good a job as they could, and why others fail dismally.

The first reason behaviour change fails is because people believe they will change more than can be realistically expected. They set expectations that are way too high.

Lesson one: set realistic expectations that are ahead of where your child is now but which are also achievable.

The second reason behaviour change fails is because after failing to reach excessively high standards people tend to give up rather than adjust to more realistic expectations.

Lesson two: if your expectations prove to be unrealistic, adjust them to a level that is more achievable but which still moves your child forward (even a touch) from where they are now.

The third reason behaviour change fails is because people expect that change will be faster and easier to make than is actually possible. When it turns out to be slower or more difficult to make, they become disappointed, lose hope, and give up trying.

Lesson three: behaviour change is not often easy or quick. Be prepared to bunker down over the medium to longer term for high quality and sustainable change to occur. This isn't to say that quick change cannot occur – but don't be disheartened if it doesn't happen as quickly as you'd like.

The fourth reason behaviour change fails is because people expect behaviour change to solve all their problems and to have benefits in other parts of their life that are not realistic. Again, when their expectations are not met, they lose heart and give up trying.

Lesson four: when your child is more motivated, other parts of your life will become more enjoyable, but it may not fulfil or completely improve all parts of your life. The fact that your child's own life is more enjoyable and manageable is reason enough for you to commit to their motivation.

The fifth reason behaviour change fails is because people set goals that focus on their failures and not on their successes. For example, parents can define their child's success in terms of not failing, not screwing up, not getting a bad report card, not getting into trouble, and so on. That is, failure becomes the focus and children succeed simply through not failing. Other parents define success in terms of the child succeeding or nearing success – such as improving, developing new skills, and personal bests. Here, success is the focus. Research shows that people are more likely to stop trying to change when the focus is on avoiding failure and are more likely to keep trying to change when the focus is on reaching success.

Lesson five: define success more in terms of your child succeeding (or approaching success) and less in terms of not failing. A positive focus is more likely to lead to behaviour change.

Chapter summary

I hope this chapter has identified one or more of your child's strengths. Sure, your child may not have scored a perfect 5 on any of the boosters (but maybe he or she did), but for some children anything above a 1 is a starting point. Here the window is ajar and this is your opportunity to fling it open, expand on this area of relative strength and perhaps develop other strengths in the process.

CHAPTER TWO TOP 5

1. Factors affecting motivation can be divided into thoughts and behaviours that boost your child's motivation and achievement, those that restrict motivation and achievement and those that reduce your child's motivation and achievement. The thoughts and behaviours that boost your child's motivation are called boosters. The thoughts and behaviours that restrict your child's motivation are mufflers. Those that reduce your child's motivation are called guzzlers.

2. Booster thoughts are self-belief, learning focus and belief in the value of school. Booster behaviours are planning, study management and persistence. Mufflers are failure avoidance and anxiety. Guzzlers are low control and self-sabotage.

3. Higher boosters and lower mufflers and guzzlers are some of your child's strengths – aim to keep these boosters high and these mufflers and guzzlers low. Lower boosters and higher mufflers and guzzlers are where your child can improve – aim to increase these boosters and reduce these mufflers and guzzlers.

4. Every child has one or more boosters that are higher than other boosters. Every child has one or more mufflers and guzzlers that are lower than others. Never lose sight of these. These are areas of strength that are very important for you and your child to recognise.

5. Motivating your child involves improving aspects of motivation that may be a problem as well as maintaining areas of strength. Pay particular attention to the chapters in this book that show you how to do both these things.

Part Two

STRATEGIES TO BOOST YOUR CHILD'S MOTIVATION

CHAPTER 3

INCREASING YOUR CHILD'S SELF-BELIEF

There is no getting around the fact that when we believe in ourselves we perform better, we are more persistent, we are better problem solvers, we enjoy what we do, we are more motivated to do it and we are better able to deal with challenges and difficulties if they arise. Exactly the same applies to students. There is simply no substitute for students liking themselves, believing in themselves and thinking positively. It is for this reason that I deal with self-belief before any other booster, muffler or guzzler.

Self-belief goes under many names, including self-esteem, self-concept and self-efficacy. Self-belief is students' belief and confidence in their ability to understand or to do well in schoolwork, to meet challenges they face and to perform to the best of their ability. Students who have a positive self-belief tend to get better results, do difficult schoolwork confidently, feel optimistic, try hard and enjoy school.

Two paths to self-belief

There are two main ways to increase your child's self-belief, and each involves specific strategies.

The first way is to *build more success into your child's life at every opportunity*. This is achieved by:

- 'chunking' schoolwork
- developing a broader view of success.

The second way to increase your child's self-belief is to *challenge his or her negative thinking*. This is achieved by:

- identifying negative-thinking traps
- developing positive self-talk
- realistic optimism
- becoming a talent scout.

How to put these strategies in place is the focus of this chapter.

They'll get their sense of worth anywhere they can

I have found in my research that students will go to incredible lengths to feel worthwhile and okay about themselves. Feeling okay about oneself is a fundamental human drive. Students are no exception and will get their sense of worth any way and anywhere they can. This is why the home and school need to provide many opportunities for a student to gain a sense of worth and self-belief. If they don't, the child will get his or her sense of worth elsewhere. He or she will spend too much time playing computer games, mucking around with mates, talking on the phone, hanging around the shopping centre, playing at the skateboard ramp or frequenting the entertainment arcade. (I hasten to add that these are all acceptable in moderation.)

Within school there are many unhelpful ways in which students may gain a sense of worth. I remember a research project a few years ago which involved IQ testing. A group of about 300 school students was administered the IQ test in the school hall. One student refused to do the test. A supervisor muttered to me that he wasn't a very good student and probably wouldn't do very well on the test anyway. After a while the student was surrounded by a scrum of teachers all demanding that he do the test. He still refused and was promptly booted out of the hall. He sat just outside the doorway and looked a lot happier out there than he did in the hall.

The students finished the test and once they had left I collected the test papers. When I got to the disgraced student's desk I saw there was a sheet of paper under the uncompleted test paper. On this sheet were amazing and breathtaking animations that he had drawn in the short space of fifteen minutes. So vivid and lifelike were the cartoons that you'd half believe they could jump off the page and walk out of the hall. In the face of a potentially demeaning experience this student had found another outlet to feel okay about himself. Believing that his sense of worth would take a pounding in that IQ test, he chose to gain some self-belief in another way. I don't know where this kid is today but he certainly was not a talentless student and I sincerely hope someone at some point seized on this strength as a means to expand other parts of his life.

Build success into your child's life at every opportunity

I want to discuss the importance of success and how to achieve it before I discuss students' negative thinking, because if students do not experience some level of success their ability to challenge their negative thinking is reduced. For this reason I suggest building success into students' lives as quickly as possible. This provides a solid foundation for increasing positive thinking. One boy told me, 'When you get good marks you want to try harder because you know you can get marks. It sort of motivates you and helps your self-esteem.'

There are *two main ways to build success* into your child's life:

- teach your child how to 'chunk' schoolwork
- broaden your own and your child's view of success.

I want to make it clear that building more success into students' lives does not mean giving them false praise or giving them all A grades. Students know when they don't deserve reward or praise and may later disbelieve it when it is deserved. Rewarding students when they don't deserve it can also create confusion in their minds about why they received that reward and this can reduce their sense of control (this will be discussed in chapter 4 when I show you how to build your child's personal control over success).

Chunking

In my work with students, a very common problem I have noticed is their tendency to see schoolwork, assignments and exams as mountains: enormous, overwhelming and daunting tasks that seem too big to even begin to tackle. When students see their schoolwork and study as mountains, they are less confident in completing tasks, tend to procrastinate because the task seems too big, or do the fastest job possible just to put the mountain behind them. All these reduce students' chances of success. The less students experience success, the lower their self-belief tends to be.

Students need to approach their schoolwork in another way, a way that maximises opportunities for success. Chunking is a very effective way of doing this. Chunking is breaking a task into smaller bite-size parts. When an assignment or study session is reduced to smaller and more manageable parts, good effects flow:

- students are more confident that they can do their school-work because smaller parts are easier to complete
- students are less inclined to put off doing their schoolwork because they see their work in bite-size and achievable parts
- students are able to plan their schoolwork more effectively and manage their study time better.

The combination of these factors means that they are also more likely to succeed.

I want to push this idea of chunking further. I also encourage students to see the completion of each chunk as a success. This means that even before students hand in their assignment and receive a mark, they have a number of cracks at success. These smaller successes have the effect of spurring students onto the next chunk. This is the ideal form of motivation because students get into the habit of rewarding themselves and propelling themselves through the task with energy and drive. This is called intrinsic, or inner, motivation – a very precious commodity indeed.

An example of chunking

To give you an idea of how chunking is done, I want to look at one of the most common tasks assigned to secondary school students – the essay. When students tell me they have an essay and I ask them how they will approach it, most say that they'll do some reading and answer the question, but are unable to tell me much more than this. Most have difficulty describing the task in terms of the more specific parts that are all important in order to complete the essay successfully.

In fact, there are at least eleven components to the essay task:

1. understanding the question/task
2. breaking the question into parts
3. performing an initial search for information (e.g. internet, library)
4. conducting a focused and detailed reading of books and other resources collected
5. undertaking a detailed summary of information
6. organising the information (e.g. putting information under each heading)
7. writing the first draft
8. tying up loose ends (e.g. a bit more reading)
9. writing the second draft
10. editing the second draft (e.g. spelling, grammar, formatting checks)
11. writing the final draft.

In theory this student, by chunking the essay task, can experience eleven successes even before the essay is submitted and before a mark is received. Not only this, but the student is being rewarded throughout the essay and this sustains persistence.

There are many tasks that can be chunked. Some examples of chunking include:

- writing a 'to do' list at the start of a homework or study session
- breaking a project or assignment into parts
- developing a detailed study timetable leading up to exams
- collecting information to select school subjects or a university course

- planning group work, a class debate, or an extracurricular activity.

There are also many tasks at home and other activities in your child's life that can be chunked. These include projects in the garden, organising a party, fixing something, planning a holiday, setting up a club, planning a training schedule for sport and putting a band together.

Notice that I am not suggesting you reduce children's mountains by removing tasks from their lives. Nor am I suggesting that you build more tasks into your child's life to increase opportunities for success. Our job as parents is to make the mountains in our children's lives more manageable and less scary by transforming tasks into bite-size chunks. When tasks are seen – and completed – in this way students are immediately exposed to many opportunities for genuine success. Genuine success builds genuine self-belief and confidence.

Before I wrap up this section on chunking I want to tell you a story from my own school days. I remember when I started the final two years of high school I found the work much more difficult than the work in the preceding years. The textbooks were a quantum leap from the descriptive and factual texts in middle high to the more analytical texts in senior high. I found this quite difficult to adjust to. I seemed to have most difficulty understanding the set text in ancient history. I'd read a few sentences, wouldn't understand what they were on about, and so move to the next paragraph and find much the same there. Very quickly the page became a hill and the chapter became a mountain.

My first few nights of trying to understand the text were soul-destroying. Ancient history had excited me in earlier years but I just couldn't crack the code in senior high. After a few nights of knocking my head against a brick wall my dad asked me how I was going with my study. With some reluctance I told him I was finding the reading in ancient history hard going. He asked if he could work through a page with me to see if he could explain it. I didn't think he (a man of science) would understand much about ancient history but agreed to give it a go. I sat next to him, he read the first couple of sentences and we talked about these until I understood them. Then we moved on to the next couple of sentences and talked about those until I understood them. I think we spent two hours reading a few paragraphs. I know this sounds like pretty basic stuff but I can assure you that this was what I seemed to need to understand what the text was on about.

We never read together again. No, not because I'd be 101 years of age before we'd read a complete chapter, but because he showed me how to tackle a sentence, analyse it, focus on key words, and even use clues from one sentence to help understand another. He helped me crack the code. It also showed me that chunking could help someone understand something that isn't even their area of strength. My dad had never studied ancient history, but chunking made the text understandable and accessible to him. Ancient history became my best subject in my finals and I went on to study it at university also.

What was the trick? Chunking. My dad was an expert chunker and I never knew it! He reduced my mountain into bite-size pieces, increasing my chances of success on not only those smaller pieces but also on the chapter as a whole. It could have been so different. Where would it have ended if he hadn't taken the time to chunk? How far would I have fallen behind? Don't underestimate how small moments like this can affect your child's study life. To this day I am still benefiting from that night my dad and I chunked a few paragraphs in an ancient history text.

Broaden your own and your child's view of success

Another very effective way of building more success into your child's life is to expand the definition of success. In my experience working with students, I have found that too many cut themselves off from genuine experiences of success by holding a very narrow view of success and what it means to be successful. This is lethal for a student's motivation because when a student thinks there is no chance of success, he or she is less likely to bother trying. A very important condition for motivation is that there be at least some chance of success.

A broader view of success is one that defines success in terms of improvement, skill development, mastery, learning new things, understanding new things, solving problems and, most importantly, personal bests. These are all aspects of success that are within reach of any student and achievable in the student's eyes. When success is seen as achievable, students are motivated to strive to reach it. Of course, getting the top mark is also an aspect of success, but too many students define success in only these terms. When students see success in such a narrow way – and so many students do – they almost immediately cut themselves off from it.

Why do students hold such a narrow and even self-defeating view of success? They need only look as far as the media to see that the achievements receiving attention and adulation are those in which the competitor is at the top of the pack. At the end of the year they only have to look at the front page of the newspaper when final school year results are published to see fifty smiling students who received a perfect score. They only have to look as far as the podium at school to see the dux presented to the rest of the school – with little or no recognition for the personal bests that others in that student's year might have achieved.

Our children are bombarded with messages that tell them that success means being the top of the pack, topping the class, beating others, knowing more than others and being the best. When they see success in this way they are almost instantly relegated to 'failure', for want of a better word, because only a few kids can be at the top of the pack. They are immediately cut off from success because their narrow view of it means that it is nearly impossible for them to achieve.

Our view of success needs to be one that increases our chances of reaching it. But it also needs to be one that is not so easy to reach that it does not extend our child. Research has shown that children are more motivated when there is a challenge before them but which is not so far beyond them that they don't try to meet it. As my discussion of chunking would imply, we don't want to make another mountain for our child to climb. Therefore our view of success also needs to be one that extends our children, always nudging them a little further than they currently are. There are many outcomes that fit these criteria for success. Some are:

- reaching personal bests
- improving on a previous performance
- developing and using new skills
- learning new things
- mastering a task

- solving a problem
- understanding something new
- working harder than before.

How many students genuinely give themselves credit for achieving these outcomes? Not enough. Those who do value these outcomes tend to be more motivated, enjoy school and study, and are high in self-belief. This is because they hold a view of success that is broad and achievable, and as a result frequently experience success. These successes are what propel them through their study with energy, interest and enthusiasm.

Most importantly, I have never met a student who is not capable of achieving these outcomes. Any student can improve in some way, develop a new skill, understand something new and even reach a personal best. It therefore follows that any student can experience success. This is not to imply that it is always easy. It's not. But it is possible and that's what matters from a motivation perspective.

Some parents, students and teachers get worried with this approach because it takes the focus off marks, and they believe that if students aren't focused on getting great marks then they won't be motivated. This is not true. What I have found and other research has shown is that focusing solely on marks can distract students' attention from the job at hand. The more they focus on marks or how their performance will be judged, the less they are able to concentrate on giving a good answer or addressing the test question properly. Furthermore, the more students focus on their marks and how their answers will be evaluated, the more anxious they feel and this, too, distracts their attention from giving a good answer.

In contrast, focusing on outcomes such as personal bests, solving problems and developing new skills is likely to lead to higher achievement. This is because all attention and energy is focused on doing the task. It will not surprise you to learn that the more students focus on the job at hand, doing a good job and providing a well thought out answer, the more likely they are to do well. Ironically, then, the less they focus on marks, the better their marks are likely to be!

I want to make it clear that this is not an argument for mediocrity. I ask excellence of students and encourage parents to do

Paul, senior high

Paul was one of those students who always passed assignments and exams but was clearly capable of more. You wouldn't say he was pessimistic but he certainly wasn't confident and he didn't think he was capable of much more. Basically, although his self-belief wasn't rock bottom, it wasn't at a level that inspired him to do as well as he could. To his parents' frustration, his self-belief was reflected in a lack of effort in assignments and exams and a string of very average performances.

In the middle of the first year in senior high, students were told about an advanced class in geography. Geography was Paul's favourite subject and the idea of doing a bit more in it was a pretty attractive one to him. Unfortunately, his grades were not good enough to give him immediate entry to the advanced class. This was a real disappointment for Paul and he decided then and there that he was going to do what it took to get into that class. His first chance was an upcoming class test. For the first time in his life he asked the teacher which topics he should cover in his study, he listened to the teacher for the entirety of each lesson, he took good notes and even thought ahead to the likely test questions and did his best to prepare for them. Even after doing all this he still wasn't sure he'd do well but he had certainly given himself a better chance at success than any other time in his high school years. He did okay in the test – not brilliantly, but better than he'd done before and it was certainly closer to what he needed to do to get into the advanced class. This modest success was all the evidence he needed to tackle the next assessment task.

This assessment task was an essay. Again, he clarified with the teacher what he had to do and also asked about good references to borrow from the library. His teacher had always been happy for students to show him drafts of essays before handing them in and Paul made the most of this opportunity. In doing so, he learnt that he hadn't presented a very balanced argument, his conclusion did not follow from the ideas he'd presented in the essay, and he used the same words a bit too often. He polished the draft, handed it in, and received a good mark for that essay – inching him closer again to the advanced class.

Paul did get into the advanced class. Without realising it, he had taken the best possible approach to getting there: biting off small chunks, taking them a step at a time and genuinely seeing the completion of each chunk as a success. Before long his success and his attitude began to play off each other – once this kicked in he was more confident and behaved in ways consistent with this confidence. Importantly, when he had started out on this journey his self-belief was not particularly strong, but chalking up small successes was enough for him to see the next task through. Then his self-belief began to grow, and when this was coupled with success, it put him into a success-oriented cycle that not only motivated him but made him resilient in the face of occasional self-doubt and pressure.

the same. Taking the focus off being the best or the top of the class does not mean you stop asking the best from your child. However, you should aim for excellence in personal terms and not relative terms. I ask students to be the best they can be. This is very different from asking students to be 'the best'. When excellence is cast in personal terms, and not in terms of how they compare with other students, success immediately becomes achievable to students. When success becomes achievable students become very motivated to strive to reach it.

To complete this section on success building, I want to emphasise the importance of success in students' lives as a solid foundation for self-belief. Without some experience of success (no matter how small), challenging negative thinking becomes increasingly difficult. Chunking and broadening students' view of success are two very effective ways to inject more success into their lives.

Challenge negative thinking

Another important way to boost your child's self-belief is to encourage them to challenge negative thinking with positive messages and 'self-talk'. Negative thinking eats away at students' self-belief and must be challenged if students are to feel okay about themselves. Ways to challenge negative thinking include:

- identifying negative thinking traps
- developing positive self-talk
- becoming a talent scout
- developing realistic optimism.

The effects of negative thinking

Research has shown that thinking negatively has a dramatic effect on students' self-esteem, feelings and behaviour. When a student thinks negatively he or she feels down, unhappy and can even become depressed. Students who think negatively tend to behave in ways that are consistent with their negative thoughts. For example, a student who thinks he or she is going to fail a test tends to do less study, does not give good answers and may even give up halfway through the test (or not show up at all). On the other hand, students who think more positively about the test do more study, do their best to answer the questions well and persist even if the test is difficult. As one girl told me, 'If I think negatively then everything turns out negative for me. Now I think about things more positively, I haven't got stressed about things, and things have worked out for the best.'

Thinking negatively can also become a vicious circle. The student who thinks he or she is going to fail does less study and does not give good answers and because of this does not do well. This confirms the student's negative thoughts and so he or she is even more likely to think negatively next time a test comes along.

Typical examples of negative thinking at school

There seems to be no end to the negative thoughts students have at their disposal. Each negative thought differs slightly from student to student and situation to situation. However, even though the details may change, there are some common themes I have found in dealing with students. Some of these themes are set out in the table on page 46 along with examples of how these themes are played out in students' minds.

These are just some of the negative ways students think that not only affect how they feel but also, sometimes, what they do. For example, a student who thinks he has no control over avoiding

Negative Thinking at School

Theme	What students think
Not being good enough to do the work	There's no way I'm going to get through science this year. It's just too hard for me.
Failing the next test or assignment	I just know I'm going to screw up on the maths test.
Feeling hopeless when receiving a bad mark	I got a D! I really suck at this subject. I don't know why I bother.
Thinking that making a mistake or failing is the end of the world	I won't be able to handle it if I fail this test. I just don't know what I'll do if I screw it up.
Thinking negatively about good marks	I know I did okay this time, but I was just lucky. Next time I know I'll stuff it up.
Not getting through the year (or the subject, assignment etc)	My God, I'm getting assignments faster than I can do them. There's no way I'm going to get through this subject.
Success and failure being beyond control	It doesn't matter whether I work hard or not, I'm going to fail anyway.

failure is more likely to feel anxious leading up to a test and is less likely to study hard or spend time trying to give a good answer.

Identifying negative thinking traps
When students think the type of thoughts described in the table above they are falling into some very common negative thinking traps. Here I describe a few of the traps that can reduce a student's self-belief.

Black and white thinking Too often students think in 'all or nothing' ways. They'll think they are really good students or really bad students; they have performed really well or they are hopeless; things are easy or impossible; there is only success or failure. This is dangerous thinking because it means that if anything negative or unpleasant happens in a student's life it will pack a big punch and may be hard to overcome. The reality is that most of life, including school, is neither black nor white, but falls somewhere in between. A more balanced, realistic view means that if something unpleasant happens your child will be able to see the silver lining to the cloud or the light at the end of the tunnel.

Biased thinking Many students filter the world in ways that can make them feel down and negative about themselves. These students tend to focus on the negatives and can screen out many or all of the positives in their lives. Even if they get a good mark on a test, they tend to think it was luck or that the pressure is now on them to do well in the next test. Their negative bias means that they are not opening their minds to success, and as I discussed earlier, success is very important to a student's self-belief.

End-of-the-worlding I find that many students low in self-belief have an almost catastrophic view of failure or mistakes. It is the end of the world if they screw up an exam. Sure, screwing up a test is not a pleasant experience, but it is not the end of the world. There are usually more tests or assignments in which the student can make up the lost marks.

Turning positives into negatives Students low in self-belief are experts at turning something positive into something negative. When they get a good mark, they're the ones who think the teacher felt sorry for them when marking their paper, or the teacher got the grades mixed up, or that there's no point doing well on one thing when they're just going to fail everything else. To enhance self-belief, students must recognise, accept and take credit for the positive things that happen in their life.

Getting sucked into scared feelings Many students feel scared and anxious when it comes to exams, tests and other performance situations. A lot of them mistake their feelings for facts, and assume that because they feel scared and anxious that must mean they are going to fail. This does not help their confidence leading up to the test. It is important to separate feelings from facts. Just because a student feels something doesn't mean it will happen.

Mega-generalising When unpleasant things happen to some students they think something similar – or worse – will take place in other parts of their lives. Disappointment in one history essay can extend to pessimism in history as a subject or extend to essays in all subjects. Negative feedback from one teacher can be translated into all teachers having it in for you. This not only eats away at a student's self-belief in the subject involved but can result in negativity across schoolwork as a whole. This is an example of a student who is not resilient – one setback knocks them off their perch. Students need to be taught how to put boundaries around things that don't go well for them. This not only protects other parts of their lives from negativity but also keeps them focused on the problem area when trying to improve it.

Mountain building Students often build negative or unpleasant events into mountains that can seem impossible to get over. For example, not getting picked for the debating team, getting a lower mark than expected, not being able to answer a question the teacher asked in class, not understanding what the teacher is saying or having difficulty in a particular subject can all be blown out of proportion. To some students these events are evidence they are hopeless, will never be able to do something, are not suited to school or are regarded by everyone as dumb. These students lack perspective, and when something unpleasant happens they feel dreadful and think negatively about themselves. With a more balanced perspective they would be able to confine the unpleasant event to a particular time and setting, and would not generalise it to themselves as a person or their life as a whole.

Recognising negative thinking
The problem with a lot of students' negative thinking is that it is automatic. This makes it difficult to detect, and if it can't be detected it can't be challenged. A negative thought can automatically flick through students' minds whenever:

- a class test is announced
- an assignment is handed back
- an essay question is assigned
- the teacher asks them a question
- the teacher looks like asking them a question

- the teacher looks at them
- they think about the homework they have to do that night
- they think about a particular teacher
- they think about schoolwork in general
- they think about school in general.

For some students, the school day can be a string of automatic negative thoughts, leaving them feeling pretty unhappy by the time the day's out. Negative thoughts chip away at a student's self-belief, gradually grinding down their confidence and motivation.

To tackle negative thinking effectively, the student must learn to recognise the negative thinking that goes on throughout the day. It is important to ask negative-thinking students what thoughts went through their minds when they received their test score, or were asked a question in class, or were told of a class test.

The first task, then, is to encourage students to become thought detectors. For some students, this may mean keeping a journal for a day in which the student records as many thoughts as possible, particularly those that occurred when something important happened, such as receiving an essay mark, being told of a class test or being asked a question in class.

Part of a student's journal may look like this:

Student 'thought' journal	
Situation	Automatic thought
Received mark for English essay	I was lucky to get that mark.
Teacher asked me a question	What happens if I don't know the answer?
Class test announced	I know I'm going to screw it up.
Given a difficult problem to do	What's the point in trying? I'll go just as badly anyway.
Saw David's mark	I'm not as smart as David.

Before challenging negative thinking, it is important for students to be fully aware of their negative thoughts. Only when the student recognises the negative thinking can he or she tackle it.

Developing positive self-talk

When students are familiar with their negative thinking and the situations in which they are most likely to think negatively, they are then in a position to tackle it.

I've heard that about 90 per cent of what we fear does not come true. I'm not sure how accurate this is, but even if it's 70 per cent it tells me that there is a lot of evidence around that can challenge negative thinking. Often students think it is difficult to find evidence to challenge their negative thoughts. What they don't realise is that commonsense usually provides evidence enough to challenge their negative thinking. If it doesn't, some good old-fashioned lateral thinking can usually come to their aid.

I want to make it clear that students should not be encouraged to think that black is white. Nor am I suggesting that you encourage your child to become blindly optimistic without regard for likely outcomes. When students challenge negative thinking with unrealistic optimism often things don't turn out as they expect. They will then doubt their positive self-talk next time around and be less likely to wage a strong attack on their negative thinking. Unrealistic optimism may set them up for a fall, and as I showed earlier, we want to maximise opportunities for success, not reduce them.

I want to show you how some common negative thinking habits of students can be challenged. The table opposite shows the same negative thoughts that were presented in the earlier table on page 49. Alongside each thought is a commonsense and realistic way to challenge the thoughts.

As you can see, the thinking that challenges the negative thoughts is not unrealistic. Because it is not unrealistic it is believable. When it is believable students are more optimistic about putting these positive thoughts into practice.

Becoming a talent scout

I sometimes get students to become their own talent scouts. Recognising their talents is another way students can challenge negative self-talk. I tell students their job is to identify five of their school-related talents – and that this job is not over until they find five. Some students can very quickly rattle off five (and more) talents. Others have a great deal of trouble and it is important to

Tackling negative thoughts

Negative thought	The challenge
There's no way I'm going to get through science this year. It's just too hard for me.	If I take it one step at a time and keep up to date with my assignments and study, I'm more likely to hang in there.
I just know I'm going to screw up on the maths test.	I can't predict the future and there are some practical steps I can take to reduce the chances of screwing up.
I got a D! I really suck at this subject. I don't know why I bother.	By reading the teacher's comments I can get an idea of how to improve next time.
I won't be able to handle it if I fail this test. I just don't know what I'll do if I screw it up.	Screwing up is not the end of the world. If I screw up, I'll find out why and use that to improve next time.
I know I did okay this time, but I was just lucky. Next time I know I'll stuff it up.	I'll look at what I did that led to my success and do this again to increase my chances of succeeding next time.
My God, I'm getting assignments faster than I can do them. There's no way I'm going to get through this subject.	If I plan ahead, prioritise and do regular homework and study I've got a good chance of keeping up with the work.
It doesn't matter whether I work hard or not, I'm going to fail anyway.	The main things that determine whether I succeed or fail are how much work I do and the way I do that work – I control these.

show them how to take a broad view of talent and how to recognise it in their lives. Too often students take talents for granted or don't even see them as talents.

Every student has talents. But I've found that they can very easily get lost among students' shortcomings or the problems they have at school or at home. You will recall that students' talents (or strengths) are your windows of opportunity as it is from students' talents that you can expand other parts of their lives. Recognising talents is essential in building self-belief and motivation.

Sure, it may be that compared to other children your child's talents are not as strong. But it is very important not to compare your child with other children. Take your child on his or her own terms and you will see that he or she has some characteristics or attributes that are stronger or better than other characteristics. These are talents. I recognise that these talents may not be as strong as his friend Sam's or his neighbour Tanya's talents, but forget about those kids – as far as your son or daughter is concerned these are his or her talents.

You'll also recall that parents and students need to broaden their view of success. The same goes for talents. Be very broad in your view of talents so that they include many different types of attributes or characteristics. A broad view of talents can include things like:

- being a good listener
- being good with numbers
- understanding how others feel
- being responsible
- being honest
- being observant
- being persistent or determined
- being organised
- sticking to a plan
- being a good reader
- doing things on time
- trying hard
- being fair
- co-operating
- playing well with others
- being a good communicator
- being creative.

This list shows that talents are many and varied.

What are your child's school-related talents? Thinking only of your child and no one else, can you list five school-related talents? I insist you find five, no matter how small or trivial you think they are. Make it your mission over the next day to let your child know that you are aware of at least some of these talents and that you value them irrespective of whether other children are higher or lower in the same talents.

Developing realistic optimism

There is recognition in psychology that reality is fuzzy. What this means is that two different people can interpret the same facts in two different ways and both be correct. A good example is two movie reviewers who agree on a description of the plot, characters and settings in a movie, but interpret the theme, messages and meaning of the movie in very different ways. In this case, reality is fuzzy because as far as these two reviewers go there are two different realities, each one correct.

The fact that reality is fuzzy means that there is a certain degree of flexibility with which we can interpret the world. It doesn't mean we can say black is white, but it does mean we can lean on the side of optimism when interpreting events in our lives and be correct in our interpretation. How often have we been told to see the cup as half full rather than half empty? This is realistic optimism.

The same applies to students. There is evidence of fuzzy reality when two students interpret the same feedback from a teacher or the same mark in two very different ways. One sees the feedback as confirmation that he lacks the ability to study the subject; the another sees the feedback as important information on where she went wrong and how to improve. Again, same facts but different reality. Cup half empty and cup half full.

There are three areas of your child's thinking in which realistic optimism can be developed:

- the way your child views past events
- the way your child views current events
- the way your child views the future.

Students develop realistic optimism by taking a more positive interpretation of events and situations that have happened in the past. These students don't dwell on past failures or difficulties. Instead, they take what they need from them to improve next time and move on. In fact, rather than wallow in self-pity or disappointment and despair, they are philosophical about unpleasant things that have happened, looking to them for lessons that will shape them into better students. This also builds resilience to future disappointments and difficulties and lays a solid foundation for realistic optimism. I can tell you honestly that some of the best things that happened to me as a student were unpleasant and disappointing at the time. Stuffing up my first general studies essay in senior high taught me that I needed to learn how to argue a case, then take a sensible position and defend it. I quickly made it my business to do just that.

The way students view their current situation also influences the extent to which they are realistic optimists. Realistic optimists are usually happy wherever they are in the moment. If they prefer to be elsewhere they accept where they are but put into action some effective steps to move on. Too often students get stuck in a moment or 'space' that they don't like, dwell on it, and soon find themselves feeling unhappy and pessimistic about the future. A common example is the student who gets stuck on a bad mark and can't shake the disappointment enough to move on. In fact, this student carries the bad mark into other subjects and soon that mark can engulf all aspects of the student's present moment. This student needs to be shown how to take some important lessons from the mark then leave it behind in order to focus on dealing with other tasks now occupying the present moment. Leaving unpleasantness behind (but taking the lessons with you) is an important part of being happy in the present moment, and this is an important part of realistic optimism.

The way your child views the future is the final factor in developing realistic optimism. There's nothing more paralysing than looking into the future with little or no hope or optimism. Your child's view of future study and school is no exception. The reality is that your child has at his or her disposal two of the most important factors that influence performance on tests, assignments and projects: effort (how much work he or she does) and strategy (the way he or she does this work). These are within your child's control and because of this your child has good reason to be optimistic that he or she has a big say in the outcome of that test or assignment. Gently directing your child's attention to these controllable factors and encouraging him or her to put them into practice will enhance optimism.

In sum, when your child views the past, present and future with at least a hint of realistic optimism, he or she begins to feel better about himself or herself as a student. This boost in self-belief creates a cyclical effect in that he or she is more likely to view the past, present and future in an optimistic way that further enhances self-belief. This is a cycle that promotes motivation and academic resilience.

Living in the real world

In the real world not everything happens like they say in the books. Here are a few things for you to think about when digesting this chapter.

- Don't expect your child to be positive and confident all the time. Research has shown that students' self-belief can differ from subject to subject and so your child is likely to be more confident and optimistic in some subjects than others.
- Don't make your child feel bad or inadequate for having low or shaky self-belief. Go easy on them and be sensitive to their feelings when guiding them into more positive thinking.
- Not every success will have magical properties. Success may be hard for your child to handle because they may think there's pressure on them to succeed next time. Recognise this and don't pin heavy expectations on them to succeed every time. Having said this, building more success into your child's life will in the long run strengthen your child's belief in him or herself and also make him or her resilient to setbacks.
- Chunking is a skill that may take a while to develop to full effect. Spending good time with your child to help them chunk effectively will be time well spent.
- Although it is ideal to develop a broad view of success, don't be surprised if your child still pins most importance on marks. In our school system most of it comes down to marks. Your child isn't thinking anything different from most other kids or from the school as a whole. Go for shifts in your child's thinking rather than radical surgery – you're likely to be more successful.

- Don't let your child lose heart if a change to more positive thinking doesn't immediately bring success. Be confident that positive thinking and a strong self-belief have many advantages not only in terms of academic outcomes but also in terms of mental and physical health.
- When identifying your child's strengths make sure you ground them in reality. Children don't feel comfortable or believe adults' praise when they think those adults aren't basing the praise on reality. Telling your child that something is black when they categorically think it is white reduces your credibility. Identify strengths that your child will (maybe grudgingly) accept.

Chapter summary

This chapter has focused on the importance of self-belief and how to increase it. Self-belief underpins a lot of very important educational outcomes such as achievement, enjoyment, confidence and interest in school. With support and guidance from you, your child's self-belief can be increased. To do this, you need to look for and seize opportunities to build more success into his or her life. Alongside this is the need to turn your child's negative thinking around by encouraging and supporting more positive messages and self-talk. The combination of these strategies will result in your child thinking more positively about himself or herself and school.

CHAPTER THREE TOP 5

1. Self-belief is one of the most important aspects of motivation. Self-belief is students' belief that they can do what they set out to do, meet challenges effectively and achieve to their potential.

2. You increase your child's self-belief by building more success into his or her life, challenging negative thinking and supporting and encouraging your child to do the same.

3. Opportunities for success are increased by chunking schoolwork into bite-size and achievable parts, broadening your child's view of success and focusing on personal bests.

4. To challenge negative thinking students need to recognise their negative thoughts and when they are likely to occur, and tackle this negative thinking with positive messages and evidence. Positive messages need to be optimistic, but also realistic and based in commonsense.

5. Recognising and valuing your child's talents (irrespective of how they compare to other children's) can be a good starting point for building and expanding other parts of your child's life. Always start with areas of strength when moving into areas that need to improve.

CHAPTER 4

BUILDING YOUR CHILD'S SENSE OF CONTROL

Having a sense of control over the things we do can be as important as having high self-belief. When we have a sense of control we believe we have some effect or impact on the things we do and the way these things turn out for us.

Students who have a sense of control know how to repeat successes they have already achieved, and also know how to improve things they don't do so well.

If your child has a sense of control, there is a belief that he or she can:

- write another good essay to follow up their previous good essay
- do well in the next test to follow up their previous success
- figure out where they went wrong on an assignment or in a test and make sure it doesn't happen again
- have a big impact on their school results.

YOU CAN CONTROL YOUR OWN DESTINY!

I FEEL DESTINED TO EAT JUNK FOOD ALL DAY

If your child doesn't have a sense of control, he or she believes that:

- there's not much they can do to improve on a poor performance
- how they do at school is almost entirely up to their teacher (as one student told me: 'If he wants me to fail, I'll fail. It doesn't matter what I do.')
- how they do in a test almost entirely depends on how easy or difficult the questions are
- how they do in an assignment almost entirely depends on good or bad luck.

Why is control important?

Put simply, students who have a sense of control over what they do and how things turn out are more optimistic, persist when the going gets tough and are more likely to try different ways to solve a problem and tackle their schoolwork. One student said to me, 'If I get results back and they're not good, I'm not shattered. I just think I haven't put enough work into it and I've got to do more. I'm still confident.'

The reason for this is clear: these students firmly believe that they have what it takes to work out a solution or to complete a task. When students believe they can repeat success or improve on a previous performance, they have every reason to feel optimistic, every reason to have positive expectations for upcoming exams or assignments, and every reason to hang in there when they are faced with a challenge or problem.

On the other hand, students feel helpless when they believe that there is not much they can do to avoid failure or repeat success. They feel helpless because there is little reason for hope, little reason to try hard ('What's the point? It doesn't matter how hard I try,' one student told me), and every reason to feel uncertain because they are at the mercy of marking, test questions or good or bad luck. One girl told me, 'You never know what's going to happen. You can work a lot harder at it, but still I find it so hard to judge how I'm going to be marked and what they expect.'

There are other reasons why low control is a problem. These

students also tend to be overly anxious when they sit for exams, are given an assignment, are asked a question in class or do a class quiz. They feel anxious because they are uncertain about their ability to pass the exam, complete the assignment successfully, answer the teacher's question or do well in the quiz. These students live in a great deal of self-doubt because they are unsure of their ability to do what is needed to improve or get a good mark again.

This self-doubt feeds into another problem: fear of failure. When students aren't sure they can repeat a previous success or can't avoid performing poorly, they begin to entertain thoughts of failure. As I discuss in chapter 10, failure is one of students' greatest fears and can lead them into dangerous territory that ultimately reduces their enjoyment and achievement at school.

You might be familiar with the term 'learned helplessness'. In the school setting, learned helplessness applies to students who have stopped trying, and in the more extreme cases have dropped out of school. One of the reasons students become like this is because they have lost their sense of control. They believe there is nothing they can do to avoid failure and so they give up trying. These students come to accept failure and helplessness as their lot in life.

You can see, then, that control is very important. The benefits of having a sense of control are optimism, hope, positive expectations, persistence and even resilience. The downside of low control is pessimism, anxiety, fear of failure and ultimately failure acceptance or helplessness.

Why do students lose their sense of control and what can we do about it?

Research shows there are common and clear reasons students lose their sense of control. Knowing these gives parents useful information about how to increase their child's sense of control. In a nutshell, the strategies you can use to increase your child's sense of control revolve around:

- the reasons your child thinks he or she succeeded or did poorly in the past
- your child's views about intelligence

- the feedback and rewards you give your child
- your expectations of your child and the boundaries set at home
- your child's input into choices and decision making.

Controllable vs uncontrollable factors in success and failure

The first reason students lose their sense of control is because they view the causes of their successes and failures as essentially external to themselves. I want you to think about the last success your child had. They may not have topped the class, but they may have done better than they've ever done before or as well as they possibly could. Why do they think they did well? My next question is: how much control do they think they had over that success? To help you think about these questions, in the table below I have listed a few common reasons students give for why they do well in school and next to each reason I indicate how controllable it is.

Controlling success at school	
Reason for doing well	Controllable?
I tried hard	YES
I practised	YES
I was lucky	NO
I planned for it	YES
I spent time figuring out the questions	YES
I made sure I presented my work well	YES
It was an easy test	NO
The teacher was a soft marker	NO

The first reason, 'I tried hard', is controllable because it is pretty much entirely up to your child how hard he or she tries.

The same goes for practice, planning and presentation. Your child is in control of these.

The third reason, 'I was lucky', is not a matter your child can control. Neither can he or she control the ease of the test, the marking or the way he or she is taught. These factors are out of your child's control. As one girl said, 'It's just her teaching style that made me do so well.'

Now, the more your child gives reasons for success that are out of his or her control the less control he or she will feel over repeating that success. So, if your child gets a good mark for a biology project and says that the teacher must have been in a good mood when she graded it, your child is likely to be uncertain as to whether he or she can repeat that success.

You might like to do the same exercise bearing in mind the last time your child didn't do well. The table below lists some reasons students commonly give for not doing well and also indicates which reasons are under students' control.

The first reason, 'I didn't try hard', is controllable because it is up to your child how much he or she tries.

Controlling poor performance at school	
Reason for doing well	Controllable?
I didn't try hard	YES
I didn't practise	YES
I was unlucky	NO
I didn't plan for it	YES
I didn't spend enough time figuring out the questions	YES
I didn't present my work very well	YES
It was a tough test	NO
The teacher was a mean marker	NO

Similarly, the second reason, 'I didn't practise', is controllable because it is up to your child how much he or she practises. The same goes for how much time he or she puts in, how much planning your child does and the effort he or she puts into presentation. Your child is in control of these factors.

The last reason, 'The teacher was a mean marker', is not something your child can control and neither can your child control the ease of the test or luck. These factors are out of your child's control.

If your child doesn't do so well and then focuses on reasons that are beyond his or her control this is likely to reduce his or her sense of control. On the other hand, if they don't do so well and focus on things within their control – such as not studying enough or not studying effectively – they are likely to feel more control over their ability to avoid failure next time.

Research clearly supports this. When students focus on factors such as luck, exam ease or difficulty, good or bad teaching and soft or tough marking, they feel less control over their ability to repeat success or avoid failure the next time they sit an exam, do an assignment or complete a project. When students focus on things like effort, practice, study skills, preparation, planning and presentation, they have a strong sense of control over their success – because they are in the driver's seat.

By now you've probably figured out the first strategy for enhancing your child's control: shifting the focus as much and as often as possible onto controllable factors in your child's life. When your child next receives a mark for a test you might like to explore their view on why they got that mark. If you hear too much emphasis on things like tough marking, bad luck, 'the teacher hates me' and the like, you will know that your child's sense of control is starting to be whittled away. Gently, and as sensitively as possible, guide the conversation towards some of the controllable things in your child's life. You might talk about improving study skills, asking you for help, getting a study buddy, spending extra time studying, engaging a tutor, studying without the radio on and typing essays rather than writing them by hand.

Now, I'm not denying that some teachers are tough markers, some teachers aren't as good as others, sometimes all the wrong questions come up on the exam paper, and sometimes the bus might break down causing your child to be late for a test – certainly these factors are all uncontrollable. Your child must hear you recognise these things when they are genuinely the case. But after listening and acknowledging their bad luck, explore how other, controllable, factors can be dealt with. Most importantly, when discussing these controllable factors, don't blame your child. Blaming and finger pointing don't necessarily improve students' motivation. Instead, be supportive and encouraging – always be helpful and constructive when searching out the more controllable aspects of your child's life.

In terms of tough marking, I know many students who take the bull by the horns and after receiving an essay question discuss with the teacher what they'll be required to do, which books would be good to read, and clarify what the question is asking. Provided this is discussed with the teacher in terms of wanting to do a good job and not just to suck up a few marks, I've found teachers are more than happy to take the time needed for clarification. Let me tell you, marking a good essay is ten times easier than marking a bad one. So if the teacher can improve the standard of essays she's receiving, she's more than happy to do so. Bottom line: teachers' grading is, to a point, uncontrollable, but there are also many controllable ways to deal with it – and motivated students do. One student told me, 'You can never justify saying a teacher is an easier or harder marker. I always find that if I put the effort in, I get the marks.'

Even 'bad teaching' doesn't faze students high in control. Talking with these students, I've found they take time to figure out 'bad' teachers' styles. If Mr Smith mumbles, they sit at the front of the room. If Ms Forsythe rattles on at breakneck speed, they develop better note-taking skills. If Mrs Frazer waffles, they learn how to select the relevant information. More generally, they listen for teacher clues. For example, when a teacher suggests the class might like to take detailed notes, that's a clue that the information is important. When a teacher says, 'This is on the test', this too is a very good clue – and one that students amazingly often ignore! Bottom line: teaching style is, to a point, uncontrollable, but there are also many controllable ways to deal with it – and motivated students do.

Mel, senior high

Mel was a great blamer, an expert at shifting responsibility away from herself and onto something or someone else. Although this may have made her feel better about herself in the short term, the ultimate cost was that she felt little control over her ability to affect outcomes. Because she felt she had little or no impact on things that had previously happened in her life, she felt little or no control over things that were happening now or would happen in the future. This was followed through in her behaviour. Believing she was at the mercy of external forces such as her teachers, exam conditions and illness, she behaved as though this was the case – not studying, not trying, and avoiding situations where she'd be evaluated.

Her saving grace was that she was sufficiently in touch with reality that she was able to see her excuses running thin and losing their effect on others around her. She saw that others no longer believed her excuses. Whether she knew it or not, she was faced with a choice: give up altogether (that is, not try at all and not even try to shift the blame elsewhere); or cop some of the responsibility for things that happened at school.

She chose the latter. She did take a bit more responsibility for things and she focused a little more on factors she had some control over (mainly how much study she did and the way she did that study). This isn't to say that she copped it all on the chin – blaming was a trademark of hers and this wasn't going to be turned around overnight. But she began to take more responsibility and began to identify her part in how things turned out. The result was that she felt a greater sense of control. More importantly, she began to behave in ways consistent with her increased control. Her parents and friends began to notice that she took on challenges and opportunities that she would have previously avoided.

Like it or not, sometimes all the wrong questions come up in an exam – even when your child has done a pretty good job of preparing. Recognise this with your child, but be emphatic that this is unlikely to happen again or at least not to the extent that it did this time. Really praise the good preparation and point out that the same level of preparation next time combined with the fact that they are unlikely to be so unlucky again should give them reason for optimism. Having said all this, you may like to gently probe how your child selected his or her study topics. Maybe they covered themselves well for the likely questions in section A but only studied for one topic in section B in the hope that it would be the topic that popped up. In doing this you are again starting to shift the focus onto the controllable factors in your child's study. Bottom line: bad luck is pretty uncontrollable, but if you dig a bit you may find that there are also some controllable ways to reduce what your child thinks is bad luck.

The bus breaking down is a real stroke of bad luck. Your child certainly had no control over that – although some parents might suspect their child was capable of sabotaging it just to get out of the test! Recognise that your child was unlucky and reassure your child that it is unlikely to happen next time. However, you might also gently suggest that catching an earlier bus could get around this risk. You might even say you'd be happy to pack the dishwasher (if it's usually their job) that morning so they can get away earlier or drive them to the bus stop to catch the earlier bus. Motivated students leave enough margin for error or mishap and would catch an earlier bus or arrange for a lift to school on the morning of a test.

The point I want to make is that there are many controllable reasons why students succeed or why they don't do so well. The more they focus on these the more control they'll feel. There are also many fuzzy or borderline reasons that may appear to be uncontrollable. You need to acknowledge the uncontrollable elements of these reasons, but gently, and without blaming your child, guide the conversation towards the improbability of it happening again. Even better, talk about the controllable ways to deal with these 'uncontrollable' factors.

Your child's view of intelligence

A second reason your child may have a low sense of control arises from his or her view of intelligence. Research has shown that students view intelligence in one of two ways. The first view is that intelligence is something that is fixed and unchangeable.

Something you're stuck with. I'll call this the fixed view of intelligence. The second view is that intelligence is something that can be improved, developed and changed. I'll call this the improvement view of intelligence.

Let's get it clear right up front. *Intelligence can be improved.* Analysis skills, problem-solving skills, critical thinking skills, decision-making skills and so on are all important parts of intelligence. All these skills are teachable and learnable and so you have every reason to encourage and promote an improvement view of intelligence at home. I'm not saying it's necessarily easy, but it is possible. It's important for students and parents to recognise this.

Think of a situation where your child gets a poor result in a subject. If your child believes the cause of that result is partly or fully his or her intelligence, *and* he or she has a fixed view of intelligence, then this can cause problems. It can reduce your child's sense of control. Why is this? Because your child believes that his or her lack of intelligence led to that result and that he or she is stuck with that level of intelligence. Therefore there's nothing he or she can do to avoid that happening again. That is, he or she has lost their sense of control.

Now let's consider the situation where your child gets a poor result in a subject, believes the cause of that result is partly or fully his or her intelligence, *and* he or she has an improvement view of intelligence. In this situation your child is likely to have a higher sense of control because he or she believes that the intelligence that led to this result can be improved – and so can the result next time round.

I've seen students' views of intelligence become either their worst enemy or one of their greatest allies. An interesting case is the student who is quite bright and gets through primary school and the early and middle years of high school without much hard work. He relies on his natural smarts and gets through on this alone. But in the senior years of high school where there's simply no getting around the fact that it takes hard and high-quality work to do well, these students can fall in a hole. Why? Because of the combination of two things: their natural smarts aren't sailing them through anymore *and* they have a fixed view of intelligence. The effect of both these is that they believe they're stuck with their poor results. They've never really had to improve their intelligence and their fixed view of it means that when the time comes that they do need to improve it, they get stuck. Essentially they feel there isn't much they can do to overcome the challenges they face. Too many bright kids simply give up at this point and achieve way below their capabilites. In a nutshell, their fixed view of intelligence has led to a low sense of control, which then feeds into helplessness.

What can you as a parent do about this? The first thing is to challenge your own beliefs and assumptions, if necessary, about intelligence. It is not something fixed and unchangeable. Countless studies show and countless teachers will tell you that students can learn to analyse information better, think more critically, become better problem solvers and develop more effective arguments. These are all components of intelligence that are central to the successful completion of essays, assignments, projects, quizzes and exams. When you work on your own assumptions you are less likely to communicate a fixed view of intelligence to your child. So, the work on this one begins with you.

Secondly, you need to listen carefully to your child if they talk about how smart they are. You may then gently explore the issue of intelligence, showing them that there are many aspects of intelligence that can be learnt and improved. Maybe you can draw on a time or situation when you developed your own intelligence in some way. You might like to talk about thinking as a skill, and note that all skills can be improved. You might also like to point out that some of the world's greatest thinkers had to work hard to get there and that this hard work actually improved their ability to analyse situations, interpret them and make sense of them – all important aspects of intelligence.

When talking to your child about intelligence you need to be careful not to communicate unrealistically high expectations. Your child can improve their intelligence, but it's not fair to tell them they can be the smartest kid in the school. Whether they can or can't, it puts immense pressure on them, and for most kids it is such an unattainable goal that they won't even try to improve their thinking skills. You will have made the mountain too big to climb. Always raise the bar just a touch ahead of where they are so they believe the goal is realistic and achievable – when they see a task this way they won't run a hundred miles. Instead, they'll give it a good bash.

Smart environments

The other day I read quite an exciting paper about intelligence. This paper proposed that intelligence does not happen in isolation. Instead, these authors suggested that how smart a person is very much depends on the context or the environment they live or operate in. Some environments really seem to bring out the best in people while other environments don't enable the person to stretch their wings and reach their potential.

This paper made a lot of sense to me because it explained why in the same subject I could perform well with one teacher and not nearly so well the next year with another teacher. One teacher created a 'smart environment' – where students were motivated to perform to their potential – the other created an environment where we weren't so smart. The same can apply to two kids of equal ability and interests from two different families. One family creates a context where a child is energised, engaged, and performing to their potential – a smart environment. The other creates a context where the child is fearful of failure, self-protective, and anxious when it comes to schoolwork – not a smart environment.

I mention this here because it is further evidence that smartness is changeable and if it is changeable then the student is not stuck with it. Importantly, the idea of a smart environment is more relevant to you than your child. It means that you and the way you create the home environment have a direct impact on your child's ability to improve themselves and reach their potential. Sure, it's not the only factor involved, but it is a factor and to this extent you should feel empowered. If you like, this entire book is about creating a smart environment at home.

The feedback you give your child

Research has shown that the type of feedback, rewards and punishment we dish out to our children can have a big impact on their sense of control. Put simply, when children know why they deserved the reward or punishment that they got, they have a greater sense of control. On the other hand, when children don't know why they were rewarded or punished, their sense of control drops. Let me explain.

Children who do a really good job on a project, get a good mark and get good feedback are receiving clear information and confirmation that what they did was on the right track and of high quality. This creates a sense of certainty about schoolwork because the child knows that by doing this, this and this, he or she will get such and such a mark and feedback. When the reward and feedback match the quality of the job, that enhances the child's sense of control and certainty about school and school-work.

Children who don't do a very good job on a project, get a low mark but get feedback on how to improve are also receiving clear information and confirmation that what they did was not on the right track and not of great quality. Even though the child doesn't like this feedback, it still gives them some sense of certainty because it tells them that if they hand in this sort of work, it will get a low mark. As awful as it sounds, this also provides a sense of control because the child knows what it takes to do poorly – and more importantly, what not to do so they won't do poorly next time.

Unfortunately, however, sometimes the reward or punishment children receive does not match the work they did. For example, it may be that sometimes their good work gets rewarded and sometimes it doesn't, or sometimes their good work might get only a very average grade and average feedback. What this does is create uncertainty in the child's mind. He or she never really knows what it takes to guarantee a good mark. That is, they have lost their sense of control. Inconsistent rewards can really reduce children's sense of control.

What do we take from this? Consistent rewards that closely match your child's performance will lay the foundation for a solid sense of control. As much as possible, try not to leave your child wondering why he or she got the particular result they did.

Closely related to consistent reward and punishment is the type of feedback you give your child. When a child does a job or task at home, parents do one of a few things. Some parents don't give their child any information about how they did the job or task. Some parents just tell their child whether they succeeded or didn't, and that's all they say. Some parents tell their child whether they succeeded or didn't and if their child didn't do so well the parents focus only on this. However, there is another group of parents that tells their child whether they succeeded or not and then talks about the things that led to that success and how to repeat the success with similar tasks. Or they talk about why the child didn't succeed and what can be learnt from that to improve next time round.

Only the last group are genuinely increasing their child's sense of control. This is because they are providing feedback to their child that is focused mostly on the task, how it was done and how to repeat their success or improve next time. The others aren't providing enough information that will help build their child's control, and some are providing no information at all.

The other thing the last group is doing is providing task-based information that helps their child do the job correctly or even better next time, whereas the other groups are providing performance-based information that tells their child how they performed but no more. You can see how one group really improves their child's sense of control whereas the others don't improve it much or at all. Whenever possible, parents need to quickly move to task-based feedback when talking with their children about how they did their schoolwork or jobs at home.

Your expectations and the boundaries at home

Even though they may not admit it, children and young people thrive on clear expectations, requirements, tasks, demands and boundaries. Although they may grumble about them, you need to be confident that clear (but fair) expectations, rules and boundaries increase your child's sense of control. When your child's world is certain and predictable, he or she has a greater sense of control.

What do I mean by clear expectations, rules and boundaries? When you ask your child to do something, be clear about what you are asking them to do and if necessary give some guidance about how to do it. When you are discussing what you expect of them in the next term at school, make sure you have clear, specific and easily identifiable standards that they can relate to and that they can realistically achieve.

I suggest you don't emphasise specific grades or marks too much, because a specific mark runs the risk of being too hit or miss. They either get that mark (or better) or they don't. Instead, I suggest you talk about your expectations for controllable actions like the amount and quality of study your child does.

Research shows that there are different parenting styles, one of which is called the permissive parenting style. With these parents it doesn't matter whether you do your homework or not, study or not, or even whether you turn up to school or not. There is not a great deal of clarity in these children's lives, no clear boundaries, and because of this the children of permissive parents don't have a strong sense of control – the only predictable thing about the world is its uncertainty.

Now I'm not suggesting you rule your child with an iron fist. Instead, you can be the authority figure your child needs in order to develop a sense of security, but be flexible and confident enough to negotiate some rules, expectations and boundaries with your child. Your child will genuinely appreciate you listening to them, respecting their opinions, and giving them a say in how they live their life. This brings me to the final way to enhance your child's sense of control: giving them choices and teaching them to be effective and responsible decision makers.

Choices and decision making

When I talk to teachers about ways they can enhance their students' sense of control I encourage them to try negotiating (within sensible limits) with their students things like essay topics, due dates and even marking criteria. When they do this, teachers are often pleasantly surprised to find that students have sensible ideas about things teachers should look for when marking an assignment. Teachers who are confident enough to loosen the reins a bit, but in a structured and clearly defined area, are doing a number of great things.

First, they empower the students. Too often students feel they're at the mercy of the teacher or school policy and this does nothing to increase their sense of control.

Secondly, they give students a sense of ownership and with it, often, a greater sense of responsibility, both of which are fundamental to a sense of control.

Thirdly, they teach their students how to make responsible and effective choices and decisions. Young people today seem to be faced with more choices than we had as kids. It may be our greatest gift to them to develop their ability to make effective choices and decisions. For example, we don't have much control over whether our children are going to be offered drugs. But what we can do is develop our children's ability to make sensible and responsible choices and decisions about their life, their health and their behaviour.

Parents also have many opportunities to involve students in choices and decision making. Allow your child some input into study times, study conditions, study buddies, subject choices and extra curricular activities. But don't forget that their input needs to have boundaries. If given a choice to do some or no study, many children will opt for no study. Whether they do study or not is not in fact an option. A good idea is for you to define the acceptable ballpark and for your child to be able to make some decisions and choices within that ballpark. For example, you might insist your child does three hours study on the weekend, but your child can choose when to put in the three hours. Or you might insist your child selects at least one science subject in senior high but he or she can choose whether it is physics, chemistry, biology or general science.

They'll get their sense of control anywhere they can

When discussing self-belief in the previous chapter I made the point that a sense of worth is so important to young people that if they don't get it in their studies or at home they'll get it somewhere else. My view is that the same goes for a sense of control. During the teenage years in particular there are many emotional, physical, intellectual, and social changes going on, and the big wide world and the choices within it seem to grow at an unbelievable rate. Teenagers who have a sense of control seem to fare better in all this apparent chaos.

Some teenagers seize control in very positive ways. They'll study, they'll exercise, and they'll seek help when they need it. However, for some teenagers who can't or won't seize control in these positive ways – maybe because they're caught in a repetitive cycle of underachievement – they'll get it in other ways. Eating disorders quickly spring to mind when thinking about teenagers' need for control. Juvenile offending is another. Indeed, research into juvenile offending is starting to look at teenagers' need for success and control and how some of them get it through crime or delinquency. I want to recount a story that touches on some of these things but which has a happy outcome mainly because the teenagers involved gained a sense of control over their lives.

I worked on a research project a couple of years ago that looked at some of the successful ways schools and community centres were helping young people who were at extreme risk of going off the rails. I remember one school in particular that was doing a great job of keeping some really tough kids at their studies. In this neighbourhood there was quite a high youth homelessness rate and these homeless young people tended to cause quite a bit of trouble in the area. They took a particular liking to some vacant housing, which they regularly vandalised and graffitied. The local school, led by an innovative and confident bunch of teachers and principal, asked the council to grant them a lease on the land so they could develop an off-site school campus there. They recruited the homeless young people, enrolled them back at school, and gave them the task of renovating the housing to be their own accommodation. Very cleverly, the school hooked into the local technical college and made sure that the skills the young people were developing in renovating their accommodation were documented so that they could gain a certificate that could be used as part completion of an apprenticeship. The kids responded so well they went on to open an internet café at the site and started gaining skills in hospitality and small business as well.

This whole exercise enhanced all the boosters I identified earlier. It increased students' self-belief, their value of schooling and their focus on the task. It also required them to plan, manage their work, monitor their progress and persist in the face of difficulty and challenge. But on top of all this, what struck me most was the sense of control these young people were developing in their lives. With appropriate guidance and support, these young people:

- decided what was to be renovated and how to go about it
- budgeted for materials and bought them

- made mistakes and were clearly shown why they happened and how to avoid them next time
- were constantly given task-based feedback
- were clearly shown that their skills and abilities could be improved
- were given choices in the rules and duties set for them and the consequences for meeting them or not meeting them were clear and consistent.

Up to this point these students felt little control in their lives. They were at the mercy of the police, the social security office and the world in general. Previously, they had seized control by antisocial means: through vandalism, graffiti, other crime and substance abuse. In the space of six to twelve months these students had become empowered and had gained a sense of control. As the list above shows, the reasons for this were clear.

Living in the real world

In the real world not everything happens like they say in the books. Here are a few things for you to think about when digesting this chapter.

- Your child's sense of control can vary from day to day and subject to subject. Don't freak out if they seem helpless sometimes – this can happen when things are a bit uncertain for them. If their helplessness becomes more ongoing and is creeping into other parts of their life, then you might want to give more emphasis to the strategies in this section. If the helplessness is still ongoing after your best attempts, maybe seek some help from a psychologist or counsellor who works well with young people.
- Research has found that a sense of control can be as effective as actual control. A sense of control is your child's belief that if they try they can soon be in control. So, control starts with the belief that they can get control.
- Some things you think are controllable your child might not. You might have to accept this and find some things that both of you agree are within their control. Avoid

getting into the blaming game – kids don't respond well to blame and it's not a basis for healthy motivation.

- Even after you agree on what's controllable, your child may resist taking control. Stick to your guns and look for opportunities to draw your child's attention to these controllable things (without beating them over the head with them).

- When looking at the things that caused your child's poor performance, don't attack or blame him or her as a person. Stick to talking about the situation and their behaviour and not about personal characteristics of your child (such as being lazy or hopeless).

- I should make the point that this chapter on control is not designed to create a generation of control freaks. Control freaks often make the mistake of trying to control things that are either uncontrollable or are so difficult to control that their time would be far better spent focusing on things more controllable or more directly relevant to the task at hand. Control is about focusing on what's controllable and which is also likely to lead to success within a reasonable period of time.

- In situations where things have been beyond your child's control (such as bad luck or bad test questions), before racing into what controllable things they could have done, fully listen to your child. In such situations they need sympathy and sensitivity. Really recognise and accept that it was bad luck and unfortunate for your child.

- When encouraging an improvement view of intelligence, I'm not suggesting you lead your child to think that they can be the top of the class. Maybe he or she can be the top of the class, but the focus should be on improvement and personal bests – goals that are realistic, believable and achievable. If your child gets to the top of the class along the way, good luck to you and them – but this shouldn't be the main or only focus.

- There are some aspects of intelligence that are more changeable than others. For example, improving an ability to solve maths problems may be easier for some children than others. Know your child, know which areas they are likely to improve in and set realistic goals that are a nudge ahead of where they are now – goals that are achievable and believable, but which move them forward.

- You're human and so you're probably not going to reward and punish your child consistently and effectively 100 per cent of the time. This does not mean you should give up trying. Aim to improve your own ability to effectively reward, punish and give feedback on things your child does.
- Sometimes you can't provide detailed task-based feedback. The usual reason is that you simply don't have enough time. This is fine – just look for opportunities whenever you can.
- There are some situations or decisions to be made where your child's input isn't appropriate or should be limited. If you show your child that in most cases their input is valued (particularly on things that affect them) and that you look for opportunities to listen to their opinion on things, they are more likely to respect your decision not to involve them on those few occasions.
- Similarly, there may be situations where you have the most say in the matter. Explain your reasons for this and look for ways to take on board your child's views. In doing this your child is more likely to respect your final decision.

Chapter summary

This chapter has focused on the importance of a child's sense of control. Control is your child's belief that he or she can repeat success and improve on a poor result. When your child has a sense of control over these things he or she feels optimistic and is more likely to hang in there when things get difficult or challenging. This is because they believe they have what it takes to overcome this challenge. On the downside, if your child doesn't feel much control over whether they can repeat success or improve on a bad result, they can feel pessimistic and helpless. When this happens they run the risk of giving up because they believe there's not much they can do to influence their results, so what's the point in trying?

It's also important to mention here that the combination of self-belief (see chapter 3) and control is one of the most powerful motivation cocktails available to students. When you hear your child say something like, 'I know that I can do it and I know how to do it,' you know they are really ready to get stuck into their schoolwork and are also likely to do well. Basically, when they say something along these lines they are saying, 'I have self-belief and I have control.'

The good news is that research has identified a number of reasons children lose their sense of control, and by identifying the reasons we are in a good position to tackle the problem. We need to encourage children to focus on the controllable aspects of why they succeeded or did not succeed, encourage them to develop an improvement view of intelligence, give them clear task-based feedback, reward them consistently and allow them to have input into decisions that affect them. All these things give children a sense of certainty and security and enhance their control.

CHAPTER FOUR TOP 5

1. In addition to self-belief, a child's sense of control is one of the most important parts of motivation. A child who is in control knows how to repeat his or her successes and also knows how to improve on poor results. This leads to optimism and persistence when things get tough.

2. You increase your child's control by emphasising the controllable things in your child's life and taking the focus away from the uncontrollable things in your child's life. The things your child can control and which also lead to better schoolwork include hard work, practice, presentation, planning, preparation, study skills, time management, organisation and so on.

3. Your child's view of intelligence can reduce his or her sense of control. Encourage the improvement view of intelligence which holds that intelligence can be improved through developing better skills in thinking, critical analysis, interpretation and problem solving.

4. Parents can build their child's control by rewarding, praising or punishing in consistent ways that match what the child did. The child needs to develop a sense that by doing this, this and this they will get such and such a reward (or punishment). When giving feedback to children on things they do it is best to focus on the task, what they did and how they did it as much as or more than on the outcome, the grade or mark.

5. Your child gains a sense of control, empowerment and ownership when they have input into the things that affect their life. This also builds effective decision-making skills – a very precious commodity in this age of seemingly limitless (good and bad) choices on offer.

CHAPTER 5

INCREASING YOUR CHILD'S BELIEF IN THE VALUE OF SCHOOL

There is no doubting the fact that when we believe that what we do is important, useful, relevant or has a purpose, we tend to be more interested in it, we tend to spend more time on it and we tend to do a better job on it. If we believe our job is useful and relevant then we tend to enjoy it, turn up on time for it, stay in it longer, do higher quality work, enjoy learning new things in it and aren't too fearful of new demands and challenges within it. Essentially, our belief in the value of our job has a really big impact on our whole experience of that job.

All of this also applies to school. When your child has a belief in the value of school, his or her experience of school is a happier and more stimulating one. The same applies to particular school subjects. When your child believes in the value of particular subjects, studying them is a happier and more stimulating experience.

Students who believe in the value of school

Students who believe in the value of school or the subjects they study believe one or more of the following:

- what they do in one subject is relevant to other subjects they study
- what they do in one lesson is related to what they do in other lessons
- what they do at school is relevant to their lives now, either in their part-time job, at home or in their hobby
- what they do at school is relevant to their lives further down the track, either at university, in their apprenticeship or in the job they want when they leave school
- what they do at school is relevant to the world as a whole
- what they do at school develops their thinking and analysis skills which help in other parts of their life, such as work or time with friends
- what they do at school gives variety so they can select the subjects to focus on in senior school, at college or at university
- what they do at school develops their people skills, and that is useful beyond their school years.

In reality, students who value school may not think all these things about school, but they'll certainly think some of them – enough to give them a sense that going to school is not such a bad thing. I should add that seeing school as a place to socialise and have fun with friends also reflects a value of school – but an ideal belief in the value of school would also include at least a couple of the other points in the list above.

In the previous chapter I discussed how researchers have found that students who are high in self-belief and who also have a sense of control tend to be more motivated and do better. Researchers have also suggested that students who value school or what they study and who also have a belief that they can do okay in it are more motivated than students who don't believe in the value of school or in themselves. So again we see the boosters don't work separately – instead, they work together, which is why it's important to look at more than just self-belief or just the value of school.

Students who don't believe in the value of school

Talking to students I often hear them say that they see school or the subjects they study as totally unrelated to anything they're interested in, anything they do now or anything they might do in the future. One girl told me, 'I'd give up a lot easier than most people. I'm not going to lock myself in a room twenty-four hours a day, seven days a week trying to master something that won't have a bearing on my future.'

These students see school as something separate from other parts of their life. Their view of school implies that it is a vacuum which they get sucked into in the morning, where they exist in dead space for six to seven hours and then get dumped out of at the end of the day. Others see school as a production line or sausage factory that trains them for sitting for a final exam and nothing else. For others school is a place to have fun with friends and nothing more. As I suggested earlier, socialising with friends contributes to the value of school but there needs to be a bit more than this to increase motivation in the classroom or to study at home each night. When school or schoolwork is seen in these ways, students are not interested in being there. As one boy told me, 'If you're not interested, then you don't learn and don't do as well as you should, whereas if you're interested in that subject then you'll say, "I like this and I'm going to study for it."'

Different types of valuing

In fact there are different types of valuing. First, there is 'achievement value'. This refers to the importance of doing well on a task or activity. For students high in achievement value, simply getting a good mark is enough for them to be motivated. Second, there is 'usefulness value'. This refers to how much of what students do or learn at school is useful to their life now or their future. Third, there is 'satisfaction value'. This relates to how much of what students do and learn at school is enjoyable, satisfying, interesting, and worthwhile. I'm quite a practical person and I'll take any sort of valuing if it will hook students into school. However, if I were to pick one, I'd aim for satisfaction value. Satisfaction value is more likely to yield the most enjoyment and delight in your child as he or she moves through the school years. However, I say again,

I'm happy with any sort of valuing and it is for this reason that I address all three in this chapter.

Why don't students value school?

There are reasons students believe that school is not very important or useful. As usual, knowing the reason something happens gives us a good idea about how to deal with it. Generally, the value your child places on school will depend on:

- your own belief in the value of school
- developing a broader view of the purpose of school
- actively linking school to your child's life
- being reasonably flexible about the school subjects your child studies.

Your own belief in the value of school

I don't have to tell you that your child watches the things you do and uses those observations to make choices and behave in particular ways – through doing much the same as you, doing the opposite to you or behaving somewhere between the two. To varying degrees your child learns attitudes, beliefs and behaviours from you in ways that are obvious and also in ways that are not so obvious. In fact, even the way they act as parents in twenty or thirty years time will be at least partly based on the way you parent them.

Your child's belief in the value of school is no exception. As an educational researcher I have witnessed first-hand the students from homes that do not value education and as a result are unmotivated, or in the more extreme cases are at risk of dropping out or being expelled. But don't be too quick to sink the boot into their parents. When researchers dig into the parents' own experience of school they trace a history of poor performance, repeated failure, helplessness, punishment as a result of these and inadequate attention to their particular needs, be they reading difficulties, numeracy troubles and so on. For many of these parents, school let them down and their own parents may not have had the resources, knowledge or skills to address their difficulties. So began what researchers call the 'intergenerational transfer of education values'.

What's the message here? Your own belief in the value of school is the starting point to building your child's belief in the value of school. Your valuing of school is communicated to your child in obvious and direct ways as well as some subtle and indirect ways. Some direct ways you foster a value of school in the home include:

- showing genuine interest in your child's study and schoolwork
- arranging the home environment so that quality time and space can be dedicated to your child's schoolwork
- going to parent–teacher nights
- taking what teachers say seriously and paying attention to school newsletters (and the like)
- spending time with your child in the early years, reading or working through arithmetic problems
- being quick to respond to problems in schoolwork by helping your child or getting some tutoring for your child
- spending time to have respectful conversations with your child about subject choice
- making sure your child has the books and materials needed to do his or her schoolwork
- seeing all your child's school subjects as important.

Some more indirect ways you communicate your belief in the value of school include:

- participating on school committees or at school fetes and the like
- doing a bit of sport coaching or getting involved in work experience and the like
- making sure your child gets to school on time – or making sure your child goes to school in the first place
- delaying the family holiday until the school term has finished and not assuming the last week of school is unimportant.

These are just a few of the ways that you communicate your belief in the value of school. There are many more. Taken together, they raise the following questions: Is school important to you and one of your highest priorities for your child? Or, are you pretty much uninterested in what happens there? Or perhaps your interest lasts only while it's convenient or until something better comes along?

If you answered yes to one or both of the last two questions then it will be more difficult for your child to develop a belief in the value of school.

The purpose of school

Your view of the purpose of school is another way you communicate your belief in the value of school to your child. Here are some reasons parents give for going to school, and their children often give pretty much the same reasons:

- to learn how to learn and think
- to learn things that can be used later – at university, in training or as part of a job
- to prepare the child for later life – at university, training or in a job
- to make friends and learn how to get along with people
- to learn how to do different things – study, play sport, play music, paint or sculpt
- to learn how to be responsible, organised and prepared.

These sorts of reasons for going to school tend to increase your child's belief in the value of school. This is because they all serve a purpose that your child sees is useful. These reasons tell children that school is getting them somewhere, improving them and keeping them interested.

I want you to compare the list above with the following list of reasons other parents (and students) give for going to school:

- to get as good a final mark as possible
- to get into university
- to keep children busy during the day
- to keep children busy until they're old enough for work
- to beat other students in exams
- to keep children off the streets or out of trouble.

These views on the purpose of school run the risk of children seeing school as:

- a sausage factory
- a dog-eat-dog place of winners and losers
- a place that is only a means to an end
- a place where you wait until real life begins
- a place that simply stops children from being bad or getting into trouble.

Students who don't believe school has much value talk about it in these sorts of ways and you can see how this sort of talk stems from their views on the purpose of school – and often these views stem from what their parents think about school.

But who am I kidding? Of course school is very much about getting marks and getting into university and so on. Certainly, parents and students who hold the view that school is about these sorts of things are quite right. However, what I suggest is that with some small adjustment you can develop more motivating reasons for going to school. For example, in the first list I mentioned that school is about *preparing* students for university. Compare this to the view that school is about *getting in* to university. There's a subtle but really important difference here. One focuses on school as a process and learning experience whereas the other runs the risk of turning school into a sausage factory. The first view ascribes a really meaningful value to school whereas the other view regards school as little more than a ticket to ride. So even though the second list might well be true to a point, it is more helpful to develop reasons along the lines of the first list if you wish to encourage a more meaningful and motivating belief in the value of school.

What I am saying here is that when we view the process of school as very important and not just the outcomes, we are also laying the ground for a more meaningful and motivating belief in the value of school. What do I mean by *process* and *outcomes*? The process of school refers to the learning, skill development, new understanding and improvement that happen along the way. The outcomes of school refer to the marks students get as a consequence of the process.

Students who have a belief in the value of school tend to focus on the process as much as or maybe more than the outcomes. For them the journey is the destination. This is not to deny that the marks they get aren't important. Of course they are. But I have noticed that motivated students see their marks not so much as the final outcome but as information that tells them about the journey. That is, the marks are information they use to tell them about their learning, problem solving and understanding. Their results or marks are a guidepost or an indicator of success and their learning and understanding are the actual success. I discuss this at length in the next chapter (on developing a learning focus) and also show that students who focus on the journey actually end up doing better. So, in fact, what I'm suggesting here does not harm students' results – it improves them.

Actively linking school to your child's life

'What's this got to do with anything?' How often do teachers and parents hear students pose this (quite reasonable) question? In research that asks students about their views on the purpose of school, one of students' biggest complaints is that school isn't relevant to their lives.

How do you hook school into your child's life? You can do it in one or more of the following ways:

- identify the usefulness of what your child studies to day-to-day issues, situations, challenges or problems
- link what your child learns at school with opportunities in their life
- draw connections between what your child learns at school and world events
- link skills developed by your child in one subject with what he or she does in other subjects
- explore skills your child learns at school that can be used to help him or her make better decisions in life

Identify the usefulness of your child's studies

Looking back at some of the subjects I studied at school I only now realise that they had an impact on ways I dealt with situations in my life at that time. For example, in general studies learning how to see two (or more) sides of an argument and then drawing a sensible conclusion helped in resolving conflict with my friends. See if anything your child does at school can help in similar ways. Can you think of ways school helped you in parts of your life?

Link learning with opportunities

If you look carefully, lots can be taken from school to help your child create opportunities in life. For example, principles learnt in commerce or business studies can help your child set up and market a rock band. Information picked up in physical education and health subjects can be used to help your child's netball team prepare for the finals. History can sow the seeds for your child's decision about which countries to visit when they do the big world trip later in life. Religious studies may stimulate your child to strike up conversation with a Hindu classmate – it may be the start of a friendship that lasts for life.

School is a place of diverse opportunities. Parents need to be mindful of these opportunities and bring them to their children's attention in enthusiastic and attractive ways. You need to realise that your child will not always make obvious connections between what they study and what they may do in the future or what happens in the world. For example, in my view history has much to tell us about what to do and what not to do, not only on a national and global scale, but also in our own lives. I was surprised to hear one girl say, 'What's history really going to do for us? I have no idea why we need to know about the past. Is that going to help us in the future? I think we should have something more relevant to the future – not the past.' In this situation, the onus is on teachers and parents to make links clear and logical. This means explaining **how** history can inform the world and our lives, not just saying **that** history informs the world and our lives.

Draw connections between your child's studies and world events

Which school subjects can help your children better understand September 11? History, religious studies, geography perhaps? The gap between rich and poor or Third World debt? History, economics? The world's population in 2050? Maths? Salinity problems in rural areas? Science, geography? The price of petrol? Economics? The 2002 World Cup? Geography, Japanese, German? Censorship in the media or of music CDs? Art, English, religious studies? How to design web pages? Information technology studies? Native title claims? Legal studies, Aboriginal studies, history? If we take the time, we'll find that every school subject provides students with a better understanding of the big

Samantha, middle high

Samantha was a student who spent most of her life in the middle of the pack but who was performing to her potential and so therefore could be considered success oriented. You'll remember that being success oriented does not necessarily mean being at the top of the class. Rather, it means achieving to one's potential, being engaged, and enjoying school and schoolwork. Probably Samantha's greatest motivational asset was her belief that school was important and involved interesting work. She had a great ability to see connections between what she learnt and other things in the world or in her life.

Her history assignment on China was a great example. Students were required to submit a major piece of research on an Asian country. She focused on China because she didn't know much about that country (real low fear of failure here – embracing challenge, not shrinking from it). She was sustained throughout this major piece of work by focusing on elements of the assignment that hooked into her interests. She was interested in travelling after she completed school and she focused on parts of China that she thought she'd like to visit. She had an inquiring mind when it came to philosophy-related ideas and concepts in Confucianism really seemed to reflect ways she approached things in her own life. She also used the flexible assessment criteria as an ideal opportunity to build some skills in website design (this is what she wanted to do after completing school) and developed a mock up of a website to present the assignment.

Her valuing of school stemmed from the core principles of linking schoolwork into her interests and things she might do after completing school. School for her was not a vacuum unconnected from the rest of the world. Essentially, she had hooked school into her present life and her future ambitions. This gave it purpose and relevance and motivated her.

issues facing the world. When students see this, school is no longer a stand-alone vacuum that has no relationship to anything else. It is a place connected to the world, and this increases your child's belief in its relevance.

Link skills developed in one subject to other subjects
Sometimes it's not just school that's unconnected to the world or students' lives. Many students firmly believe that the subjects they study aren't connected to each other. So, not only is school a vacuum but the subjects within it are stand-alone, isolated vacuums too. On the other hand, when your child sees connections between subjects, these subjects immediately become more meaningful and useful. There's a reason to study the subject over and above the fact that your child has to study six subjects in senior high to get through to university or college. Schools are now recognising this and government education departments are developing what are called 'cross-curriculum statements'. These statements require schools to see a student's collection of subjects as a package, and to develop skills across subjects and make links between subjects as much as possible.

As a parent, also, you can recognise and show your child that across their range of subjects they learn new things about topics as diverse as:

- the environment
- skills needed for work
- dealing with technology and the speed of technological change
- dealing with and analysing information
- writing better
- working with people
- gender and issues relevant to men and women.

When students see their school subjects come together as a package that builds skills and knowledge, they have a better sense that the subjects are meaningful, useful and relevant. That is, they have a greater belief in the value of school.

Explore skills your child can use to make decisions
My view is that young people have more choices available to them than I did. I also hold the view that in many ways they have more pressures and challenges than I did. School has a lot of impact on how they make effective decisions and choices in the face of these challenges and situations. One girl told me, 'School's the dress rehearsal you need for the rest of your life.'

As much as we may like to, we can't stop the world reaching into our child's life. The internet exists and even if we aren't connected at home, schools are and so are our child's friends. Drug dealers hang around train stations, and even if we drop our kids at school they're encountered perhaps at shopping centres or in amusement arcades. Alcohol is accessible to young people even though you might not have any at home. Like it or not, sex is an option for teenagers no matter how much we keep a close eye on our children and their girlfriends or boyfriends. Bottom line: you can't structure the world so that your child doesn't face any temptation or tough life decisions. So what do you do?

First, of course, you can set sensible limits on your children if only to demonstrate your own principles on the matter. You may clearly communicate your views and expectations on drugs and alcohol, you may make sure an adult is in the house when your son and his girlfriend are there, you don't accept all-night partying, and you may restrict access to particular sites on the internet at home.

Secondly, before, during and maybe after these limits are set you also teach your child to be a good decision maker – this is the best defence against the world's nasties. You can't stop the world from knocking at your child's door, but you can have an impact on whether your child opens the door, to whom and on what basis.

The previous chapter on building your child's control discussed the value of giving your child some input into matters that affect his or her life. This builds decision-making skills. Your children also watch you making decisions and choices and learn from this. You should explain to them why you make the decisions you do: outline the pros and cons and why you went with one course of action rather than another. You might like to ask your children what they would have done in a similar situation.

Finally – and getting back to my original point – school has a very big impact on your child's decision-making skills. School is a place where your child has the opportunity to learn how to think, look at alternative courses of action and solve problems. Talk with your child about this. You might like to draw on your own experience. For example, talk about how one teacher really got you thinking about other parts of the world and inspired you to travel after university, or got you interested in how parts of a machine worked and set you on the path to becoming a diesel mechanic or an engineer.

Being flexible about the subjects your child studies

Increasingly, schools are doing a better job of making school more relevant to different groups of students. When I was at school most of the subjects available were academic subjects, and by the time you were in senior high they were pretty much all academic. What I mean by academic subjects are those traditional, bookish-type subjects that require a lot more thinking than doing – subjects like maths, English, history, economics and so on. At best, you got a few days of work experience in middle high school.

More and more these days vocational subjects are offered at school, even in senior high. More and more, schools are linking what students do to the community, the world of work and training organisations. Vocational subjects include business studies, information technology studies, hospitality, legal studies and so on. Having these subjects available to students means that a larger part of school is relevant to the world of work and further training, and is therefore seen as useful. This gives students a reason to be at school. One boy told me, 'I reckon it's just good knowing that you are working to get yourself a decent job and a decent lifestyle and things. Like if you didn't come to school, you'd be nowhere.' What this has also meant is that more students stay on to senior high school, and given the research showing that staying at school is a good predictor of positive events later in life, this vocational curriculum is also having a long-term impact simply by keeping kids at school.

Unfortunately, these vocational subjects have had an image problem. Many students don't respect them as much as the academic subjects. The assumption is that if you study these subjects you're not smart enough to study the academic ones. Hopefully this belief is changing as more students study vocational subjects. Another problem is that many parents also don't value vocational subjects as much as academic subjects. Students' choices of school subjects should not be diminished in this way.

Of course, the opposite can be the case. Some parents do not value academic subjects as much as vocational subjects and think that studying history is a waste of time compared with something like business studies. Again, students' choices in school subjects should not be diminished in this way.

My advice is that as a general rule if your child shows an interest in a school subject, don't stand in the way. If your child is interested in a subject, the confidence and control gained in that subject can have a knock-on effect in other areas. Finding out that you can prepare a balance sheet for business studies increases confidence in numbers generally, and who knows, maybe your daughter will stick at a maths problem ten minutes longer than she normally would.

I used the words 'as a general rule' because there are always exceptions, and a balanced subject choice may mean that your child has more options available than if all their subjects are academic or pretty much all vocational.

The message from all of this is:

- respect your child's choice of subjects
- be flexible about the subjects he or she can study
- if your child shows an interest in a subject, take this very seriously and have very good reasons for deciding to override that preference
- if you are concerned your child's choices are not balanced or that the choices may significantly limit his or her options, aim to negotiate to a point where things are minimally acceptable to you (that is, you might not love the idea but you can live with it).

Living in the real world

In the real world not everything happens like they say in the books. Here are a few things for you to think about when digesting this chapter.

- Don't expect your child to value school 100 per cent of the time or value every subject – or at least don't expect it to happen too quickly. Start small. If there is a valuing of any aspect of school that's a great starting point. If your child never comes to value any other aspect of school, thank goodness there was at least something about school that gave them a reason to be there – this is more than some kids can say for school.

- Don't expect your child to value school as much as you do. Remember that the longer we're out of school the more fondly many of us look back on it. Your child hasn't got the luxury of thirty years hindsight – they're still in the thick of it!

- There may well be some subjects that you don't value much. They may be academic or vocational. Keep this to yourself, but remember to listen when your child whinges about them. Just don't add fuel to the fire.

- Don't be a broken record when going on about the value of school; your child will get sick of you glorifying it. Choose your windows of opportunity when talking about the value of school or particular subjects within it.

- Remember that sometimes you have to live with what's minimally acceptable – you may not like some subject choices your child makes, but you can live with them. Sometimes bigger battles are won by giving a bit of smaller ground.

- Remember that sometimes your child has to live with what's minimally acceptable – he or she may not want to do a particular subject, but they can live with it. Sometimes they can get a bit of leeway in other areas of their life by doing something you want them to do.

- Some subjects are very hard to relate to the real world and your child may question their relevance. This is a tough one and may be a case where a 'grin and bear it' approach to these subjects is the only realistic option available.

Chapter summary

This chapter has focused on how important it is for students to have a belief in the value of school. Students who believe school is useful, relevant, meaningful and interesting tend to enjoy being there, are more enthusiastic and persist when things get tough. They will also carry this valuing of education into their own children's lives. There are some clear ways to increase your child's belief in the value of school which not only require you to check your own beliefs about school and its purpose, but also to link school to your child's life now or his or her life further down the track whenever possible, and to take a broad and supportive view of the subjects he or she wants to study.

CHAPTER FIVE TOP 5

1. Your child's belief in the value of school is the extent to which he or she thinks school is useful, relevant, meaningful and interesting.

2. You increase your child's belief in the value of school by first looking at your own view of school. You'd be amazed at the many ways parents unknowingly pass on their own attitudes and beliefs about school.

3. Developing a broader view of the purpose of school is important. Although schools are a place where marks are gained to get into a job or university they are also so much more. Very important life skills are learnt there, lifelong friendships are made there, choices in sporting and hobby involvement may never be wider and opportunities to test new ideas and understanding are ever present.

4. Always look for ways to link school to world events generally, topical current affairs, other parts of your child's life, and your child's ability to make better decisions in life.

5. Recognise and respect the diversity of subjects on offer to students today. Recognise and respect your child's preferences because your child's interest in school-related things is precious and can have some great knock-on effects in other parts of his or her schooling. Learn how to recognise and then live with what is minimally acceptable to you – this means you might not love some subjects your child wants to do at school but you can live with them.

CHAPTER 6

INCREASING YOUR CHILD'S LEARNING FOCUS

When doing their schoolwork, some students focus on doing the job as well as they can and direct most or all of their attention to getting it done. Other students are mainly focused on what mark they'll get, how their schoolwork will be judged by the teacher and how they compare with other students. The difference I'm describing here is the difference between a *learning focus* and a *performance (or competition) focus*.

Students who are *learning focused* are mainly focused on:

- doing the schoolwork
- developing new skills
- improvement
- personal bests
- understanding new things
- doing a good job for its own sake and not just for rewards.

Students who are *performance or competition* focused are mainly focused on:

- how their schoolwork will be evaluated or judged

- the marks they will get
- how they compare with other students
- doing better than other students
- knowing more than other students.

Students who are *learning focused* tend to enjoy school, be enthusiastic in class and study, be reasonably relaxed in their study, persist when things get challenging and get better marks.

Students who are *performance or competition focused* are more likely to find school stressful, pay less attention to their schoolwork, are more anxious, fear failure and don't do as well as learning-focused students.

Because of this, we want to increase our child's learning focus and reduce our child's performance focus.

But isn't competition a good thing?

When I describe these two types of students to parents and teachers, many are surprised to learn that a performance or competition focus is not such a good thing. Some of the questions they ask me include:

- Doesn't competition bring out the best in students?
- Wouldn't students stop trying if there was no competition?
- Isn't competition energising?
- Don't students need competition to stay interested?

'Not necessarily' is the answer to all these questions.

I will later describe the parts of competition that are okay to keep and how students can cope better with competition. But first let me explain some of the problems of competition.

Performance- or competition-focused students don't pay enough attention to schoolwork. This is because part or a lot of their attention is focused on things that aren't central to schoolwork, such as how they compare with other students, how the schoolwork will be marked and whether they know enough to pass. The more their minds fan around thinking about all these things the less they can focus on doing the schoolwork. Students who don't pay enough attention to their schoolwork don't do so well. On the other hand, most of learning-focused students' attention is on doing the job. This means they tend to do better schoolwork.

Secondly, performance- or competition-focused students have a narrow view of success. They view success as getting better marks than other students, being the top of the class, knowing more than other students or being the best. Students who see success in this way make it very hard for themselves to succeed. Like it or not, only a few students can get to the top of the pack – this means that most of the class 'fail'. One girl said to me, 'You try your hardest to do something, but there's always someone ahead of you.' When students cut themselves off from success like this, their self-belief and control start to drop and their fear of failure starts to rise. Another girl said, 'There's a particular class that's very competitive against each other. They have to do better than one another and they get really upset if they don't get in the top five.' This can lead them to stop trying. On the other hand, learning-focused students have a broad view of success. Sure, their view of success includes getting good marks but they also see success in terms of learning new things, improving, reaching personal bests and developing new skills. Because these can be achieved by anyone, learning-focused students open up more opportunities for success and this feeds straight into a healthy self-belief and a sense of control.

Thirdly, performance- or competition-focused students tend to have a view of intelligence that can make life more difficult for themselves. They have a fixed view of intelligence. In chapter 4, I defined a fixed view of intelligence as one in which intelligence can't be improved – you're stuck with how smart you are. So, when competitive students don't do so well, they run the risk of feeling helpless because they don't think they can improve their thinking, analysis or problem-solving skills (all aspects of intelligence). On the other hand, learning-focused students have an improvement view of intelligence – for example, by improving thinking skills, analysis skills and problem-solving skills. This means that learning-focused students are more optimistic and hopeful.

Finally, when competitive students don't do well at school they tend to blame their lack of intelligence whereas learning-focused students tend to blame things like the effort they put in and their study skills. Because competitive students see their intelligence as fixed they don't feel they have much control over improving next time – because their lack of intelligence is the reason they screwed up and they are stuck with their lack of intelligence. On the other hand, because learning-focused students focus on effort and study skills (which are within their control), they respond to a poor performance much better than competitive students – they respond with optimism, hope, control and persistence.

These are the main ways that competition is not such a great thing. But before you throw competition out the window, I want to make three points:

- competition can be energising if developed by parents and teachers in particular ways
- there are many students who don't have a problem with competition
- competition is a reality of life and students need to be prepared to deal with it.

Later in the chapter I talk about how to:

- encourage friendly and supportive competition and discourage dog-eat-dog competition
- help your child cope better with competition
- take the helpful parts of competition and leave the unhelpful parts.

But first, let's look at how to increase your child's learning focus.

Six ways to increase your child's learning focus

A learning focus is a very effective and positive alternative to a performance or competition focus. There are six direct ways to increase your child's learning focus. They are:

- increasing the emphasis on personal bests
- reducing comparisons with other children
- arousing curiosity whenever possible
- encouraging active learning
- recognising the journey as much as the destination
- focusing on effort and strategy more than ability or intelligence.

Increasing the emphasis on personal bests

I've mentioned personal bests a couple of times. They are very important because they are achievable for all students. A student gets a personal best when their level of performance, skill or knowledge is higher than or is as good as their previous best level of performance, skill or knowledge.

Focusing on personal bests is a very clever strategy because although the student focuses on his or her own standards and performance, it also evokes the sort of energy that friendly competition can provide. This is because the student competes with himself or herself. Personal bests provide a great way to get the most out of a learning focus and yet capture the best of a performance or competition focus.

I've found that students really like the idea of personal bests. They feel a bit like an academic athlete racing against themselves and this is exciting for them and energises them. Instead of looking around at everyone else's marks and how they compared, they are focused on their own game and trying hard for personal reasons rather than competitive ones.

To argue the case for personal bests I need look no further than our elite sportspeople. You will see that personal bests are high on their lists of priorities. You will find for many sportspeople that a personal best will draw just as big a smile as a medal or a place. Importantly, it is these athletes who are the most mentally tough. When they are in a slump, it is only a focus on improvement and personal bests that will get them through because it might be some time before they are back on the winner's podium. I encourage you to tune in to what elite sportspeople say as they climb out of the pool or stagger off the track after a race. See what they have to say about personal bests, improving, doing the best they can under the circumstances and putting in a good technical performance – all outcomes that are successes even though they may not have won the race.

In fact, even very competitive schools that hold traditional views of success along the lines of being the best and beating others find the idea of personal bests appealing. These schools accept a focus on personal bests because they allow for a bit of competition in that the student competes with his or her own previous performance, but also allow for a personalised marker of success in that one's own standards are the most important. One boy I spoke to gained great satisfaction in 'doing or knowing something that I've never done before'.

What athletes will tell you is that taking a broader view of success – such as focusing on personal bests and improvement – does not in any way harm performance. Similarly, focusing on personal bests in no way compromises your child's performance because you are asking excellence of your child – but importantly it is excellence in personal and achievable terms. One girl got it right when she said, 'I know what I'm aiming for and other people might not be aiming for the same thing. If I get what I'm aiming for then that's what matters.'

I should point out that simply telling a child to do their best is not necessarily helpful if you don't give them some specific direction about where they should be headed and how they should get there. That is, children actually do their best when they have a specific and clear and achievable goal to aim for and are given some good guidance about how to get there. Telling them to do their best without this direction and guidance leaves them in a bit of a no-man's land: knowing that they have to do something but not too sure about what it is exactly or how to get there. Personal bests are good because they create a clear benchmark to aim for – bettering a previous grade, or technique, or strategy, or whatever. But personal bests don't provide information about how to get there – this is where some task-based guidance from you or a coach or tutor or teacher is needed.

Reducing comparisons with other children

As I discussed above, the more students have their minds fanning around how they compare with others, the less attention they can pay to their schoolwork. Comparing themselves with others also takes the focus off their own standards and personal bests and places it on others' standards. And when students don't match up to others successfully they can get really deflated and lose their motivation to try next time.

I can find it hard to convince students that they shouldn't compare themselves with other students. Sometimes this is because their parents compare them with others – their brother or sister,

Ben, senior high

Ben had real trouble coping in competitive situations and competitive classrooms. He constantly compared himself to other students – usually ones ahead of him – and this made him quite anxious and often disappointed when he didn't match up to them. In his first year of senior high he struck a chemistry teacher who spent a lot of time focusing on how Ben (and the other students) compared with their own previous performances and not so much on how they compared with each other's.

At a few key points in the year, this teacher provided students with an individualised graph of their own performance tracked over the year. Through tracking Ben and the rest of the class, two things happened. First, Ben paid less attention to how he compared with others and more attention to his own performance and benchmarks. This isn't to say that he was able to completely eliminate comparisons from his life, but the comparisons weren't so dominant that they overwhelmed him. Secondly, the class climate changed from one in which students were mainly focused on outperforming others to one in which students dug deep to do better than they had previously. You couldn't call it an uncompetitive environment, but the focus of the competition had shifted from a comparative one to a more personalised one. In becoming a more positively energised classroom, students (including Ben) were finding a capacity in themselves they never knew existed, and the end-of-year aggregate level of achievement for this class was very high.

their friends or other children. You can literally see children slump their shoulders as their parents point out how other students do things better than they do. Even when parents point out how they have outperformed other students, the child senses that he or she is on the favoured list only so long as they continue to outperform others.

So, the first thing you need to do is reduce the extent to which you compare your child to other children and increase the extent to which your child is his or her own benchmark. Sure, you may privately know how your child compares with other kids but avoid pointing this out to your child. Instead, focus on the task, what can be learnt from the mark or feedback they got from the teacher, how their mark or feedback compares with their previous performance, and the best ways to improve next time.

Now, I know as a parent how hard it is to not look over at other children to see how your own child is travelling. This leads me to an important point. Being aware of other children can give you information about whether your child needs important clinical, medical, psychological or educational intervention. If this is the case, of course you need to use other children as your guide. This isn't the same as constantly telling your child that he or she doesn't do as much study as Tim or doesn't do as well in maths as Claire.

The next thing to do is stop your child putting himself or herself down compared to other students. This won't do much to help them next time they have to do an exam or assignment. You should gently encourage your child to see themselves as their own benchmark and show them that your focus is on them and their potential – and not on how much better or worse they do than another child.

Arousing curiosity whenever possible

What's the best way to fast-track a learning focus? In a word, curiosity. Curiosity immediately puts the entire focus on the task, causes little reason for students to think about how others are performing, doesn't make the student think about how he or she will be marked and generally doesn't cause the student to worry about failure. Curiosity is a truly magical thing.

I've seen teachers walk into a classroom and hook the entire class within one minute by posing an intriguing question, describing an engaging situation or raising an interesting issue. Some are so expert at arousing curiosity that simply the tone of their voice or a raised eyebrow can hook students.

After school as a kid I often flicked through TV channels looking for 'Batman' or 'Get Smart' or whatever. As I cycled through the channels I sometimes landed on 'The Curiosity Show', which I absolutely was not looking for. Just in that instant I'd hear one of the hosts ask a question like, 'Have you ever wondered how you get a boiled egg into a bottle?' No I hadn't, but now that he'd mentioned it, how *do* you get a boiled egg into a bottle, I'd wonder. Just one simple question and they had me engaged for five minutes. Invariably, they'd then ask another quick, punchy and intriguing question, and I'd sit and watch for the solution. Sometimes I'd miss the entire episode of 'Get Smart' to watch this show. How did this show compete with the other shows in the timeslot? Its name said it all.

You should encourage and celebrate your child's curiosity. You do this by showing your child that you are a curious person. Think about some questions you'd like to answer. Why did Van Gogh cut off his ear? Why does the lawnmower splutter in cold weather? Why do plants die when planted in the back corner of the yard? What does perpetual motion mean? Where's Pago Pago? Can humans spontaneously combust? How come some popes in the old days had children?

When time is available, don't let questions like this pass. Make this an opportunity to spend time with your child. Make it a fun activity over the following few weeks to find answers to some intriguing questions. Try to draw on many sources: the internet, an encyclopaedia, a teacher, someone you know who works in the topic area, the library, and even some of your own experience which might not be directly related but might give some clues. There are also heaps of books that deal with lots of quirky topics that teachers often use in class themselves.

Students need to value curiosity, not just marks or results. They need to learn that the journey, the challenge and the unsolved problem is as important as the solution, the discovery or the answer. This leads me to the fourth way to increase a student's learning focus: focusing as much on the journey as the destination.

Recognising the journey as much as the destination
Although learning-focused students know that at the end of the day they have to perform, they also realise that their performance is only as good as the time, energy and effort put in along the way. What's more, they often find the time, energy and effort just as satisfying as getting a good mark.

Recently a university lecturer was telling me he had a black-tie dinner to go to that night at a swish restaurant. When I asked him about the occasion, he told me that the students in that faculty had got halfway through their course and that the staff – from the dean all the way down – made a point of turning that into a special event. I thought it was a wonderful way of celebrating the journey. They were celebrating irrespective of whether the students would graduate or not, get through that year or not, or were high, middling or borderline in achievement.

Think about celebrating your child getting halfway through the school year. Think about giving your child a treat for the hard work put into study for the exams – before your child receives his or her results. Think about giving genuine recognition to a weekend spent on an assignment or project. Think about recognising when your child learns something new. Think about acknowledging when your child gets interested in something they are doing at school. Think about telling your child that it was great that they looked at a difficult schoolwork problem in a new way or spent extra time looking for information.

If your child has travelled well (that is, studied hard, tried a new study technique, read an extra book for an assignment, put aside a weekend for schoolwork and so on), never let the journey go by without genuinely recognising it.

What's more, the journey is often filled with many achievements and it's important that your child recognises them. These successes are what a learning focus is all about. Although marks and grades are a very important part of your child's achievements, there are usually other achievements on the way to getting those marks or grades. These include developing skills, solving problems and learning new things. The table on page 107 contains an exercise you could work through with your child or you could take its central message and discuss it informally with your child.

As you can see, the journey holds opportunities for your child to achieve and succeed. Recognise your child's journey as much as his or her destination and encourage your child to do the same.

Focusing on effort and strategy more than ability

Performance- or competition-focused students often believe that how well they do at school depends on their ability or intelligence. Although this may be true to a point, we saw the dangers of this if performance-focused students also see their ability or

Achievements in the school journey

Achievement	Describe the last time this happened to you	Why is this an achievement?
e.g. *What I learnt helped me in another subject*	*What I learnt in history last week helped me understand a poem in English*	*I was able to understand a poem that I usually would have trouble with*
I understood something that seemed difficult at first		
I got really interested in something I was taught		
I learnt something new		
I looked at an issue/ situation in a new way		

intelligence as fixed – if they don't do well, they don't think they can do much to avoid that happening again. This means they are less motivated for the next test or assignment.

Your child develops more of a learning focus when they focus less on ability and intelligence and more on things like how hard they work (effort) and their study skills (strategy). This is because hard work and study skills are all about doing the schoolwork which immediately means your child is focused on the task and not so much on how it will be marked or how their mark will compare with others. Another way to develop more of a focus on the task is to encourage active learning.

Encouraging active learning

I discussed how curiosity is one of the best ways to fast-track a learning focus. Another way to get your child really hooked into the job at hand is through active learning. When I say 'active learning' I don't necessarily mean building things or measuring or weighing things, although it can include these. What I really mean is getting students to do something to or act on what they read, see or hear. Examples of active learning are when your child:

- summarises what they learnt in class in their own words
- makes notes in the margin of a textbook
- reduces the class notes to a page of the main points
- expands on an important idea learnt in class
- underlines key words in a text book
- gets the key ideas of what was studied for tomorrow's test onto one page
- draws up a 'mindmap' or 'spidergram' – for example, writing the name of a book they've read in the middle of a page and around that writing out key characters, a summary of the plot, strengths and weaknesses, theme and what they like or dislike about the book (look at the example on page 109).

Active learning means that your child is not a passive, inactive listener, reader or viewer. It means that your child must stop and think about what he or she is reading, hearing or seeing. It also means that they take the time to try to understand what they are reading, hearing or seeing. Active learning demands that your child focuses on the task at hand and tries to make sense of it. As much as possible, encourage your child to do something to the information they receive.

Helping your child to deal with competition more effectively

It's my understanding that the word 'competition' has its origins in the idea of a group of people 'searching together' to perform to their potential. That is, it was based on the idea that you get a bunch of people around you to bring out your best. Originally competition was not about beating other people but about using other people as an inspiration to dig deep and maybe deeper than you ever have before. Can school be like this? Recently I spoke to a group of school students who believe that friendly competition is possible. One boy told me, 'In English it's a bit of motivation if your friends get an A or something. It's good to get close to their mark. There's no hard feelings or anything afterwards, it's all good.'

EXAMPLE OF A MINDMAP

What is this book about?

Who are the main characters?

Describe two of the main characters.

Describe the main theme/s of the book.

Write the name of a book you have finished reading recently

....

....

....

Describe the style of writing. What do you think of the style?

What do you think of the book overall?

What was your favourite part of the book?

Write out two strengths of the book.

Write out two weaknesses of the book.

As discussed earlier, competition is here to stay and competition can be energising. The question, then, is how we can take the best parts of competition or create conditions where students can deal with competition better. Research and my experience with schools and students suggest that the following are ways to help students better deal with competition:

- Encourage your child to compete with their own previous performance or strive to reach personal bests even when engaged in conventional competition – this keeps them energised but also keeps the focus on their own standards by seeing themselves as their own benchmark.
- Encourage your child to see others as an inspiration to bring out their best rather than seeing others as people to beat – this creates friendly competition and reduces dog-eat-dog competition which can arouse a fear of failure.
- If your child doesn't compete successfully, encourage them to see their effort (how hard they work) and strategy (their study skills, preparation, planning and so on), more than their ability or intelligence as the keys to doing better next time – this keeps them in control and increases optimism.
- Make it clear to your child that if they don't compete successfully, this doesn't mean they are less of a person or you think they are less worthwhile – this will reduce their fear of failure in competition.
- If your child doesn't do so well in competition show them how to look for lessons or clues in the competition to use to improve next time – this, too, will reduce their fear of failure in competition.

There are other reasons for learning

In this chapter I've really only focused on two reasons for learning: to improve, develop skills, and learn new things (a learning reason) or to beat others, know more than others, and the like (a competitive reason). I emphasise a learning focus as the best way to develop high quality motivation.

I probably don't have to tell you that there are other reasons for learning. Some students have *social* reasons for learning. This involves learning in order to please parents and teachers or it may involve not working in order to gain peer approval. Other students have *avoidance* reasons for doing what they do. This might involve working really hard to avoid being seen to be dumb.

Again, however, I encourage more *learning* or *mastery* reasons for doing what they do because this puts the focus on what matters most: the task at hand and the importance of becoming absorbed in that task.

Having said this, I should also recognise that students can have multiple reasons for doing what they do. For example, research has shown that some students can balance a learning focus with a competitive focus and know when to focus on mastery and when to get a bit hungry for success. I suggest that personal bests are the most effective way to balance multiple goals and navigate a sensible path between a learning and competitive focus. Personal bests enable students to do this because they require students to compete with their own benchmarks but do so by having them focus on the task at hand and not so much on their competition.

Living in the real world

In the real world not everything happens like they say in the books. Here are a few things for you to think about when digesting this chapter:

- Don't expect your child to only ever do things in order to improve or develop new skills. This would be nice but probably not realistic.
- Don't expect your child never to be competitive or never to compare himself or herself to others. They probably will. Your job is to help them deal with competition more effectively.
- Don't expect your child not to have social reasons for learning. We're social creatures and expecting your child not to care what others think is an unrealistic expectation.
- It is entirely possible that your child can have a learning focus and also be very interested in getting a good mark or outperforming others. Some students are able to co-ordinate the two very well. They know when to have a learning focus and when to be competitive.

- Celebrate good marks. A learning focus does not mean you don't praise your child for getting good marks, but don't forget to also celebrate the effort and study skills that got them there.
- Don't beat yourself up if you find yourself comparing your child to other children. The important thing is not to let your child know about your comparisons.
- Don't let curiosity amble along too far at the expense of other schoolwork. Children need to learn that they have a number of other schoolwork commitments, not just the thing that is really engaging them. Like it or not, some schoolwork is less interesting but it still has to be done. However, don't put a lid on curiosity too quickly – it is a precious commodity so maybe give your child a bit of leeway if something is really getting them in.
- Like it or not, some outcomes (such as final year results or the end of school exams) carry a lot of weight. Some exams have a big impact on students' futures. Don't deny this to your child because you'll be flying in the face of everything he or she reads in the newspaper and is told at school. Instead, encourage your child to see that the best way to enhance these outcomes is to focus on really getting the processes right – this involves effective study skills, hard work, good preparation and good planning.
- The reality is that the world celebrates those who are the best and so it can be hard for your child not to see this as the mark of success. To deal with this narrow view of success there needs to be a quiet revolution that begins in the home. Celebrate broad indicators of success – not just the marks but also the hard work put in, the development of new skills and personal bests if your child reaches them.
- Fully recognise that high school is competitive. Don't go telling your child how bad competition is. Competition is here to stay and telling your child it's no good leaves them in a pretty unwinnable position: this tells them that it's no good but they're stuck with it! This is bound to make your child feel somewhat helpless. In any case, competition can be energising and motivating if the conditions are right. Rather than dwell on all the possible nasties of competi-

tion, shift the spotlight onto the merits and advantages of a learning focus and talk about how to develop more of a learning focus.

Chapter summary

In this chapter I've discussed how a learning focus increases students' motivation. I've also discussed some of the dangers of a performance or competition focus but have described ways to help students deal better with competition and harness some of the motivating properties of competition. Ways to increase your child's learning focus include encouraging your child to reach personal bests, avoiding comparisons between your child and other children, harnessing the power of curiosity and active learning and recognising that what your child does on the way to getting his or her marks can be just as or more important than the marks themselves.

CHAPTER SIX TOP 5

1. A learning focus is your child's focus on learning and understanding new things, developing skills, reaching personal bests, solving problems and improving.

2. You increase your child's learning focus by encouraging personal bests as one of the main goals of learning. Personal bests are also a good way of harnessing the energy that some students get from competition. When promoting personal bests, remember to be clear about what a personal best is, provide some guidance about how to get there, and give some good feedback along the way if possible.

3. Comparing your child with other children and telling them how they compare with other children can reduce your child's motivation. Avoid comparing your child with others.

4. Arousing and encouraging your child's curiosity is a very powerful way to hook him or her into a learning focus. Another way to get your child focused on schoolwork is to support active learning by encouraging your child to act on or do something to what he or she reads, sees or hears.

5. You foster a learning focus by encouraging your child to enjoy and focus on the journey and not just the destination. The journey includes using different sources of information for an essay, studying for an extra couple of hours, trying hard on an assignment and using an effective study technique. Research shows that the more students get into and enjoy the journey, the more they hit the mark when it comes time to perform – whether in a test, assignment or project.

CHAPTER 7

ASSISTING YOUR CHILD'S SCHOOLWORK AND STUDY

There's no getting around the fact that no matter how motivated your child is, at some stage he or she actually needs to do some study. There's also no getting around the fact that you can't study for them – and believe me, many parents wish they could! It's probably no comfort to you that at this very moment, across the world, there are countless parents tearing out their hair over their child's lack of study.

In response to parents' frustrations, I've often told them, 'Well, you can lead a horse to water, but you can't make it drink.' Truthfully, I've always been dissatisfied with this last-ditch response to a difficult situation. In fact, I used this response recently at a workshop for teachers, only to have one astute teacher respond with, 'No you can't make it drink, but you can salt the oats.' Got it in one! This really sums up a lot of our job as parents and teachers. Salting our children's oats to develop their thirst to learn and improve. As I suggested at the beginning, this book is very much about how to salt the oats.

I'LL DO THE WASHING UP IF I DON'T HAVE TO HELP WITH YOUR HOMEWORK

Liz, senior high

Liz is a great example of someone who planned her approach to schoolwork and carefully monitored her progress. This was most evident in her approach to taking major exams. Many weeks before the exams she would look at past test papers and put together a list of likely questions (and variations of these questions). She would check with the teacher how many sections would be in the exam, how many questions she was required to do in each section, and then prepared for enough of these questions to maximise her chances of covering all bases for each section. As you can see, her planning began very early in the process.

In the actual exam, her planning was just as efficient and this had very important benefits for her ability to monitor her progress. In the first two minutes of an essay question she would sketch out her answer on a blank sheet of paper and map out the relevant points under each part of the question. She would also write the first couple of words to each quotation she planned to include in the essay. After every page of her answer she re-read the question. If she was at risk of drifting off track this was the best way to make sure she would stick to the point. Throughout the essay, she followed the essay sketch and added points to the sketch if new ideas came to her as she wrote the answer. She would also regularly check the time and would rarely go over the time she had allotted for that answer. If she did go over time, she would only do so on answers that were worth more marks.

For Liz, planning and monitoring went hand-in-hand. The better she planned, the more likely she was to stick to the question and complete it in the time required.

This chapter is about how to make the job of studying easier for your child. It is not a chapter on study skills. There are lots of books around that tell students how to study. This chapter is more about the motivation to study and the organisation, management and planning that need to happen to lay a good foundation for study.

In particular, I want to talk about things that I've found are really important to children's homework and study. They are:

- planning schoolwork
- understanding what needs to be done
- monitoring schoolwork and answers
- studying under ideal conditions
- managing study time.

Planning schoolwork

Of all the things students need to do for effective study, I've found that they spend least time and pay the least attention to planning their schoolwork. Students who do plan their schoolwork:

- get clear in their minds what an assignment is asking
- spend time thinking about how to do an essay or project
- spend a couple of minutes at the start of an exam planning their answers
- prepare a plan for an assignment before getting stuck into it
- think through the steps involved in preparing for an upcoming test
- plan a study timetable for the week.

Planning an assignment or another task

The best advice I can give about planning schoolwork is to encourage your child to chunk. Remember, chunking is where your child breaks schoolwork into smaller, bite-sized parts and sees the completion of each chunk as a success. When your child sees the completion of each chunk as a success, he or she is immediately injecting success into the process of schoolwork – this is very motivating and boosts your child's self-belief.

But not only is chunking important for ongoing motivation and self-belief, it also has very obvious benefits for study. Chunking:

- provides a plan for action and the steps needed to complete schoolwork
- helps your child monitor his or her progress as the schoolwork is done
- helps your child make better use of his or her study time.

I want to again work on the list presented in chapter 3 as an example of chunking. This time I want to extend that list by asking your child to think more carefully about what he or she has to do for each chunk, how long each chunk will take to complete and the precise actions needed to complete each chunk.

The table on page 119 provides an example of how your child can better plan each part of an assignment. I've provided details for the first couple of chunks. Of course, your child can be flexible about the exact way he or she thinks through and performs each chunk. Indeed, the details in this table will change depending on the nature of the schoolwork he or she has been asked to do.

You will also see that there's a column for your child to tick when each chunk is completed. When your child sees half a page of ticks halfway through the assignment, it is both satisfying in the present moment and spurs him or her on to tackle the next half page.

Planning a schoolwork timetable

The previous section described a way to plan an assignment. There is also a need to plan for more extended activities and schoolwork. Probably the most important planning along these lines is planning a weekly study timetable.

Planning an effective study timetable is a difficult thing to do. It requires quite a bit of juggling, allowing enough space for unexpected interruptions, balancing what you know you should do with what you are capable of doing and balancing those with what you want to do and so on.

The table on page 121 is an example of a senior high school student's study timetable. As you can see, it allows time for sport, music and part-time work in addition to schoolwork.

It also allows for:

- free study periods for extra study in a subject that might get priority that week (for example, if a test is coming up)
- a free day on Sunday, but with a bit of time to prepare for the following week (for example, packing the schoolbag etc)
- three hours study for each subject
- a study-free night during the week.

A detailed example of chunking

Steps involved	Time to do	Brief description of what you will do	✓ when done
Understand the question/task	*5 mins*	*Read question carefully; take note of and underline key words like 'compare', 'contrast' and 'discuss'*	✓
Break question into parts	*15 mins*	*List sections of assignment by themes relevant to the question*	✓
Initial search for information (e.g. internet, library etc)			
Focused and detailed reading of books and other resources collected			
Detailed summary of information			
Organise information (e.g. put information under each heading)			
Write first draft			
Tie up loose ends (e.g. do a bit more reading)			
Write second draft			
Edit (e.g. spelling, grammar, formatting checks)			
Final draft			
Reward yourself for completing the assignment			

How many hours of study should your child do? To be honest, I don't know exactly. Most researchers are reluctant to recommend a specific number of hours. What they say is that as a general rule students who do more study and study more effectively tend to perform better.

For those who aren't happy with this vague response to a perfectly reasonable question, here's a guide to the minimum number of study hours each night recommended to me by a few school principals and head teachers:

- Junior high (e.g. Years 7 and 8)   ➔ 1.5 hours each night

- Middle high (e.g. Years 9 and 10)   ➔ 2.5 hours each night

- Early senior high (e.g. Year 11)   ➔ 3.5 hours each night

- Final year of senior high (e.g. Year 12) ➔ 4 hours each night

Some of you may be horrified at the large number of hours your child should be studying – particularly in senior high. You won't be so horrified when you do a few calculations. Say your child is in senior high and studies six days of the week (let's give them a day a week free of study). Say he or she has six school subjects: this allows for four hours for each subject each week. That's not a lot when you consider how much they'll be examined on in their finals. It's even less when you take out the time they'll need to do their homework. But remember that this is a guide only. Some students need more study time while others get away with less. You should talk to your child's teachers about what they think is appropriate for your child.

When helping plan a study timetable, I ask the student:

- How many subjects do you study?
- For each subject, how many hours do you need to do the homework and revision of the week's work?
- How much sport, music, part-time work etc. do you do?
- What other activities – church, hobbies, interests, socialising etc – do you have each week?
- Which TV shows do you watch; how many friends do you phone in a week; how much time do you spend on the internet etc?
- What weekly family commitments do you have?

An example of a study timetable for senior high

	MON	TUES	WED	THURS
Before school			1 hour (My pick of subject)	
School				
Before dinner	Sport practice	Music lesson	1.5 hours study (Japanese)	1.5 hours study (Japanese)
After dinner	3 hours (Maths, English)	3 hours (Science, geography)	Free night (Catch up with friends, TV or the net)	3 hours (Maths, English)

	FRI	SAT	SUN	
Before school	1 hour (My pick of subject)	Morning: part-time work/sport		
School		Afternoon: 3 hours (Science, geography)	Night: Prep for next school week e.g. pack schoolbag	
Before dinner	Part-time work/sport			
After dinner	3 hours (Economics)			

Knowing all this is important when developing a realistic study timetable. Remember, the less realistic it is, the less effective it will be.

The number of study hours will also depend on:

• the time of year – later in the year more study may be required
• the type of subjects – some subjects may need more time

- the subjects your child is good or not so good at – subjects your child is not so good at may need more time, or your child may choose to spend more time on his or her good subjects to really consolidate strengths
- what's coming up in the near future – there may be a test at the end of the week that needs more study time.

Here are some general rules for planning and then sticking to a study timetable:

- It shouldn't be too tough or demanding because your child will be unlikely to stick to it.
- It shouldn't be so slack and undemanding that it is almost useless.
- If your child has real trouble getting into the study, first develop a timetable that is on the easy side. This will maximise the chances of success, better ensure that your child sticks to the timetable, and from there your child will be more willing to expand the study hours a bit.
- Allow for free spots that can be used when an unforeseen disruption occurs.
- Allow for free nights or blocks of time that can be used to catch up with friends, watch a favourite TV show or surf the net.
- If your child doesn't stick to the timetable one week, this doesn't mean he or she should abandon it.
- If your child doesn't stick to the timetable for a number of weeks, you should talk about whether it needs to be adjusted or whether other parts of your child's life need to be adjusted (for example, fewer hours in the part-time job).

Understanding what needs to be done

I've read many students' essays in which I'd swear they were answering a completely different question to the one they'd been set. Often their answer is a pretty good one – but it's a good answer for a completely different question. How does this happen? Aside from the students who haven't prepared properly for answering the question, I find students hurtle off in the wrong direction on an answer for two reasons: they misread the instructions or the question, or they don't understand what the question means.

Misreading the instructions or the question

Instructions are important because they provide information about how many questions to answer in a section, how many words to write, maybe how many marks are awarded for each part of the answer, whether to provide examples in the answer and so on.

When talking with students I insist that they do not read test questions until all instructions relating to those questions have been read. I also insist that they underline and understand the key words in the instructions. As I described in chapter 6, underlining is a form of active learning which demands that the student think about what he or she is reading, understand it and decide if it's important or not.

If students are not sure what to do part way through a test, I tell them to read the instructions again and not to rely on their assumptions. The cost of not following instructions is too high – I tell students that reading (and maybe rereading) instructions can be easy marks because the consequences of not carefully reading instructions can be a drastically lower mark.

Misreading assignment and test questions is tackled in two ways. First, if it's a test question that's worth a lot of marks or requires a long answer, students should dedicate one whole minute (or longer if it's a complex or multi-part question) to reading and understanding the question. Even if after 45 seconds they think they know what it means, I insist that they spend the remaining 15 seconds checking that the entire question and all its parts are understood and that there are no other possible points the question is raising.

Secondly, during this minute, the student should underline or circle key words in the question. As I described above, this is a form of active learning or thinking and is a great way to ensure the student does his or her best to understand the question. Some students develop a system whereby they underline the words that tell them what to do in the answer (for example, discuss, summarise, compare, contrast etc) and circle the words that tell them what their answer should refer to (for example, Julius Caesar, World War II, Darcy and Elizabeth, the tundra, Caucus etc).

Not understanding the question

Another reason students' answers aren't that great is because they don't understand the question or some of the words in the question. There are two main things your child can do to reduce the chances of this happening:

- understand key words that often appear in questions
- use some logical thinking to understand difficult parts of the question.

If your child thinks about the words that appear in exam or assignment questions, he or she would find that some pop up more than others. Some of these frequently appearing words are:

Analyse	Discuss
Compare	Evaluate
Contrast	Justify
Define	Summarise

Understanding these key words is very important to understanding the question as a whole. I ask students to write out an explanation of each word and then to check their explanation with a teacher. Are there any other words your child can think of that often appear in assignments or tests?

In other cases, your child may not understand all parts of the question. For example, there may be three parts to the question and your child only really understands two of them. There are a couple of ways to deal with this. First, your child can use clues from the other two parts and words within the difficult part to try to understand it. Secondly, your child can focus on writing a really good answer to the first two parts. They can then deal with the third part in a more general way that doesn't expose their ignorance but which is sufficient to give them credit for answering the whole question. If your child has absolutely no clue about the third part and can't even give a ballpark answer, it's probably best to give a high-quality answer to the two parts that are understood and leave it at that.

Most importantly, if your child doesn't understand part of a question, tell them not to freak out. They must not let it interfere with their answer on the other two parts because providing a high-quality answer on those parts will probably be enough to get them through the test and maybe even enough to get a decent mark.

I remember in one of my finals at school the word 'impunity' came up in a question. For the life of me, I didn't know what this word meant. I didn't even know if the word referred to something good or something bad. Because it was a key word in the question it was really important that I knew, at least vaguely, what it meant. I decided that at the absolute minimum I needed to know whether it was a word which in the context of the topic referred to something good or something bad, and then knowing this I could spin an argument together revolving around a general theme of 'this is a good thing blah, blah, blah' or 'this is a bad thing blah, blah, blah'.

I looked at the characters mentioned in the question and knew that they weren't the most popular figures in history. I looked at a few of the other words in the question and they were pretty negative too. I thought the word 'impunity' looked a bit like 'punitive' – a word I knew very well, sadly! Because I was a desperate student and had no option other than calculated guess-work, I decided that in the context of the essay topic 'impunity' was not a good thing and wrote the essay accordingly. As it turned out, I was right. The message here is that there are some times when a question must be attempted but your child does not have a clear idea on how to answer it. Using clues from other parts of the question, links with other words or characters, and some amateur detective work your child increases his or her chances of giving a half decent answer.

Monitoring schoolwork and answers

Above, I described students who seem to answer a completely different question to the one asked. Other students start answering the question but slowly wander further and further away from it so that by the end of their answer they are in a completely different galaxy to the question. Why do they do this? Basically, they don't monitor their progress and don't check that they are on track.

Along with not planning an answer, I've found that students spend too little time monitoring their answers and checking their progress. This is a real shame because monitoring and checking can be really easy marks too. How many times have you double-checked something to find an error or miscalculation?

I ask students to think about the different monitoring and checking strategies they can use and then ask them the subjects in which they are required. The table on page 127 shows one way I get students to do this. You can work through the table with your child or just talk about it informally with him or her. Can you and your child think of two more checking strategies?

Studying under ideal conditions

I'm often stunned at when, where and with whom students try to study. It is clear that some conditions are not the most ideal in which to concentrate, and yet students persist in trying to work under them. To get the most out of study, students should aim to study under conditions that will bring out their best. Common problems with the choice of study times and conditions include:

- studying too late at night
- studying with the radio on
- studying with (too many) friends
- studying with the wrong friends
- studying in cramped, hot, cold, messy or dark areas
- studying at places where it's difficult to concentrate
- studying with too few or too many breaks.

As a general rule, these aren't great conditions in which to study. Having said this and before you throw this list at your son or daughter, I want you to consider a few points:

- Some students can study quite effectively with a radio on or a TV in the background. Living in a cramped apartment, I wrote my PhD in the lounge room with the TV on a good part of the time.
- It is better that your child studies with the radio on than do no study with it off.
- Some students can study in a messy room. A colleague of mine has the messiest office I've ever seen but he knows

Examples of checking strategies

Checking strategies	I need to do this in these subjects
Example: Reread the question after each paragraph I write	*English, history, geography*
1. Reread my answer/essay when I have finished writing	
2. Double-check my calculations	
3. Check a dictionary or thesaurus if I don't understand a word	
4. Check that each part of the question has been answered	
5. Pause a moment to think before I write the first thing that comes to mind	
6.	
7.	

that a reference list for first year educational psychology is in pile number 37 about half a metre down.

- It is better that your child studies in a messy room than does no study because he or she won't clean it.
- Some students can study quite effectively with friends.
- It is better that your child studies with friends than does no study on their own.
- Some students can study quite effectively at odd hours.

I suppose what I'm suggesting is that if a student is prepared to study, try not to get in the way too much. But this isn't to say that you can't gently direct or guide your child to times, places and company that might enhance their study and concentration.

This may take some negotiation between you and your child. Some examples of negotiation around study are as follows:

- allowing the radio on while your child works on schoolwork that doesn't need much concentration (for example, typing up a handwritten essay, covering books, planning next week's schoolwork, surfing the net), but turning it off when revision for an upcoming test is needed
- working with friends two or three days of the week and studying alone on the other days
- studying late into the night two or three nights of the week and getting an early night's sleep on the other nights.

You might not love the arrangement, but if it is acceptable and you can live with it, then maybe let it ride for a while or until you have an opportunity to negotiate again. It may be more important to start small, allow for some success, allow some positive habits to develop and then talk about expanding the study timetable or improving the study conditions once these are in place.

I try to encourage students to think about the conditions that bring out their best. The table on page 129 is something I present to students. I tell them that the more they respond 'Yes' to the study conditions the more they become a 'study all-rounder'. I also tell them that it is a good thing to expand their ideal study conditions to include conditions they previously might have thought were not suited to them. So, if a student only ever studies during the week, it's a good thing to expand his or her ideal study conditions to also include a few hours of study on Saturday or Sunday.

Managing study time

In addition to studying under effective study conditions, your child will also benefit from making better use of time. Three effective ways to make better use of time are:

- prioritising
- multi-tasking
- using in-between time.

Prioritising

Students often have competing deadlines and demands during the school term. How do they handle these competing demands?

Broadening ideal study conditions

I study well under these conditions (circle YES or NO)

At home	YES (which room? _____)	NO
At the library	YES (which library? _____)	NO
Somewhere else	YES (where? _____)	NO
Weekdays	YES (which days?) _____)	NO
Weekends	YES (which days?) _____)	NO
In the morning	YES (at this time: _____)	NO
In the afternoon	YES (at this time: _____)	NO
At night	YES (at this time: _____)	NO
Alone	YES	NO
With a friend (select him/her carefully but ask yourself if studying with others is genuinely helpful)	YES (which friend? _____)	NO
In a group (select the group carefully but ask yourself if studying with others is genuinely helpful)	YES (names: _____)	NO
In a quiet room, no distractions	YES	NO
With background activity (e.g. radio; but ask yourself if background activity is genuinely helpful)	YES	NO
With a break every 30 minutes	YES	NO
With a break every hour	YES	NO
With a break every two hours	YES	NO

Some handle them very well, others not so well. The difference between the two types of student is in part due to the fact that the first type prioritises their work. The other type seems to work on assignments that aren't due immediately or that are worth fewer marks before they work on things that are due the next day or are worth a lot of marks. According to one girl, 'It's a lot of work and a lot to focus on and sometimes I find myself under so much stress because I've got all these things building up and I don't know what to prioritise.' Whereas, according to another, 'If there's a harder assignment, I get started on it earlier because if there's an easier one you can leave it to a few days before and still get something that's worth an A grade.' This student knows how to prioritise.

To get students thinking about prioritising, I ask them to consider the schoolwork they have to do that night. I then get them to go through the following exercise:

- Write a list of the things they have to do for homework, assignments and study that night.
- Put the number 1 next to the most important item (important in terms of marks or due date – the student can choose).
- Put the number 2 on the next most important item, and so on.
- That night start working at number 1 and work through to the last number.

In the senior years of high school prioritising becomes increasingly important. Students who prioritise make better use of their time and as a result are more able to hand work in on time. They are also able to do higher quality work because they are less likely to rush and do last-minute study.

Multi-tasking

There are a number of times during the day that students are able to multi-task, or do two things at once. It is quite simple to achieve and can add up to quite a lot of 'extra' time by the end of the school term. Great times for your child to multi-task are while he or she is doing something that doesn't take much concentration. Examples of multi-tasking are:

- being quizzed for the next day's test while doing the dishes or packing the dishwasher
- going over quotes for English while jogging
- rehearsing French vocabulary while swimming
- listening to an audiotape of a Shakespeare play while at the gym.

Using in-between time

Also throughout the day there are small breaks that can be used to do bits of schoolwork that don't take much time. These breaks are called in-between time. Examples of using in-between time are:

- packing the schoolbag in TV ad breaks
- making a quick call to a friend just before dinner is served
- rereading an essay while waiting for the school bus
- preparing the assignment's cover page while connecting to the net or downloading a program or e-mails.

Using in-between time also has the advantage of saving the night's study session for schoolwork that really takes concentration. This is because much of the menial work has been done and the night's study is reserved for the hard stuff. Your child can hit the ground running when he or she begins study that night.

Once when I talked to students about multi-tasking and using in-between time, one pointed out that if she used in-between time and multi-tasked all the time, her entire life would be filled with schoolwork. Most of her class nodded in agreement. Quite understandably they did not like this idea. I quickly told them that balance is the secret in life and if she used in-between time or engaged in multi-tasking just a few times in the week, this would buy her quite a bit of extra quality study time by the end of the year or some free time later that week. She was happier knowing this. I tell this story because even though using lots of in-between time and multi-tasking is very appealing to us as parents, it is not necessarily an easy thing for students to do. If your child uses his or her time more effectively than usual a few times in a week you should be proud of them – and let them know this.

Living in the real world

In the real world not everything happens like they say in the books. Here are a few things for you to think about when digesting this chapter:

- At some stage your child must sit down and study and you can't do it for them. You may need to go for small gains at first. If your child is easily frightened off study then don't go in hard. Start small and give due credit when your child gives it a good shot – even if it's not quite as much study as you'd have liked them to do.

- It may take a while for your child to develop effective chunking skills. Spending time with your child to help them chunk will be time well spent.

- Developing an effective study timetable is a skill. I can't emphasise enough how important it is to develop a realistic timetable. It is a precious commitment your child is making when they agree to a study timetable – don't waste it by making it so ambitious that they give up or so easy that it's useless. Maybe start off modestly and then when your child is succeeding with that talk at an opportune moment about extending the timetable a little.

- If your child isn't doing the recommended number of hours studying, you'll need to tread carefully. Going in too hard can scare them off, yet going too easy may not communicate to them how important quality study is. I suggest you don't raise the bar too high. If your senior high son or daughter is only doing one hour a night, don't aim for three hours straightaway. Building up gradually is more realistic and will be seen by your child as achievable. Talk about the rewards they can give themselves after an extra half-hour study on a given night. Talk about how you can make it easier for them to do more study. Try to take more notice of when they get close to or reach the three hours than when they miss the mark. This isn't to say you ignore it when they miss the mark. Rather, let them know you believe they can do better and remind them that they have done three hours before. Maybe they'll never get to three hours, or get there only every now and then – if this is the case, don't forget that some study is better than none and if they are doing more than they were before, then give credit where credit's due.

- Your child won't always monitor or plan their schoolwork. Aim for them to do this more often than they do right now and if they come to the party even a little, be proud of them. This may be the building block for more planning and monitoring in the future.

- Remember that your child may not always study under the most ideal conditions. Maybe you can agree that they may work under their preferred conditions for more straightforward schoolwork, but that they work under ideal conditions when serious and demanding study is needed.

- Prioritising, multi-tasking and using in-between time are skills that take time and practice to develop. Give your child good time and guidance to develop these skills.

Chapter summary

Unfortunately, it is not enough to simply have a strong self-belief or sense of control – at some point your child needs to *behave in motivated ways*. Planning, checking, monitoring and more effectively managing study are good examples of motivated behaviour. This chapter has discussed how your child can plan and monitor their schoolwork, study under conditions that help them concentrate better, and use their time more effectively. Important skills to develop include identifying the steps in doing schoolwork or an assignment, understanding instructions and questions, planning a study timetable, understanding key words often used in assignment and exam questions, double-checking answers, prioritising, multi-tasking and using in-between time. All these are tangible skills that are part of the motivated student's school and study life.

CHAPTER SEVEN TOP 5

1. In addition to booster thinking such as self-belief, value of schooling and learning focus, your child needs to develop booster behaviours. These include planning, monitoring and study management.

2. Chunking schoolwork into smaller, bite-sized parts is a great way to plan schoolwork more effectively. Developing a challenging but realistic study timetable can be a good way to plan the school week and the study that needs to be done in that week.

3. Monitoring progress is an important booster behaviour. To more effectively monitor schoolwork and progress, your child needs to understand the question first. This obviously requires preparation before an assignment or exam, but also requires your child to understand instructions and questions, and understand particular words and concepts that often arise in exams and assignments.

4. Monitoring requires your child to double-check answers, consult a dictionary or thesaurus for words that are not understood, reread essay questions a number of times while doing an essay, pause to think before answering a question, and check that each part of the question has been answered.

5. Effective study management is a booster behaviour that's important to develop. It involves identifying ideal study conditions and aiming to become a 'study all-rounder', prioritising, multi-tasking and using in-between time.

CHAPTER 8

ENHANCING YOUR CHILD'S PERSISTENCE

How does your child respond to difficult or challenging school-work? Some children answer or write the first thing that comes to mind. Some don't bother even doing that, they just give up. Some will immediately ask for help before giving it a good shot themselves. However, there are others who spend time figuring out an answer, do a bit more reading, try some alternative ways to do the schoolwork, and if they can't figure it out after that, will then go and ask for help. These children are persistent.

School is filled with difficult and challenging situations – as well as academic challenges there are social, sporting and emotional challenges to face. To effectively deal with these challenges, children need persistence. In a way, persistence is a very important part of resilience. Persistence can make the difference between a child who gets stuck academically and maybe runs the risk of never quite catching up again and the child who pushes through to the next level and an ever upward journey through school and study.

Persistence can be a real protective

factor for future challenges your child may face. In fact, lessons learnt from persisting in some challenging schoolwork can be applied to difficult personal challenges such as a fallout with a friend. Persistence can encourage your child to be solution-focused and deal with situations in new and perhaps better ways.

The good news is that there are some very effective ways to develop persistence. To a large extent we come to learn particular ways of dealing with challenge. The ultimate learning at the wrong end of the spectrum is learned helplessness. You'll recall that this is where the child learns that no matter what he or she does there's nothing he or she can do to avoid failure or attain success. That is, he or she learns to become helpless. One girl told me, 'Every day I want to give up. I just can't see the end and you just get more work.' Importantly, the opposite is also the case. Your child can learn to do things that increase control over events in his or her life.

Ways to increase persistence

There are a number of ways to increase your child's persistence. Some boosters will increase your child's persistence, especially:

- *Self-belief* Your child will persist with challenging work when they have a belief that they can master the school-work given to them.
- *Control* Your child will be more persistent and less likely to lapse into helplessness when they have a sense that they can avoid poor performance or repeat a previous success.
- *Value of schooling* Your child will stick at schoolwork that they believe is relevant, useful, important and meaningful.
- *Learning focus* When your child is focused on problem solving, improving and doing a good job, there is greater motivation to persist at schoolwork that is difficult or challenging.

Previous chapters have dealt with each of these boosters. Additionally, there are other ways to build your child's persistence, including:

- chunking schoolwork into time slots
- examining times when your child has previously persisted in the face of challenge

- developing a plan for when schoolwork is difficult or challenging
- effective goal setting.

Chunking schoolwork into time slots

Now, I know you're probably tired of this chunking business so I promise I'll look at it differently in this chapter. But I can't emphasise enough how important it is for us as parents to break down the mountains that exist in our children's minds or in the reality of their lives. One reason students don't persist at schoolwork is because they see it as too difficult or think there's too much of it. When they start viewing their schoolwork this way, they are likely to write the first thing that comes to mind, not try at all or race to you to ask for help before giving it a good try.

In the previous chapters I've talked about chunking in terms of the task itself. That is, I've talked about how to break an assignment or essay into bite-sized parts and to see the completion of each part as a success. Your child can chunk in another way. He or she can chunk in terms of the time needed to do his or her schoolwork.

The table on page 138 is an example of what I get students to do when thinking about chunking using *time* as the chunking factor. I ask them to see their essay or assignment or study in terms of 30-minute chunks and to approach a night's work in terms of bite-sized 30-minute blocks. If 30 minutes is too long for some children, I change it to 15-minute chunks.

I insist that students see the completion of each 30-minute chunk as a success (requiring them to tick the chunk when finished). I also build in a two-minute break after the first chunk in the hour and then a five-minute break after the second chunk in the hour.

Some parts of the assignment may take longer than 30 minutes, and in that case the student writes the word 'continued' on the next line of the table to show that the task is a continuing one.

As you can see, there are eight slots in the table and so this example would take care of a four-hour study session. Obviously, if your child studies in blocks of two hours, only four slots would be needed.

How does setting up and following through a table like this one build persistence? It does so in five ways:

- Experiencing frequent mini-successes along the way spurs your child onto the next time slot.
- Preparing a schoolwork session ahead means your child knows where he or she is going, and there is less chance of getting lost along the way or stopping altogether.
- It is a way of requiring your child to commit to a set period of time. When your child is given a specified amount of time to solve a problem, he or she is more likely to use it effectively.

Time chunking

What I need to do	Start	Finish	Finished
e.g. Read and fully understand essay question	6.00	6.28	✓ (then 2-minute break)
e.g. Do rough essay plan	6.30	6.55	✓ (then 5-minute break)
e.g. Do rough essay plan (continued)	7.00	7.28	✓ (then 2-minute break)
1.			
2.			
3.			
4.			
5.			
6.			
7.			
8.			

- It is a way of asking your child to commit to a specific destination – as we shall see shortly, this is a form of effective goal setting and is motivating for students.
- It builds in small breaks that are rewarding and energising.

Examining times when your child has persisted previously

I've yet to meet a child (or person for that matter) who has not successfully dealt with some challenge in life. Even if a child doesn't successfully cope with challenge at school, he or she might be pretty good at sticking at tough football training sessions, or learning a new piece of music, or fixing a broken toy, or mastering a difficult computer game, or swimming a long distance, or dealing with a personal loss, or resisting negative peer pressure – you get the picture.

Life is difficult and the fact that your child even exists in the here and now means they're doing something right at least some part of the time. When you and your child recognise this, you start to tap into another key to persistence: using lessons learnt from previous challenges to help deal with present challenges.

I talked not so long ago with a student in middle high school. He was struggling with schoolwork and was certainly not a persister. All he wanted to do was play professional football. In fact, this was a real possibility because he was in a junior representative side. He saw absolutely no point in being at school; he thought of nothing but football. He didn't stick at anything at school and when I asked him why, he told me nothing was worth sticking at, he didn't have what it took to do the schoolwork and schoolwork was boring anyway.

I asked him whether he got all the football moves right first go, or whether he could lift the required weights all the time first go, or whether his kicking game was perfect. He was quick to tell me that of course he didn't get everything right first go. We then talked about how he approached these challenges. It soon become clear that in fact he was very persistent in his football and that he was an expert in mastering challenges in that arena. I told him that some kids in his class did exactly the same sort of thing in maths or science or whatever. It was a surprise to him that in ways he never suspected he was similar to the kids he always thought were geeks (his word, not mine).

They identified challenges and took persistent steps to overcome them.

I then asked him what he'd do if he became a professional footballer. How would he understand his contract? How would he use his substantial salary? How would he make effective decisions? How would he take care of his body? How would he deal with coaches he might not like? He began to see that school was one of the few places he could prepare himself for these sorts of challenges. Nowhere else would he learn how to read and interpret complex documents, deal with numbers and budgeting, learn about the human body and deal with people in positions of authority.

He told me that it was easy to persist with football because it was fun – whereas school wasn't. This was a little tougher to deal with because a lot of school is not fun. I asked him if there were any parts of school that were fun or interesting. He promptly told me that there weren't. I took another tack. I asked him to describe the teacher who brought out his best work or made him most interested in the subject. He described one teacher who aroused his curiosity, who had a sense of humour, who used different techniques in lessons (a bit of hands-on work, a bit of book-work, some discussion, some group work etc), who didn't hammer him for making mistakes, and who respected and listened to him. I then talked about how this lesson sounded a lot like his football training session. Again, he was surprised to find himself agreeing.

I must confess I don't know what effect our discussion had on this kid. To have an impact, it was probably important for someone to take an ongoing guiding and supportive role with this student, to hook him into schoolwork and to enhance persistence through using the most precious thing in his life – football. Maybe our discussion was at least a starting point for the student and showed him that:

- he had what it takes to deal with challenging schoolwork because he was an expert in persistence at football training – he already had persistence skills.
- school has the potential to be interesting and engaging through effective teaching – just as a good coach keeps all players interested, engaged and energised.

- school was a training ground for his future career – if he became a professional footballer – it would help him make effective decisions and make the most of his success.

If I was smarter at the time I would have talked about personal bests, how students become academic athletes by competing with their own previous performance, and how he could become an athlete in respect to his schoolwork as well as on the football field. I suspect this sporting analogy would have worked really well.

So what can you do when your child is at risk of throwing in the towel? You may like to talk about previous times that he or she has broken through to succeed at something challenging. It may not be schoolwork; it may be in sport or music, at his or her club, or with his or her friends. You may then like to ask your child to:

1   describe that situation in detail
2   say why it was difficult
3   identify the things they were thinking or the things they said to themselves to help them get through the situation
4   identify the things they did to help them get through the situation
5   describe how the things they thought and did helped them in that difficult situation
6   suggest things they can think in this present situation to help get them through
7   suggest things they can do in the present situation to help get them through.

The purpose of the exercise is to show your child that they have dealt with tough times before, and that there are identifiable reasons why they got through. They were thinking and doing things that were helpful – and they can think and do things in this situation that can help too.

Developing a plan for when schoolwork is difficult or challenging

Often students can 'hit the wall' and see no way around, under, or over it. This can be really hard to deal with, can be quite discouraging and can lead the student to feel helpless.

Cathy, junior high

In Cathy's first year of junior high she found she was quite good at German. In her second year of junior high, Cathy started at a new school. Before leaving her old school her German teacher told her she had a talent for the language and that she should continue it at her new school. Cathy started German at her new school quite a confident student. However, because this school used a different text book from the one she'd used previously, because the students had learnt a somewhat different set of vocabulary, and because the teacher had a different method of teaching the language, Cathy didn't perform as well as she had hoped. This was a disappointment to her, so much so that she wanted to drop German. In fact, her confidence was so shattered that she convinced herself that her previous strong performance in German was just good luck. Her parents, on the other hand, were pretty clued in to what was happening and believed that this was a bit of a teething period and that she would bounce back.

They dealt with the situation by talking about why she'd done well the year before and why the teacher had said what he did about her talent. They focused on the specific things Cathy was good at. As they talked, Cathy was able to identify that she was pretty good at getting on top of the rules of grammar, had a skill in getting the accent right and was able to memorise lots of words. These were all skills that she still possessed no matter what school she was at. The main problem was that there was a gap in knowledge (not skill), but she would be able to draw on her existing skills to plug this gap. It took longer than expected to plug the gap, but plug it Cathy eventually did. The secret to her persistence was to draw on previous times she had successfully applied her skill and use this to work through her current challenges.

A reason hitting the wall is so discouraging – and why students throw up their hands in surrender when it happens – is because they don't anticipate it. Because they don't anticipate it, they aren't prepared for it. It hits them like a bolt from the blue, which can be paralysing and not very helpful to one's persistence.

If your child is easily unsettled when they hit the wall, you might encourage them to become a troubleshooter, identifying potholes they might hit along their way and how they'll deal with them. You might like to talk through some of these potholes when your child has a project or an assignment to do. Some common potholes are listed in the table below, together with examples of anticipatory thinking and action required to overcome them.

Overcoming 'potholes'	
Pothole	How to get around it
Not being able to find relevant information	Ask a librarian for help
Finding too much information	Focus on information from the last five years
Key books missing from the library	Get an inter-library loan or visit another library
Not understanding important concepts	Ask the teacher or refer to a dictionary or thesaurus
Competing deadlines	Develop a priority list and chunk your schoolwork
Taking longer than expected	Begin the assignment early or build flexi-time into your timetable which can be used to spend extra time on it
Losing files from a computer crash	Back up files on a regular basis and keep a hard copy of most important files

Brainstorming some of these scenarios with your child gets them thinking in solution-focused ways. It shows them that problems are possible, even likely, and that there are usually sensible ways to deal with them. This means that your child isn't paralysed from the shock of the challenge or difficulty, and retains a sense of control and a belief that challenges and difficulties are surmountable.

Is preparing your child for potholes teaching your child to be a pessimist? I don't think so. The fact is you are focusing on solutions, not problems. Ask any successful business person and they'll tell you that knowing the lie of the land and developing contingency plans is a factor in their success. Being prepared involves more than knowing the successful steps in a process or task; it's also about being able to recognise and deal with the potholes, the dead-ends and the bolts from the blue.

Effective goal setting

Effective goal setting is another way to enhance persistence. Good students don't just have goals, they have effective goals. Many goals students set are not very effective. One girl told me, 'I've tried to set goals and say, "I'll have so much done by this time," but it never happens. So I don't do it anymore – there's no point.' Ineffective goals are:

- unrealistic
- unachievable
- not attractive to the student
- not specific enough to lead to action
- not measurable, so students don't know when they have been achieved or how close they are to achieving them
- not clear, so students don't know exactly what they are aiming for
- too easy and not stimulating
- not time-bound, so students don't have a timetable for action and results.

Goals that are effective are more likely to lead to persistence and success. Effective goals are:

- realistic
- achievable
- attractive and desirable to the student
- clear and specific
- measurable, so students know when they are achieved or how close they are to achieving them

- sufficiently challenging to draw students forward but not so challenging that they are unachievable
- time-bound, so that students have a clear timetable for action and results.

The table below gives some examples of goals that are effective and some that are not so effective. As you can see, the more effective goals are the ones that are clear and specific, reasonably measurable, and involve a time frame. It is assumed that the students setting these goals see them as achievable and attractive, and that the goals are reasonably challenging for the students but realistically within the students' capabilities. When these conditions are met, you can be sure that your child has set effective goals.

Setting effective goals

Ineffective goals	Neither here nor there goals	Effective goals
I must improve in history.	I must improve my essay writing in history.	For the next history essay I will read the question carefully, ask the librarian for help to find good books, spend an extra day reading, take detailed notes when reading and write one draft before handing it in.
I must be better behaved.	I must improve my behaviour in history and French.	I will sit away from Andy in history and Jo in French; I will not talk while the teacher is talking.
I must do better in science.	I must improve my practical work in science.	I will carefully plan and prepare for each science practical; I will ask questions if I'm unsure what to do; I will write up the practical on the same day that I do it.

Your child can set goals in any area of his or her life, including:

- goals for that week's study
- goals for sport
- goals for saving money for a holiday
- goals for losing or gaining weight
- goals for reducing the amount of television watched in a week.

Some other hints for effective goal setting include writing the goals down, not being discouraged if they aren't met (have a good look at why they weren't met – was it anything your child did or was it an ineffective goal?) and rewarding oneself when the goal is met.

Effective goals increase opportunities for success in a student's life because they serve as a road map: students with effective goals have a clear idea of where they are going, a clear idea of how they are going to get there, a clear idea of why they want to get there and a clear idea of how they will know when they are there. Any good business person or sportsperson will tell you that knowing all this is a blueprint for persistence and success – and also provides a light in the darkness when things get difficult.

More on effective goal setting

Because goal setting is a very important part of persistence and also an important part of success, I want to spend more time on it and run another idea by you.

Research suggests that goals can be *product* related or *process* related. Product-related goals are goals that refer to the student producing something or creating an output. Examples are: reading ten pages of a text book, doing half the essay that night, memorising three formulas, memorising some literary quotes, finishing the novel by the end of the week, and answering all the questions at the back of the book. Process-related goals are not so much concerned about the destination as they are about how you get there. They include:

- understanding something
- learning a new strategy
- solving problems
- developing new skills

- improving skills
- trying a new approach or technique.

Research suggests that product and process goals can give students confidence and lead to success. However, the process goals are the ones that are most related to motivation – this is because these goals enable students to become totally absorbed by the journey.

I also want to briefly talk about two things that increase the chances of students reaching their goals. These are goal commitment and good feedback. I mention these two because you have a direct part in building both of them into your child's life.

Students are more likely to reach their goal when they are committed to the goal. In fact, commitment is most important when goals or tasks are challenging or difficult. There are two ways to get students more committed to goals.

The first way to increase goal commitment is to negotiate goals with your child, or, at the very least, give good reasons why you have decided on the goals for them that you have. My preference is for the former – negotiating goals with your child. There must be some aspect of the goals your child pursues that is desirable to them.

The second way to increase your child's goal commitment is to communicate to them that they can reach their goals. When your child believes that they can reach their goal, they are more committed to reaching them. You increase your child's belief in their ability to meet goals by giving them good training or the opportunity to master tasks. Another way to build their ability to reach goals is to show them how you reach your goals and wrestle with challenging tasks or situations.

In addition to goal commitment, your child needs to receive feedback on their progress. If they don't know where they are, where they are going, and how to get there, they are less likely to get there. Good feedback involves telling them where they are at in relation to their goal, information about what they have done and how they have done it, and guidance about where they need to go from here and how to get there.

By negotiating goals with your child, building their belief in their ability to reach their goals, and providing good feedback, your child is more likely to reach their goals.

Effective help seeking

I want to say a few words on help seeking. Many students believe that if they get help from a teacher or a parent that means they aren't persistent – they think it means they've given up. There are others who won't seek help because they fear being seen as dumb. However, of those who seek help some seek it at appropriate times and in appropriate ways, while others seek help in not so appropriate ways. That is, there is effective help seeking and there is ineffective help seeking. Let me explain.

Some students ask for help even before they've given something a fair shot. They take one look at the problem or question, make a quick decision that they can't do it and shoot their hand up to ask their teacher for help or run to their parents or older brother or sister. These students aren't persistent and aren't likely to be so in the future because they aren't learning the skills of persistence described above. Nor are they developing a sense of control or self-belief because they aren't giving themselves a chance to succeed through their own efforts. Moreover, research has found that these students ask ineffective questions. They'll look at a problem and ask an unfocused and general question like, 'How do I do algebra?' As we'll see below, the persistent help seeker asks more focused and useful questions.

In contrast, persistent students first spend time trying to understand a problem. They'll try to get at it from a few directions. They'll look for more information. They'll figure out all the things they know about the problem and bits of the solution that they are confident about. Then they'll go to the teacher or their parent with focused questions about parts of the problem they haven't yet figured out. That is, they are effective help seekers. They enhance their persistence for next time because they have gained a sense of control and self-belief by getting part of the way themselves without help and by asking effective and useful questions.

Knowing when to stop persisting

I also tell students that there are effective persisters and ineffective persisters. Effective persisters know when to stop trying to figure out a solution and ask for help or move on to something else and maybe later come back to the problem fresh. Ineffective persisters can keep working at the problem so long that other schoolwork suffers. In extreme cases, no other schoolwork gets done at all.

Knowing when to pull out of a problem is a skill. A common situation I deal with in schools and universities concerns perfectionists. They will keep working at something until it's perfect, often missing other deadlines and letting their guard down in other subjects. In some cases, they'll not even hand in the work they've been doing because they're still not satisfied with it. This is not effective persistence. In many cases, it means dealing with a fear of failure and this I discuss in chapter 10. This issue of perfectionism is also discussed in chapter 14 on motivating the gifted and talented.

Living in the real world
In the real world not everything happens like they say in the books. Here are a few things for you to think about when digesting this chapter:

- Sometimes your child may give up sooner than they should. Don't make them feel bad about this. If after gentle encouragement they still won't budge, you don't need to be alarmed. Accept that in this instance they are not persistent. It's more of a concern when this happens frequently.
- Knowing when to pull out of a difficult challenge is tough. My rule of thumb is to decide when enough is enough, then do a bit more and then stop.
- Sometimes persistence won't pay off. Sometimes your child will not meet with success after persisting long and hard. Sometimes he or she will persist only to get the answer wrong. This happens and your child needs to understand that more often than not persistence pays off.
- Even with effective goal setting, sometimes your child might not reach his or her goal. Don't let your child lose hope if this happens. Take another look at the goal to see if it needs to be revised and look at the controllable factors that made it difficult to reach the goal. If this doesn't provide any clue, remember that setting effective goals increases the likelihood of success next time – so keep plugging away.

- Remember what I said earlier about chunking: it is a skill that may take time and support to develop.
- Just as your child is encouraged to call on previous times they have toughed things out, they may also need to remember times they haven't dealt with things so well to see why things didn't work out. Remind them that the fact they've handled things before is proof they have the skills required for persistence.
- When talking about possible potholes ahead remember to be solution focused and not problem focused. This means your child won't tip into fear and pessimism. Don't dwell on the potholes; just spend a little time talking about them so your child won't be shell-shocked if they come along but will have the confidence needed to deal with them. If talking about potholes freaks your child out too much, don't dwell on them in advance but be supportive when they arise.
- Don't let your child get discouraged if their goal setting doesn't lead to success. Check the goals they set, check there's nothing else they could have done to reach the goals, and make it clear to them that effective goal setting increases the chances of success.

Chapter summary

At some stage in your child's school life – and probably quite often – he or she will need to deal with difficult or challenging school-work. To successfully overcome the challenge, which may be frequent or recurring, your child needs to be persistent. Persistence is also important in terms of resilience and the ability to weather tough times. To help build your child's persistence you should encourage him or her to chunk (either in terms of time slots or in terms of work to be done), draw on previous times he or she has dealt with challenge, set effective goals, anticipate obstacles that may arise down the track and think through contingency action. Indeed, these are skills that are not only important for dealing with challenging schoolwork, they are important for coping with tough times in other parts of your child's personal life.

CHAPTER EIGHT TOP 5

1. Effective persistence is your child's ability to work through difficult schoolwork, seek help at appropriate times and in useful ways and know when to take a breather or pull out to attend to some other work.

2. As with many other parts of your child's school life, chunking is a great way to increase persistence: breaking schoolwork into bite-sized parts lays out a plan that keeps students on track and helps your child commit to seeing the task through.

3. Without doubt, your child will have weathered tough times in the past (either in sport, music, socially or at school). Talk about the things he or she thought and did that helped get him or her through. Lessons learnt from previous episodes of persistence can help your child persist this time.

4. Effective persisters are not shell-shocked or discouraged if they hit the wall. They anticipate potholes and have a plan for dealing with them. In any assignment at school there will be potholes. Talk with your child about how these may be handled.

5. Effective persisters are effective goal setters. Effective goals are achievable, believable, realistic, clear and specific, desirable, measurable and time-bound.

CHAPTER 9

REDUCING YOUR CHILD'S TEST ANXIETY

Leading up to and during tests is when students' anxiety is usually at its peak, and also when anxiety has its worst effects. According to one girl, 'I just quiver in exams. I just fall to pieces.' Novelty and fear of failure are the two main reasons students experience test anxiety. That is, tests are not a usual day-to-day occurrence that your child can get used to and there is often a lot riding on this novel and high-pressure event.

Test anxiety is a strange thing. A small amount doesn't seem to interfere with performance. In fact it may improve it. One girl told me, 'I love getting stressed. I need to feel the pressure on me when I'm doing things.' But too much can really get in the way of performance. This chapter, therefore, is not necessarily about eliminating anxiety from your child's life, it's about reducing it to more comfortable levels that won't interfere with your child's functioning.

I want to make it clear that I'm not talking about clinical levels of anxiety or anxiety disorders in this chapter. It is

IF YOU FORGET TO WAKE ME UP FOR THE EXAM, I'LL FORGIVE YOU

about test anxiety and school-specific anxiety. Certainly, some suggestions in this chapter are helpful for reducing any sort of anxiety. However, if your child's anxiety is significantly interfering with their functioning, they may need specialist assistance from a psychologist, counsellor or psychiatrist.

Test anxiety affects different students in different ways. I've found that anxiety can lead some students to become overstrivers. That is, they respond to their fears by doing their very best not to screw up. Others respond to their anxiety in less helpful ways. In fact, some can respond to their anxiety in ways that almost guarantee they will fail. The next chapter talks about these types of students in some detail.

Many would say that the overstrivers don't need any help. Sure they're anxious, but they're getting the results. To some extent, this is true. But the risk with these students is that they aren't resilient if they don't do well. This can confirm their self doubt and focus them on failure. Then, instead of responding to their fears with overstriving, they may respond with avoidance or self-sabotage. Because of this, I suggest that all students can benefit from a reduction in test anxiety and this chapter is about how to help them do this.

It is important to recognise that in our highly competitive school system, a certain level of test anxiety is to be expected. As I mentioned earlier, a low level of anxiety is not necessarily going to interfere with your child's performance. A student who experiences butterflies going into an exam does not necessarily freeze at the first question on the paper. This low level of test anxiety is not a problem for most students.

How do you know when test anxiety is a problem? Simple. When it starts impairing your child's functioning and performance. Examples of anxiety interfering with functioning include:

- freezing in the exam
- having distracting thoughts that reduce concentration
- avoiding the exam altogether
- avoiding study
- not writing clear answers
- having difficulty focusing
- having difficulty paying attention
- making mistakes in calculations.

If this is happening as a result of feeling nervous or worrying too much, then you know anxiety is a problem and needs to be reduced.

What is test anxiety?

Test anxiety has two parts: a thinking part that is often called 'worry' and a feeling part that is often called 'nervousness'.

Worry involves thinking things like:

- What happens if I fail?
- What if I'm not good enough?
- What if Sam beats me?
- What if bad questions come up in the exam?
- What if I can't get into university?
- What will my parents say if I screw this up?
- What if I don't know the answers to the test questions?
- What if I don't have enough time to answer the questions?

A quick way to tell if your child is a worrier is to see how many 'what if' questions they ask you or themselves. Worriers are more focused on the future than the present, so to help reduce your child's worrying you need to address their negative or fearful thinking and bring them back to the here and now as much as possible. One girl told me, 'From the beginning I see the assignments and I go, "Oh my God, what am I going to do?" Every second it's on my mind, "What am I going to do? What am I going to do?"'

Nervousness involves physical symptoms like:

- a churning stomach (more severe than butterflies) and maybe vomiting
- palpitating heart
- giddiness
- sweating
- pins and needles
- numbness in body parts
- a dry mouth.

Often, students will start experiencing these sensations in response to their worried thinking. So obviously to address these feelings, students need to tackle their worrying. But there are also practical things students can do to reduce their nervous feelings and this chapter explores some of these.

If you suspect that these feelings or symptoms are not because of your child's anxiety, ask a doctor to check them out.

Why are students anxious?

There are many reasons students are anxious. I want to focus on just a handful which I've found have a big impact on whether a student experiences anxiety that is getting in the way of his or her functioning.

I propose five main reasons why students worry and feel nervous. These students tend to:

- think negatively
- live in the future too much and not enough in the here and now
- have trouble effectively dealing with stress and pressure
- find the novelty or unusualness of test situations disturbing
- have a high fear of failure.

To address these problems I focus on five strategies, as follows:

- tackling negative thinking
- grounding your child in the here and now
- developing effective relaxation techniques
- preparing for tests and exams
- developing test-taking skills.

Tackling negative thinking

If you asked an anxious student what was going through their mind when thinking about an upcoming test or exam, the answer would involve a lot of negative thoughts.

You'll recall from chapter 3 on self-belief that negative thinking erodes students' confidence, optimism and self-belief. It also affects their behaviour. Students who think negatively are less likely to persist at schoolwork, less likely to try to solve problems and give less effective answers to questions. On the other hand, students who think positively tend to persist at schoolwork longer, try harder to solve problems, write clearer and more effective answers, and as a result tend to do better in their schoolwork.

Students who think negatively are also more likely to feel anxious. More specifically, they tend to worry more than other students and as a result start feeling pretty nervous. It's no wonder they feel anxious when thinking along the following lines about an upcoming test:

- failing
- not being good enough
- other students beating them
- impossible exam questions
- disappointing their parents
- not knowing the answer to a question
- running out of time.

Anyone dwelling on these sorts of things is not going to feel good about going into the exam room. According to one girl, 'I can't eat the night before an exam. All night I have nightmares I'm going to fail and that Dad's going to come after me.'

Students low in anxiety don't dwell on these things. Sure, these things might run through their minds at some stage but they are able to put them into perspective and not let them overwhelm them or impair their performance. If any of these things start to take a hold on these students, they are quick to challenge the thought with some commonsense thinking. As we learnt in chapter 3 on self-belief, they do this through:

- identifying negative thinking traps
- developing positive self-talk
- developing realistic optimism.

Let's quickly recap the essence of these points.

Identifying negative thinking traps There are some common negative thinking traps students fall into including:

- black and white thinking (things are either easy or impossible)
- biased thinking (taking a negative interpretation of events)
- end-of-the-worlding (thinking it's the end of the world if they fail a test)
- turning positives into negatives (if they succeed on an exam they only see it as more pressure to succeed next time)
- getting sucked into scared feelings (assuming that because you feel nervous it means you are going to fail the test)

- mega-generalising (if something unpleasant happens in one subject, it's going to happen in other subjects)
- mountain building (a bad mark means you're hopeless and you're never going to get through the term).

Developing positive self-talk Developing positive self-talk requires students to challenge their negative thoughts. Usually this involves nothing more than some commonsense thinking. Commonsense tells students that if they take their study a step at a time, if they put in some hard work, if they take more notice of teachers' feedback on their work, and if they get organised and plan ahead, they will increase their chances of doing well in the test.

Developing realistic optimism There are three areas of your child's thinking in which realistic optimism can be developed:

- the way he or she views past events (not dwelling on poor performance or mistakes but taking the lesson to be learnt and then moving on)
- the way he or she views current events (being happy with where they are in the moment and not dwelling on what's happened in the past or what might happen in the future)
- the way he or she views the future (thinking that whatever comes up in the future, he or she has the ability to deal with it). The worrier spends too much time in the future and thinks about it in negative ways.

You may wish to go back to chapter 3 to look at some of the specifics involved in each of these three areas.

Using the principles from these three areas (identifying negative thinking traps, developing positive self-talk and developing realistic optimism), the table on page 158 shows some ways of dealing with worrying thoughts. You can sit with your child and go through these, or you might like to chat informally when the opportunity arises.

As you can see, there's nothing unrealistic about the challenges in the table on page 158 to worrying thoughts. It's all commonsense and therefore has the advantage of being believable and achievable in your child's mind.

Overcoming worrying thoughts

Worrying thought	The challenging thought
What happens if I fail?	If I do regular revision I'm less likely to fail.
What if I'm not good enough?	The main things that will get me through are hard work and effective study – I can increase these.
What if Alex beats me?	What Alex does or doesn't do is none of my business. Anyway, I'm likely to do better if I focus on the schoolwork and not on Alex.
What if bad questions come up in the exam?	If bad questions come up, everyone else will have to deal with them too, so I'm no worse off than them).
What if I can't get into university?	There are lots of universities and if I can't get into one I'll try to get into another. Anyway, there are alternative entry paths and lots of ways for older students to get into university later.
What will my parents say if I screw this up?	Sure I'd like my parents to be happy with me, but I'll deal with it if they're not and I'll think about what I can do next time to do better.
What if I don't know the answer to the test questions?	I'm more likely to know the answer if I'm well prepared. If the worst comes to the worst, I'll try hard to do better on the other questions.
What if I can't answer the teacher's question?	Students often don't know the answer to the teacher's question and it's not the end of the world if I don't.
What if I don't have enough time to answer the questions?	Before I start the test, I'll make a quick plan of how much time I'll spend on each section. If I've got spare time at the end I can go back and build on a section if I want.

The difference between worriers and positively motivated students is not so much in whether they think negative thoughts, but more in how often they think them and the extent to which they are able to deal with them. The thought of failure crosses many students' minds, but most of them are able to draw on previous successes and lessons learnt and use this to challenge their worrying thoughts.

Grounding your child in the here and now

You saw above that worriers do a lot of 'what if' thinking. This type of thinking is almost totally focused on the future – and in a negative way. 'Future' thinking wouldn't be so debilitating if it was optimistic.

I've dealt with the positive thinking side of the equation in the previous section and in chapter 3. The future thinking side of the equation is what we'll deal with here.

To cut to the chase, there's usually no better way to deal with the future than to live in the present. You can only ever do something in the here and now. You can't do something in the future until you arrive at it in the here and now. What's happened in the past has happened and what will happen in the future hasn't arrived yet.

Any psychiatrist, psychologist, counsellor or practising Buddhist will tell you that your child is less likely to worry the more they live in the here and now. This is because:

- dealing with the here and now reduces your child's load – trying to deal with the present and the future as well can be too much of a mountain. (Remember, you need to reduce the mountains in your child's life.)
- the known is often less scary than the unknown – the present focuses on the known and the future focuses on the unknown.
- trying to predict future events can be wasted energy because they may not eventuate, whereas dealing with the here and now is likely to be energy well spent.

Now for an important qualification to the above. This isn't to say that your child should have no regard for the future – of course they have to plan, develop contingency plans and prepare for things like exams that are coming up. But what they need to do is see what's coming up and spend their here and now moments preparing for this; not spend their here and now moments worrying about the outcome and its consequences. As parents you need to encourage your child to have responsible regard for the future, but support them in recognising that the best place to effectively deal with future challenge is in the here and now.

Some techniques to ground your child in the here and now include:

- encouraging them to think, 'What can I do now to reduce the chances of that happening?'
- encouraging them to immerse themselves in the tasks or schoolwork they are doing right now
- encouraging them to go for a goal in the next 15 minutes; for example, 'In 15 minutes time I'll have this sum worked out.'
- encouraging them to focus on their environment in the here and now; noticing everything about where they are or what they are looking at or hearing. This can be particularly helpful when your child can't turn off racing, worrying thoughts about the future.
- encouraging them to recognise that they can't predict the future and that all they can know and deal with is where they are in the here and now.

You may be able to think of some other ways to ground your child in the here and now. Do any work for you when you start worrying about the future? Maybe talk with your child about some effective ways you deal with your own worry.

Developing effective relaxation techniques

Dealing with anxiety is not just about tackling the negative worrying thoughts that make your child feel unpleasant, it's also about dealing with the feelings and physical symptoms of anxiety. One very effective way of doing this is to help your child develop a relaxation technique or process that suits him or her.

There are many different relaxation techniques your child can choose from. These range from very formal and disciplined meditation through to yoga and swimming laps.

Christie, senior high

Christie was a chronic worrier. She spent most of her time worrying about unpleasant things that might happen to her in the future. She was absolutely guilty of 'what if' thinking and she would continually play out worst-case scenarios in her mind, often working herself into quite a panic. It was not uncommon for her to go into the exam room with a churning stomach and a racing mind – both draining her concentration, attention and memory. Her parents were concerned about this and encouraged Christie to see the school counsellor. Through her work with the counsellor, she developed an ability to focus more on the present moment. Together, they figured out a strategy to deal with her 'what if' thinking. When future worry thinking entered her mind, she would tell herself, 'I'm not there now and when I get there I'll deal with it.' She also developed an ability to really focus on the here and now by actively noticing and immersing herself in her present environment.

For Christie, these were effective ways of grounding herself in the here and now. In fact, she found that she was always able to deal with what she encountered in the present moment and that it never seemed to be as bad as her worry thoughts told her it would be. She learnt that the best way to deal with the future was to do a good job of focusing on the present. Was that the end of her anxiety? Of course not. She'd been a worrier for as long as she could remember and this wasn't going to be reversed overnight. However, she did reduce her anxiety enough that she was able to function more effectively in the exam room. Christie, her parents and her counsellor agreed that this was a great result and a great start to tackling something that had plagued her for most of her life.

One thing I will say about relaxation is that it's horses for courses. Your child needs to find or develop a technique that really suits him or her. If it's not a suitable technique it's not likely to be very effective. Some children can't sit in one spot for more than two minutes and so formal meditation might not be their scene. Instead they might benefit from a more active form of yoga or repetitive exercise of some description (such as swimming, jogging or walking).

On the other hand, just because your child can't sit still for two minutes doesn't mean they can't discipline themselves into sitting quietly for longer periods of time. I've spoken to a number of teachers who through individualised attention have encouraged even their disrupters into sitting quietly.

What are the advantages of developing a relaxation technique? Many have found that:

- Relaxation is a great way to reduce the unpleasant physical symptoms of anxiety.
- Relaxation is not only about reducing unpleasant feelings, it also increases pleasant feelings.
- Relaxation is a great way of stilling the mind, emptying it of worry thinking.
- The effects of relaxation carry on even after the relaxation session has finished.
- People can get quite expert at quickly putting their body into relaxation mode and use this in pressure situations such as exams or job interviews.
- People can get quite expert at quickly stilling their worry thinking and can use this skill in pressure situations also.

There are literally hundreds of books proposing different ways to relax and you can find many of these in the health or personal development section of any bookstore. However, to give you a quick introduction to relaxation, I've set out on pages 164–5 a relaxation technique that I've found works well. This exercise can be completed in just fifteen minutes.

Before your child does the suggested relaxation exercise (or any similar relaxation exercise) you need to tell them the following things:

- Find somewhere quiet, not too cold, not too hot and not too bright.
- Don't get frustrated if it takes a few goes before you start relaxing.
- Don't get discouraged if you only feel relaxed for a couple of minutes in the session – a couple of minutes of relaxation is better than no relaxation at all.
- Don't worry if distracting thoughts enter your mind (some call this 'monkey mind'); just gently turn your attention back to your breathing or that peaceful place.
- Don't finish your relaxation session abruptly; just as you gently went into the relaxation, you need to gently come out of it.
- Don't jump up straight after the session; get up slowly and take it easy for a few minutes.
- The more you practise the better you'll get at relaxing and the quicker you can turn on your relaxation mode when you're in a pressure situation.
- If your relaxation technique makes you feel unpleasant or uncomfortable then you might want to consider another technique that's more suited to you – remember, repetitive and rhythmic exercise such as jogging, swimming or walking can be equally effective in relaxing you.

Preparing for tests and exams

Up to now I've discussed how to tackle worry thinking and also how to develop an effective relaxation technique. In this section and the next I want to describe some practical ways to reduce your child's anxiety leading up to tests and exams and also some practical ways to deal with the actual test situation better.

What I'll do in this and the next section is briefly describe each strategy and then present a checklist that you might like to work through with your child as tests or exams are approaching. This checklist is a summary of what I present below but it's also a quick way for your child to identify the different issues that arise leading up to a test. This has two advantages. First, they won't freak out if the issue arises – it's not a nasty surprise that unsettles them before a test. Secondly, it's a way of better preparing for the test.

Something you may notice is that there's no one thing that

RELAXATION IN FIFTEEN MINUTES

- Step 1. Expect to relax. (Calmly tell yourself, 'I am going to relax now.')

- Step 2. Find somewhere quiet to sit or lie down. (Try to avoid places where you might go to sleep.)

- Step 3. Make sure you are comfortable and close your eyes.

- Step 4. Concentrate on your breathing.

  – Breathe deeply down into your belly.

  – With your first in-breath count 'one' in your mind; with your second breath count 'two' and so on up to 'five', and then start again at 'one'.

  – Each time you breathe out, say "relaaaxxx" in your mind.

- Step 5. After a few minutes of this you then progressively relax each part of your body.

  – Focus on your right foot, clench the toes tightly for a few seconds and then slowly release them.

  – Now do the same with your left foot.

  – Now clench your right thigh muscles for a few seconds and then slowly release them.

  – Now do the same with your left thigh muscles.

  – Do the same with your right hand, left hand, right arm, left arm, stomach, neck, shoulders and your face.

- Step 6. Now your body is more relaxed, turn your mind to the most peaceful place you know. It might be a beach, it might be a garden, it might be a particular room or a bush setting. When your mind is →

there, take special notice of every part of that place and all the peaceful things about it. Spend time looking around that place. Take notice of other things such as the smells, the sounds, or the feel of the ground under you. If distracting thoughts enter your mind, that's okay – gently focus on your counting or that peaceful place.

- Step 7. When you are ready, come back gradually, slowly taking notice of your body again. Before opening your eyes take notice of the sounds in the room, then – open your eyes slowly, flex your arms and legs, and get up very slowly. (You may feel a bit light-headed, so don't jump up.)

- Step 8. Set a day, time and place for your next relaxation session.

Practise as often as you can.

reduces anxiety leading up to a test or exam. Rather, it's the accumulation of a number of actions which means your child is more relaxed going into a test. But your child doesn't have to do everything suggested in order to be less anxious. Instead, he or she can identify, say, five or six things that are relevant and target those.

Start study early in the term and do it regularly
There is no substitute for getting into study early in the term and no substitute for doing it regularly. This avoids last-minute panicking and cramming. The early study doesn't need to be intense, but it's good to keep up with material as it's given. But remember that late study is better than no study at all, so never let your child say it's too late to do any study.

Develop a study timetable and stick to it
Your child will be able to prioritise, plan and prepare better for study if he or she has a timetable. An example timetable was presented in chapter 7.

Hand in work on time
Students tend to be anxious when they get behind in assignments and other schoolwork. Handing work in on time is the most effective way to deal with this.

Look at past test papers; set your own test; hand in practice mini-essays
A major problem with tests and exams is that they are novel – that is, your child doesn't do them every day and so they aren't something he or she gets used to. Another problem is that students aren't prepared for questions that come up in the test. Looking at and doing past test papers under test conditions can be a good way to become more comfortable with the test situation and questions in it. Your child might like to ask a teacher if they will read a couple of practice exam essays and give him or her some feedback.

Look for teacher clues
Often material in a test is predictable. It'll be the stuff on which the teacher asked the class to take detailed notes, the material the teacher emphasised in class or about which the teacher said, 'This is on the test.' You'd be amazed at how many students miss these clues and cues. Encourage your child to recognise them.

Know as much about the test as possible
This means knowing:

- the material to be covered in the test
- the proportion of the term/year mark allocated to the test
- the time allowed
- the venue
- the types of questions (multi-choice, essay, short answer, true/false etc)
- the materials allowed in the exam room.

Students who know these things are better prepared and less distracted by the novelty or unusualness of the test situation.

Identify the distractions that can arise leading up to an exam
Even the best-intentioned students can get distracted leading up to the exam. It's a good idea to identify the potholes your child

might hit as the exam approaches, and discuss with him or her how these might be dealt with. Distractions can range from friends to sporting commitments to part-time work. How is your child going to handle these when they threaten to get in the way of exam preparation? Remember that flexibility and balance are essential, and so totally cutting your child off from the outside world, for example, is not the most balanced way to deal with the outside world's distractions.

Avoid making major life decisions before a test

One of the most important ways to reduce anxiety leading up to the test is to keep the ship steady for your child. This means not making major decisions as your child approaches the test day. For your part, this means not announcing selling the house, putting down the old pet cat, changing jobs, and so on. For your child's part it means, for example, not deciding one week out from the economics exam that he or she doesn't want to be an accountant anymore so there's no longer any reason to study economics. This is probably not a great decision given the fact that he or she has wanted to be an accountant for the previous two years. Discuss with your child how major decisions are not best made under pressure, and suggest they see through the next week as planned and keep their options open before making that major decision.

Keep relationships intact leading up to the test

To keep the ship steady before an exam it's a good idea to keep relationships intact as much as possible. It's not uncommon for students under stress to break up with their girlfriend or boyfriend or pick a fight with friends in study week and this does nothing to reduce their anxiety. Again, discuss with your child how this is not the best time to make major decisions and suggest they see through the next week as planned and keep their options open before making that major decision.

Try to get good sleep in the week leading up to the exam

Getting good sleep is important. With good sleep your child is likely to be less stressed and more energised. Of course, some students will be studying later into the night than usual, but try to ensure a bit of balance during the week before the test. Maybe have four late study sessions and three earlier nights of sleep.

Avoid too much caffeine and maintain a balanced diet in the week leading up to the exam

Try to encourage a reasonably healthy intake of food and drink leading up to the exam. But don't forget balance. For example, coffee drinkers will want their coffee – but go easy on it; choco-holics will want their chocolate – but don't overdo it.

Try to do a bit of exercise to burn off excess anxiety

Exercise is a great way to burn off tension. Again, however, remember balance. You don't want your child overdoing exercise in the week before the test and crawling to the exam room exhausted and aching.

Practise relaxation as often as possible

As discussed in the previous section, relaxation is a great way to reduce anxiety leading up to a test. Students relax in different ways. Some go for formal and disciplined meditation, some for more active relaxation such as yoga, and others for physical exercise. Let your child do whatever works best.

On page 170–1 is a checklist of these anxiety-reducing actions. Work through it with your child if you like. Which actions do they think are most relevant to their preparation? Maybe target a handful that your child thinks will help reduce their anxiety most. Can your child identify any other things he or she can do to reduce anxiety leading up to the exam? You might also recognise some of the things he or she does better than others. Recognising your child's strengths is important.

Developing test-taking skills

Well, the test day has arrived. With a bit of luck your child has tackled a few of the pointers described above to reduce anxiety. But dealing with anxiety doesn't stop here. Your child still has to survive the pre-test nerves and then sit the test. There is still work to be done. This work starts as your child wakes up, continues as he or she waits to be let into the exam room, and is completed once the supervisor says, 'Pens down.'

Again, I'll briefly describe each action your child can take to reduce anxiety on the day of the test and then conclude with a checklist you and your child might like to work through. Identify only a handful of actions that your child thinks will really make a difference to his or her anxiety. Remember, doing fewer things better is more desirable than doing everything on the list not very well.

If you're a heavy sleeper, set two alarm clocks or get someone to wake you

This may be news to some students, but you need to be awake to sit an exam and you also need to be there on time. This means your child has to wake up in good time to get to the exam. You may like to wake them or set two alarm clocks some distance from the bed. I spoke to one student who can walk across the room to turn off alarms in his sleep. He has to rely on his mother to wake him up. Yes, I know children must be responsible for themselves, but exams are too important to use to teach lessons like that – teach lessons during activities in which your child gets a chance to do it again if they stuff up.

Have all your materials ready the night before

Your child's anxiety tends to be on the higher side when they are running around like a mad thing trying to find pens, a calculator, a ruler or their watch the morning of the exam. Get everything ready the night before and spend the morning being focused and relaxed.

Have something to eat before the exam

Try to get something into your child's stomach. If he or she is feeling sick from worry, encourage them to have a few mouthfuls at least – just sufficient that their stomach won't be empty in the exam room. Within ten minutes of the exam starting, your child's anxiety is likely to be lower than it was before the exam and suddenly they'll be starving. It's hard to concentrate when your belly's grumbling. If your child can't face even a mouthful then let it go – don't get into an argument the morning of an exam. Alternatively, your child may be able to take some food into the exam room and this may satisfy their hunger during the exam.

Aim to arrive at the venue a touch early

Rushing to the test venue is stressful. Getting there late is throwing away marks. Help your child get there a touch early to maybe find a quiet place to sit and get psyched for the test.

Checklist of anxiety-reducing activities

Tick which ones need special attention, then add two more

☐ Start your study early in the term and do it regularly – but remember that late study is better than no study.

☐ Develop a study timetable and stick to it (see chapter 7).

☐ Hand in work on time.

☐ Look at past test papers; set your own test; hand in practice mini-essays (say, 250 words).

☐ Look for teacher clues (material repeated in class; teacher saying 'This is in the test'; teacher asking the class to take detailed notes).

☐ Know the following: the material to be covered in the test; the percentage of term/year marks allocated; the time allowed; the venue; the types of questions (multi-choice, essay, short answer, true/false etc); the materials allowed in the exam room.

☐ Write down the distractions that can arise leading up to an exam (e.g. part-time work, friends). How will you deal with these?

☐ Avoid making major life decisions before a test.

☐ Keep your relationships intact leading up to a test.

☐ Try to get good sleep in the week leading up to an exam.

☐ Avoid too much caffeine and maintain a balanced diet in the week leading up to the exam.

☐ Leading up to the week of the test, try to do a bit of exercise to burn off excess anxiety.

→

☐ Practise your relaxation as often as possible (see the previous section).

☐

☐

Avoid panickers before the exam

Just before the exam, rumours can race through the class or year group at the speed of light. Whispers of what's on and what's not on the paper ripple through the crowd. Encourage your child to avoid students who do this. If they happen to hear a rumour, tell them not to become unsettled. They need to be like the swimmer who focuses solely on the lane and the clock – in the exam it comes down to the student, the paper and the clock; they should forget about the rest.

Take no notice of other students in the exam room

I'm always fascinated by the behaviour and posturing that goes on in an exam room. For some students it's a race to write as many pages as possible. For others it's a matter of looking really cool and relaxed as though everything's under control. Other students just act silly, dropping pens, shuffling papers and making stupid noises. Others try to finish as quickly as possible and then sit there looking pleased with themselves. A teacher once told me that exam supervisors registered a complaint from students that one student was distracting them because he was acting so confidently! What's the message in all this? Forget about the other students in the exam room. Remember, it all comes down to the student, the test paper and the clock. Nothing else matters.

Read instructions very carefully

One of the most common – and fatal – mistakes students make in exams is that they don't read instructions carefully. I've lost count of the number of students who answer questions 1, 2, 3 and 4 in section A when they were only required to answer one of the four questions. This is lethal. It's marks down the drain. Students get so focused on answering the questions they've prepared for that they glance quickly at the instructions, think they know what they say and dive into the paper. Insist that your child spends good time reading the instructions very carefully.

Know the mark and time allocation

If section A is worth 10 per cent of the test marks, section B is worth 30 per cent and section C is worth 60 per cent, it is critical that your child spends most time on section C, less on section B, and less again on section A. It's all about prioritising. Too many students get sucked in to spending too much time on section A simply because that's where they happen to know the most. As much as I sympathise with this, they can only get 10 per cent of their marks from this section and so must move on.

Look through the test paper so you know what's ahead

It's often a good idea to know what's coming up in the test. This is another way of allocating time. For example, if each of the four sections in the exam are worth equal marks and having looked at sections B, C, and D your child finds they know these better than section A, then they might spend a bit less time on section A and go for better marks in the last three sections. If they hadn't looked ahead, they would have spent too much time on a question they weren't comfortable with and lost their advantage in the other three sections.

Read questions very carefully and underline key words

Just as students don't read instructions carefully enough, they sometimes spend too little time reading the questions. This sounds crazy but students go into exams pumped up to answer questions and so focus entirely on the answering and not on understanding what's being asked. At best, some will glance at the question, see some key words and assume they know what the question's asking. Then away they go, hurtling off into the wide blue yonder. There are often subtle issues and sub-questions within questions that may be overlooked unless the student reads them very carefully. You might also encourage your child to underline key words.

For long answers, look back at the question frequently

For long answers, not only is it important to read the question carefully at the start, it's also important for your child to look back at the question as they go along. This ensures that they stay on track. Too many students slowly and gradually wander off the track and by the end of the answer are completely lost.

For long answers, spend time at the start to sketch an answer plan

In addition to regularly looking back at the question in long answers, it's a good idea for your child to spend a minute or so sketching an answer plan. This minute may be the most effective and valuable minute of the exam.

If the answer to a question isn't known, don't freak out

It's quite common to not know the answer to a question or questions in the exam. Unfortunately, this can really unsettle some students and can interfere with their answers to the rest of the paper. It's important that they don't freak out. Instead, they should calmly move to the next question or a question they can answer. It's not unusual for the answer (or part of an answer) to come to them while they are answering another question. If there's time left at the end of the paper, then they can ponder what the question is asking. Even if they can't answer the question at all, your child's overall performance will be better if they handle the other questions in a relaxed and focused manner.

Know which method of test taking suits

Different students have different ways of doing tests. Talk with your child about whether they prefer working from the beginning to the end of the paper, doing the easiest questions first or doing the most difficult questions first. This may depend on which subject is being tested, whether it's an easy or difficult paper and whether it's a multi-choice, true/false, short answer or essays-based exam. Sitting in the test is probably not the best time to decide these things. It is good if your child figures out an approach based on their past experience of tests. But remember to be flexible – if it doesn't work in a particular exam then change it.

Write neatly

I know you think the third grade was when your child last got marks for writing neatly, but like it or not his or her handwriting may also affect the marks your child gets today. He or she needs to remember that the examiner has read forty answers, it's late, he or she is tired – and your child's answer is the next one up for marking. If the examiner has to reread things your child has written because they're almost illegible, this is not going to make him or her happy. He or she may choose not to try reading that part of the answer at all. If important things your child has written can't or won't be read then they're throwing away marks. Maybe in your child's practice tests at home he or she can focus on writing neatly.

Use all the time available

Some students throw away marks by not using all the exam time available. In fact, some seem to see it as a status symbol to finish early and let everyone know it. More effective students double-check their answers or reread an essay if they finish early – they're sometimes surprised to find they've made a mistake somewhere. Using all the time available is yet another way to do as well as one can.

What all this adds up to is that test taking is a skill. There are clear strategies and behaviours that improve students' ability to take tests. The more your child has some or many of these strategies and behaviours under their belt, the less anxious they will be and the better they will do in that test.

On page 176–7 is a checklist of test-taking strategies. Work through it with your child if you like. What does he or she think is most relevant to their test taking? Maybe target a handful of strategies that your child thinks will help reduce their anxiety most. Can your child identify any other things he or she can do to reduce anxiety during the exam? As before, you might like to recognise some of the things they do better than others. Recognising your child's strengths is important.

Living in the real world

In the real world not everything happens like they say in the books. Here are a few things for you to think about when digesting this chapter.

- Anxiety is not necessarily going to impair your child's performance and in small doses may increase his or her performance. But it can escalate quickly and get in the way of your child's functioning. When it does, it needs to be reduced.

- If your child's anxiety is extreme, significantly impairing his or her functioning, or is a concern to you in any way, then seek professional assistance from a psychologist, counsellor or psychiatrist. Make sure they work well with young people.

- It is not unusual to worry about tests and exams. Most students at some stage wonder whether they're up to the test and how they'll do on the day. It becomes a concern when the worry starts impacting on your child's functioning.

- Your child may not always tackle his or her worry thinking successfully. Go for small gains and changes in thinking. Take it slowly; don't go for radical thought change in one go – it will probably only scare your child off.

- Don't expect your child to completely eliminate 'what if' thinking from his or her life. Often 'what if' thinking is a habit that has developed over time and so needs to be slowly turned around as with any other habit.

- Be flexible about which way of relaxing suits your child best. For some children physical exercise is their scene, whereas for others meditation is very effective.

- Doing good preparation and developing test-taking skills are great ways to reduce test anxiety. This chapter has presented many small ways to reduce anxiety and it is too big an ask for students to tackle all of them. Instead identify some suitable strategies and do a good job of addressing those. Remember, doing fewer things better is preferable to doing many things not so well.

Checklist of test-taking strategies

Tick which ones need special attention, then add two more

☐ If you're a heavy sleeper, set two alarm clocks (some distance from the bed) or get someone to wake you.

☐ Have all your materials ready the night before (including a watch).

☐ Have breakfast.

☐ Aim to arrive at the venue a touch early.

☐ Avoid panickers before the exam. Also avoid people who might unsettle or distract you.

☐ Read instructions *very* carefully.

☐ Know the marks allocated to the test, the number of sections/questions, and allocate your time at the start.

☐ Look through the test paper so you know what's ahead.

☐ Read questions *very* carefully, perhaps underlining key words.

☐ For long answers, look back at the question frequently – this keeps you on track.

☐ Pace yourself – know how much time is available for each question.

☐ For long answers (e.g. essays), spend 1 or 2 minutes at the start to sketch an answer plan.

→

☐ Take no notice of other students in the exam room.

☐ If you don't know the answer to a question, don't freak out; go on to another question and go back to the difficult question last – sometimes the answer comes to you as you're doing another question.

☐ Know which method of test taking suits you (but be flexible depending on the exam). Do you prefer working from the beginning to the end of the paper? Doing the easiest questions first? Doing the most difficult questions first?

☐ Write neatly.

☐ Use all the time available – if you finish early, check your answers.

☐

☐

Chapter summary

Anxiety not only makes the journey a less pleasant one, it can also impair your child's performance in tests or exams. Although a low level of anxiety is not necessarily a bad thing, anxiety can quickly escalate – particularly in competitive situations. It is therefore important to support your child in developing effective ways to reduce the anxiety in his or her life. This chapter focused on five ways in which this can be done: tackling worry thinking, grounding your child in the here and now, developing effective relaxation techniques, preparing for tests and exams and developing effective test-taking skills. Through some or all of these strategies your child will be able to reduce his or her anxiety and also provide better answers in test situations.

CHAPTER NINE TOP 5

1. Test anxiety has two main components: worry and nervousness. Worry is the negative and fearful thinking that happens leading up to a test or exam. Nervousness involves the unpleasant feelings and symptoms (such as churning stomach, giddiness, sweating) that result.

2. Tackling worry involves tackling your child's negative thinking about tests. This means identifying the various negative thinking patterns that students fall into and challenging this thinking with some common-sense optimism.

3. Another major part of worry is the future-based 'what if' thinking that accompanies negative thoughts. Your child needs to develop techniques to ground him or herself in the here and now.

4. Relaxation is an effective way to deal with the symptoms of anxiety. Different relaxation techniques suit different students. They can range from formal and disciplined meditation to yoga to relaxed breath training to repetitive exercise such as swimming, jogging or walking.

5. There are some practical steps your child can take to reduce test anxiety. These can be separated into those taken leading up to the exam beginning with early and regular revision through to a balanced diet and adequate sleep in the week before the exam, and those taken on the day of the test such as arriving early, focusing on the test and not on others in the room and reading instructions and questions very carefully.

CHAPTER 10

REDUCING YOUR CHILD'S FEAR OF FAILURE

Through the last ten years of research and work with schools and students, I have come to the conclusion that fear of failure is one of the most pervasive and dangerous features of our school system. Fear of failure has some wide-ranging effects on students. At one end of the continuum it can lead to overstriving or perfectionism. At the other end it can lead to self-sabotage, cheating and dropping out. Fear of failure has some very powerful effects on students' motivation and must be dealt with if your child is to be positively motivated.

In this chapter I describe some of the common ways fear of failure manifests itself in students' lives. These are:

- overstriving
- perfectionism
- defensive pessimism
- self-sabotage
- giving up or disengaging from school.

After I describe each of these will I look at what needs to be done to eliminate them from your child's life. It is first important that you know if your child is a failure fearer, and if so which type, as then you will be able to identify the most effective ways to support your child towards more positive motivation.

Overstriving

Some students deal with their fear of failure by succeeding! These students study really hard, are extremely well prepared and often do quite well – some of them exceptionally well. In fact, there's been many a school dux who has been a failure fearer but dealt with it through overstriving. The thing that drives them is their intense fear of screwing up, performing poorly, disappointing parents, letting teachers down or being seen as dumb. That is, they are dominated by their fear of failure and their drive to avoid it. They bust their butts trying to avoid failure.

These students don't spend much time looking forward towards success, reaching goals or improving themselves. Instead, they spend a lot of time looking back at past failures or close calls and are mainly focused on making sure these don't happen again. They feel they are only as good as their last success, and often a feeling of achievement lasts only twenty-four hours before they're worrying about their next exam or assignment. They are terrified of challenge because it is just another chance that they might screw up.

But if they get good marks, who cares if they're failure fearers? Surely a bit of fear and worry is a small price to pay for success. Unfortunately it's not this simple. For a start, they don't have a great time at school because it's filled with anxiety, stress, pessimism, self-doubt and fear. So there's a personal price to pay. Secondly, this can get too much for some students. I could recount a number of stories about incredibly bright students who haven't coped with their fear of failure and dropped out of school (some as late as a few weeks before the final exams) never to return. This is an absolute tragedy, and in my view it should never have come to that.

It is clear, then, that overstrivers may not have a very happy journey and they are not academically resilient – they can buckle under their fear, particularly if they start experiencing a few setbacks such as bad marks or criticism from teachers or parents. Of course, many overstrivers don't buckle. They cope and they get by. But they certainly could be supported to enjoy the journey a bit more.

Perfectionism

Perfectionism can be a response to a fear of failure. Some students become so intent on not doing anything wrong that they try to do everything perfectly. Unfortunately, as with the overstrivers, these students can be anxious, stressed, pessimistic and fearful. These students won't hand in any work that is not perfect and many hand in no work at all because they are not perfectly happy with what they've done.

Perfection is pretty hard to reach and if your child is to attain it, it will probably be at the expense of other things. Often these are assignments or projects in other subjects. In fact, it is not uncommon for perfectionists to spend all weekend on an essay at the expense of other schoolwork due on Monday, only to decide on Sunday night that the essay isn't good enough – so nothing is handed in on the Monday.

Defensive pessimism

At some point overstrivers may start to doubt themselves a bit more. After all, constantly worrying about failure can be draining, and when the fear of failure starts tipping into more extreme territory students may reach for self-protective ways to deal with their fear. Defensive pessimism is one such strategy.

Defensive pessimists set unrealistically low expectations leading up to exams and assignments. These are the students who swear to you that they're going to fail the exam. They're the ones who say they'll only barely get a pass grade. They're the ones who have a really bad feeling about the upcoming test.

What possible advantage does this offer and how does it deal with their fear of failure? There are three main advantages to this strategy and each is a way to deal with a fear of failure. When I say 'advantage' I mean that the student sees it as an advantage – but as I'll discuss shortly, it's not really an advantage at all.

The first 'advantage' (in the student's eyes) is that the student lowers the bar, so to speak, so that it is easier to jump over. That is, a lower mark is easier to get and therefore by setting a lower acceptable mark the student is reducing the chances of failure.

The second 'advantage' is that it is a way of mentally preparing themselves for the possibility of failure. Students have told me that when they expect the worst this reduces the disappointment if the worst actually happens. That is, they cushion the blow of failure. Students also tell me that if they do okay it's a really nice surprise. In a way, they see their defensive pessimism as a no-lose situation – it protects them if they don't do so well and gives them a buzz if they do okay. One boy told me, 'I try to be pessimistic . . . then if I do better than expected it's a pleasant surprise and if I do worse than expected then it's less of a fall.'

The third 'advantage' of defensive pessimism is that it is a way of preparing others – friends, parents, even teachers – for the possibility that a student won't do so well and may even fail. According to students, this is a way of reducing their parents' disappointment in them. I find that the defensive pessimists are the ones who say, 'I told you I'd fail. Didn't I tell you I'd fail?' after they get a poor result. One girl told me, 'It's so people don't say "Oh look at you, you said you were going to do well and look what happened." So I tend to be cautious.'

What's the problem with defensive pessimism? Well, after a while students tend to do as much as they expect of themselves. As students downwardly revise their expectations they run the risk of achieving in a downward spiral also. And so the bar gets set lower and lower until it serves no self-protective purpose at all. When this happens, students may start reaching for more drastic strategies to deal with their fear of failure. One of the classic ones is self-sabotage.

Self-sabotage

Students self-sabotage when they put obstacles in their path to success. Some of the more classic self-sabotage strategies are procrastination, wasting time and doing no study. One girl told me, 'Pointless time wasting? Yeah, I'm the queen of pointless time wasting.' Why do students self-sabotage? They do it so they have an alibi in case they fail. These students are the ones who say something like, 'Well, I suppose I should have done more study' or, 'I suppose I shouldn't have stuffed around the night before the exam.'

Why do students need an alibi? Because as many students will tell you, anything is better than failing because you're dumb. In our competitive school system, there's nothing more damaging to students' self-worth than feeling or looking dumb. So, what students do is establish alibis or excuses so they can shift the cause of failure away from the fact they might be dumb and onto something that's not so threatening to their self-esteem, such as procrastinating or wasting time. It's better to be seen as a procrastinator than a dummy.

Hang on a minute! If they're so frightened of failure, why do they do things that almost guarantee failure? Research shows that some students will accept failure if they can arrange it so they can come out of the failure with their dignity or self-worth intact. Therefore even though they don't avoid failure itself, they can avoid the implications of that failure.

Some of my research has focused specifically on self-sabotage and I've been amazed at the diversity of ways students go about it. To give you a sense of this, here are just some of the techniques of self-sabotage I've come across:

- procrastinating
- wasting time
- not studying
- going to a party the night before the exam
- binge drinking the night before the exam
- visiting Granny more often during study week
- signing up for extra hours in the part-time job
- cleaning the bedroom, fish tank or garage
- alphabetising the video collection
- leaving books at home or at school when they are needed for study
- clowning around in class
- disrupting other students.

In fact, some students are very crafty about what they use as their alibi. In one study I spoke to a girl who I'd selected because she scored high in self-sabotage. She told me about her elaborate study preparation and spent some time telling me about the study timetable she'd developed. In this timetable, she had all the days organised, sorted into half-hour blocks, and colour coded. At this point I was thinking I'd got her self-sabotage score wrong because she certainly seemed to have her act together. Then she told me that she put all this information onto the computer and after it was entered she turned the days from columns into rows and proceeded to go through the whole exercise again. At this point I asked her how much study she'd done that week. Looking exasperated, she said, 'None! By the time I'd finished my study timetable there wasn't any time left to study.' I realised her high self-sabotage score was dead right. Another student who was more honest about things told me, 'Planning a timetable is a brilliant time waster.' This isn't to suggest that students should not develop a study timetable. What I'm saying is that this should be developed efficiently and then the student should get into study.

Self-sabotage is a very seductive strategy for students. This is because it is a protective way of dealing with failure. That is, students' dignity and self-worth live to see another day. It is also seductive because if students do well after having procrastinated then they look really smart. They're the ones saying, 'Wow, how smart am I? I got an A after doing no study at all!' So not only can self-sabotage have protective properties if students don't do well, it can also have enhancing or elevating properties if they do well after all.

Before you go running into your son's room (yes, boys self-sabotage more than girls – but girls do it too) slapping the 'self-sabotage' label on him, I want you to remember that just because he procrastinates does not mean he is self-sabotaging. We all procrastinate and we all waste time but it doesn't mean we are self-saboteurs. How can you tell if your child is a self-saboteur? Through three clues:

- if the behaviour is habitual and routine (that is, it's done a lot)
- if the behaviour arises out of a fear of failure
- if the behaviour seems to be used as an excuse if they don't do well.

Even if your child is a self-saboteur, I wouldn't use this label for them. Instead, talk about the behaviour rather than slapping this alarming and depressing tag on them. They don't need to carry around these sorts of negative labels in their minds.

After a while the excuses of the self-sabotaging student start to lose their credibility. Students' friends sympathised the first couple of times they did no study, but soon they start suspecting that the student isn't up to the job. After a while failure hits students so often that they become numb to it and the excuses have long run out. Eventually not only do they not try to avoid failure, they don't even bother to avoid the implications of failure by reaching for an alibi. When students get to this point there is a strong possibility that they will simply give up and disengage from their schoolwork. They become failure acceptors.

Giving up or disengaging from schoolwork

At the end of the slide from overstriving through defensive pessimism and self-sabotage is failure acceptance. Failure acceptors have given up trying and are completely uninterested in school and learning. They aren't necessarily the troublemakers – in some cases they couldn't even be bothered trying to make trouble. These are the students who are at risk of truancy or dropping out of school altogether. They have come to accept that failure is their lot in life and there is nothing they can do to avoid it – so why should they bother trying?

These are the truly unmotivated students. Some call them the fringe dwellers because many exist at the outer edges of the class, never involved and never interested.

It is at this point that parents and teachers and perhaps other professionals need to dig deep. Having said this, it is far better to help these students before they become failure acceptors. In chapter 12 I deal with failure acceptance and disengagement in detail.

There are some clear reasons why students slide down the continuum of failure fearing through to failure acceptance. Some key factors that seem to have a significant impact are:

- the way students view failure and mistakes
- the reasons students learn
- the way students deal with their fears
- the way students view trying hard in their schoolwork
- students' ability to distinguish excellence from perfection
- the extent to which students pin their self-worth on their achievement

- the extent to which parents link their child's worth to his or her achievement
- the extent to which parents link their own worth to their child's achievement.

I'll tackle each of these factors now and introduce strategies to turn negative influences into positive ones.

Taking a fresh look at mistakes

One reason students develop a fear of failure is because their view of failure, poor performance and mistakes is a flawed one. My research has found that students who fear failure see mistakes as evidence that they are hopeless, useless, or worthless. Mistakes tell these students that they are dumb and lack intelligence. As one student told me, 'Failure means you're a loser.' For these reasons, they are at pains to avoid failure. They live in terror of challenge or difficulty – because that's just another chance they'll fail.

When students see failure or mistakes in this way, is it any wonder that they are fearful of making mistakes or failing? Is it any wonder they reach for any strategy that will protect them if they fail? If students interpret failure in such a horrible way, is it any wonder that they give up trying altogether?

Motivated students see mistakes and failure in a very different way. They see mistakes as important information that tells them how to improve next time. They believe mistakes are their launch pad to success. Mistakes tell them that they need to work harder or need to develop better study skills. Believe it or not, some actually talk about mistakes as an opportunity to break through their existing level of performance into a higher one.

Motivated students' view of mistakes, poor performance and failure means that they don't live in fear of mistakes. Does this mean they don't care about making mistakes? Absolutely not. They care about them a great deal. But they don't dwell on them. Instead, they take what they need from the mistake or poor performance and move into the future. They ask themselves, 'What's the lesson to be learnt here?' and then use the answer next time round. These students have parents who encourage them to see mistakes this way. One girl said, 'When they see my report, for the bad scores they say, "Do you see where you could have improved?" then so they'd help me work on it for next year.'

When your child doesn't live in fear of mistakes, challenging schoolwork is not a worry to them, they aren't terrified of the teacher asking them a question in class, they aren't scared sick of tests and exams and they don't try to sabotage their chances of success. One boy told me, 'I actually like challenging things, things that test my abilities. If you get a real hard challenge and you struggle with it, it's good that you can learn from it.'

Elite athletes are a great example of how students can look at poor performance at school. The athletes who are mentally tough don't endlessly beat themselves up after a dropped pass, a poor swim, a fall in the race or a missed goal. Sure they're disappointed, but they don't wallow in feelings of worthlessness and self-pity. They're quick to pick themselves up and then they make it their mission not to let this happen again. They spend extra time practising receiving passes or kicking goals. The mentally tough swimmer who mucks up a swim is quick to dissect his or her race to see exactly where things went wrong. If it's the tumble turn they're quick to recognise that improving it is their leg-up to a better level of performance next time.

Below is an exercise for you to work through with your child next time he or she screws up. You can have a relaxed chat about the things in the exercise or you can sit down with your child and work through it more formally.

1. Describe a mistake you made in your schoolwork recently – the bigger the mistake the better! (e.g. *'I failed my history essay.'*)

2. What did you do or think that is under your control that led to that mistake? (e.g. *'I left it to the last minute so I rushed and didn't read the question properly.'*)

3. What can you learn from this to improve next time? (e.g. *'I'll get onto assignments earlier and I'll read the question carefully next time.'*)

This exercise is aimed at showing your child how to take lessons from mistakes. It asks your child to focus on things in his or her control that contributed to that mistake. These are the clues for how to improve next time. The strength of this approach is that:

- it does not allow thoughts of being hopeless, useless, or dumb
- it empowers your child by focusing on things in their control
- it makes clear that your child can improve
- it insists that your child looks forward to improving next time and doesn't dwell on what went wrong in the past.

Developing helpful reasons for learning

For the student who fears failure, the main reason he or she does any work at school is for avoidance purposes. They work hard to:

- avoid looking dumb
- avoid disappointing parents or teachers
- avoid other people thinking bad things about them
- avoid getting bad marks.

These are all unhelpful reasons for learning. This is because they make students anxious, fearful and less resilient in the face of difficulty, stress or setbacks.

It is better for students to develop more helpful reasons for learning. These include:

- improving
- developing new skills
- reaching personal bests
- understanding new things
- solving problems
- overcoming challenging schoolwork.

On page 190 there is an exercise you could work through with your child. It is aimed at identifying unhelpful reasons for learning and then challenging those reasons with a more positive success focus. You may wish to chat informally with your child about these reasons or you could sit together and work through them in more detail.

Unhelpful reasons for learning	Challenging with a positive success focus
E.g. *The main reason I work hard is because I don't want people to think I'm dumb.*	*What people think of me is none of my business. My job is to focus on studying hard and well and doing the best I can.*
The main reason I learn is because I don't want to get bad marks.	
The main reason I learn is because I don't want people to think bad things about me.	
The main reason I learn is because I don't want to disappoint people.	

As I've said a few times before, you don't need to develop unrealistic challenges to your child's problematic thinking – common sense usually provides the best challenge because it is believable and achievable. The trick to any attitude change is to:

- first identify the problematic thinking or attitude
- find some commonsense approach or evidence to challenge the thinking
- be quick to challenge negative thoughts whenever they arise
- don't underestimate how automatic negative thinking can be – always be on the lookout for it
- be especially on the lookout in situations in which a performance is required (such as a test, whenever an essay or project is assigned, when the teacher asks a question in class) or there is competition.

Dealing with fears more effectively

Dealing with fear is a skill that can be learnt. Maybe it should be part of the school curriculum because many educational, personal and social problems can be traced back to young people's inability to deal with fear effectively.

Richard, middle high

The main reasons Richard did any schoolwork were so that he wouldn't screw up and so people wouldn't think he was dumb. In middle high, Richard was assigned an English teacher who made a special effort to focus on the students' strengths. Up to then, most people had focused more on things Richard wasn't good at and provided feedback mainly on these negative things – often without any feedback on things he did well.

When he did schoolwork for his English teacher he often felt a bit more motivated because he knew she wouldn't make him feel bad if he didn't do things so well. Richard found that this made him do more work because this teacher made English a reasonably stress-free subject to spend time on. In fact, she made him interested to find out more of his strengths and in so doing drew him to more work and persistence. Importantly, she didn't ignore areas of weakness, but she managed to tackle his weaknesses through his areas of strength. She made him want to be a better student – and he became that by behaving in ways that confirmed her positive expectations for him. This didn't mean she never cracked the proverbial whip. Sometimes the students needed to be driven a bit, either because the work was not so stimulating, or they seemed plain lazy or uninterested on the day. But she got the mix just right, with a greater focus on their strengths than their weaknesses. The result was a group of students who were not so fearful of failure, were not frightened to tackle a few challenges, and who were prepared to put in a bit more work than they did in other subjects.

First things first. Everyone has fears. Sure, some have more than others but there is fear in everyone's life. Indeed, fear has played a very important role in our survival. The old fight or flight response has saved many a skin.

When we look at successful students, athletes or businesspeople, they aren't successful because they have no fear. They are successful because of the way they deal with their fears. We saw earlier that many students deal with their fears in a way that reduces their achievement. On the other hand, motivated students deal with their fears in more productive ways. One way is to see their mistakes as opportunities to improve, rather than something to avoid or dread.

So, if you can't eliminate fear from your child's life, the obvious thing to do is teach them how to deal with fear more effectively – in ways that move them forward, and don't hold them back.

On page 193 there is an exercise that sets out one way to look at fears more effectively. It focuses on one worry, fear or concern your child may have about school and works through it constructively.

'What if' brainstorming
Another way you can help your child deal with fear more effectively is to do a bit of 'what if' brainstorming. This involves taking a fear right to the end of the line so that your child can see that we can deal with a lot of what we fear when the time comes, and that the worst of our fears is often the fear itself and not the reality.

An example of a 'what if' brainstorming session is set out on page 194. When doing 'what if' brainstorming you can focus on something your child fears now such as failing a maths test or you can lighten it up a bit and pick something more comical like going to school in his or her pyjamas.

Taking a healthy view of effort
Some students believe effort and hard work are very dangerous things. They believe that the more effort they put into their school-work the dumber they'll look if they fail. Remember that students are at great pains not to look dumb, because looking dumb is a great blow to their dignity and self-worth.

I have found that some students strategically plan how much hard work they put in. Many will put in just enough to give them-selves a chance to do okay, but hold back enough so that if they fail they can say they didn't try hard enough. Then no one can accuse them of being dumb – just of not trying hard enough.

A sports coach once told me of an athlete who was ranked third in the country in her sport. This athlete came to her one day

Working through fear

1. What is causing you most concern at school?

e.g. I'm worried that I won't figure out how to do my science assignment.

2. Write down two things that you can THINK to start tackling the worry.

e.g. I've done difficult assignments before. If I get stuck I can ask for help.

3. Write down two things that you can DO to start tackling the worry.

e.g. I'll ask my teacher if I have a problem. I'll spend more time at the library reading.

4. Write down a short, positive and strong statement about your belief in yourself to do the assignment.

e.g. I believe I can figure out a way to deal with this assignment – all I need is time and effort and maybe a bit of help.

5. Write a realistic solution or outcome that you can aim for. Having a goal will make you more committed to dealing with the fear.

e.g. I'll aim to spend as much time on the assignment as possible, will read widely and think of different ways of solving problems as they arise.

for advice. She said that she'd only ever given 95 per cent in training and competition. She was scared of giving 100 per cent in case she didn't make number 1. Holding back a bit of effort was her way of never being faced with the possibility that she didn't have what it took to get to the top. The coach convinced her to give 100 per cent and to be proud of doing that no matter

'WHAT IF' BRAINSTORMING

- What if I don't know the answers in the maths test?
- Then I might fail the maths test.

- What if I fail the maths test?
- Then my parents will think I'm hopeless.

- What if my parents think I'm hopeless?
- They might get a maths tutor for me.

- What if I have to get a maths tutor?
- Then I'll have to spend more time studying.

- What if I have to spend more time studying?
- I'll spend less time mucking around with my mates.

- What if I spend less time with my mates?
- It won't be as much fun but I might do better in maths.

- What if I do better in maths?
- I might be able to spend a bit more time with my mates again or I might enjoy doing well in maths and keep studying a bit harder.

what the outcome. Happily in this instance it paid off. She was at the top by year-end.

But 100 per cent effort may not always pay off and it's for this reason that children can live in fear of hard work – it can have a real sting if they try and fail. I remember a scene in 'The Simpsons' in which Bart was devastated by failing after studying hard. The teacher was surprised, remarking that she thought he'd be used to failure by now. He replied that this time it was different. This time he'd tried. "Now I know I'm dumb!" was his conclusion.

A healthy view of effort is achieved by doing three things:

- Reducing your child's fear of failure by having them see that failure provides information about how to improve. Failure is not a reflection of them as a person. Reducing your child's fear in this way will mean it's not so dangerous to try hard.
- Downplaying the link between effort and ability or intelligence. Even the smart kids need to try hard to do the best they can.
- Making it clear to your child that if he or she doesn't do well after trying hard, this usually means they need to develop more effective study and schoolwork skills. This is within their control. It does not mean that they are dumb.

Motivated students have a healthy view of effort. They don't hold back in order to have an alibi in case they don't do so well. They give it all they've got. If they still don't do well, they look at their study skills to see how they can improve. That is, they recognise that to bring out their best it's not only the quantity of the study they do but also the quality of that study that is important.

Recognising the difference between excellence and perfection

Of particular relevance to the perfectionists is the important difference between excellence and perfection. Effective students recognise this difference and are satisfied with excellence. This means that they can get on with other assignments and study and do their best across all subjects. Perfectionists don't often recognise the difference, or if they do recognise it they ignore it.

The table on page 196 gives some examples of how excellence and perfection differ.

A first way to address your child's perfectionism is to address their fear of failure. The previous sections and the next few sections tackle this fear of failure head on.

A second way to reduce perfectionism is to get your child to set strict time limits – reading limits, writing limits and double-checking limits – for themselves. They might say for example,

Excellence vs perfection

Excellence	Perfection
Rereading an essay once or twice before handing it in	Reworking an essay until it is absolutely perfect then sometimes not handing it in
Double-checking calculations and then getting onto the next task	Checking calculations over and over and sometimes not getting through all the other tasks
Preparing for three possible topics in the history exam in which you are required to write on one	Preparing for every possible topic in the history exam in which you are required to write on one
Spending an hour on the design of the project's title page	Spending a day on the title page and sometimes screwing it up at the end and deciding it's not worth handing in
Writing 2,900 words for the 3,000 word essay	Writing exactly 3000 words for the 3000 word essay
Handing in a science project with a reference list of books read and maybe one appendix if it has been requested	Handing in a science project with a reference list of books read and multiple appendices for good measure (even if not requested)
Reading a sensible selection of good books for the assignment	Reading all possible books written on the subject for the assignment
Consulting the teacher about a project only when clarification is needed	Constantly consulting the teacher to check a task is being done correctly

'At 9pm tonight I will stop working on my project, I'll read it once and make the required changes, then I'll staple it together and put it in my bag to hand in tomorrow.' Most importantly, your child must then commit to handing it in, no matter how he or she feels about it. You might like to build in 30 minutes flexitime, so that if they get to 9pm and are still not happy, they may spend 30 'power minutes' knocking it off. Other examples of setting limits include:

- reading only six of the ten books on the reading list (provided your child is not instructed to read them all)

- checking calculations only once before moving onto the next problem

- attaching only one appendix to the science project (unless more were requested by the teacher)

- taking the 3,000-word limit as an approximate value and letting their essay go at 2,900 words.

A third way to tackle perfectionism is to get your child to aim to become more of an all-rounder. That is, to get really good at lots of things rather than being perfect in one or two subjects. When students relax their perfectionism and start spending more balanced time across all subjects they are often pleasantly surprised to find that their overall school grades go up. Becoming an all-rounder requires students to have a broader focus and allocate sensible time to all areas of schoolwork. If your child gets stuck on perfecting a particular piece of work, encourage the all-rounder in him or her to move on. If there's time left after all the other work has been done, then he or she can go back to it.

A fourth way to reduce perfectionism is to insist that your child gets more balance in their life. This means they must see that life is more than a perfect score in maths, for example. One thing perfectionists are short on is balance. Balance might involve becoming a study all-rounder as described above or it may mean signing up to a sport or social club. You may even want to cheekily suggest that they perfect the skill of balance in life!

Before I finish with perfectionism I want to make the point that maybe your child is a perfectionist in every aspect of school and actually pulls it off. Good luck to you and them and maybe you don't want to interfere with that. But if areas of schoolwork are suffering or your child is having a bit of an unpleasant journey through school, then there may be a need to tackle his or her perfectionism.

Reducing the link between your child's worth and his or her achievement

I've mentioned a couple of times in this book that one of our highest priorities is to feel okay about ourselves. Our self-worth is one of our most precious assets. Because of this we can sometimes go to great lengths to protect it and keep it intact. Students are no different.

In our highly competitive school system, many students' self-worth is pinned completely on their ability to do well at school. They feel okay about themselves when they do well, and feel hopeless and no good if they don't do very well. These students make a direct link between their worth as a person and their achievement.

This can be very dangerous because every assignment, exam, project or essay becomes a test of their worth as a person. In fact for many students, walking into the maths exam is as much a test of their worth as a test of their maths. Is it any wonder that they have been dreading the maths exam for the past week? Is it any wonder that they live in terror of failing the exam? To fail means that they have also failed as a person.

Linking self-worth to success is also why so many students fear competition. This is why competition crushes some students.

But competition is here to stay, and so we need to support our children in coping better with it. This was discussed in detail in chapter 6 on developing your child's learning focus. What wasn't discussed in that chapter and which I'll discuss here is the need to reduce the link between your child's worth and his or her achievement. I say 'reduce' because I don't think it's possible to eliminate the link completely. This is because society will continue to celebrate achievement and link achievement to students' worth. One girl told me, 'I know people who don't go to university and people see them as less of a person than people who do go to university. It's stupid but that's the way the world works.' But the more the link is reduced, the less threatening competition and failure are to students.

To reduce the link between your child's worth and his or her achievement, it is important that you understand that your child's worth is a given. Their value as a person is not to be questioned.

Here's the important bit: no matter whether they top the class or score rock bottom, their dignity and worth must be protected and preserved at all cost. How do you do this?

One way to protect your child's dignity is to separate the behaviour from the person. It is your child's study skills, hard work (or lack of it) and answers to the test paper that are under the spotlight – not your child as a person. If they didn't do so well, it is their behaviour and effort that are on the line and not their intelligence or character. One girl said, 'I'd probably be cross with myself, but I don't think I'd be less of a person for it.' So, if your child doesn't do so well, focus on messages involving:

- spending a bit more time preparing
- not going out the night before the next test
- getting a bit of tutoring next term
- asking for help if they need it
- doing some practice questions next time
- dropping a couple of hours at the part-time job to do more study
- turning off the radio when revising for exams.

Do not send your child messages such as:

- You're useless.
- You're no good at it anyway.
- I don't know why we bother with you.
- All this money for school fees is just a waste.
- You're just going nowhere.

The first approach focuses on your child's behaviour and is not so threatening to his or her worth. As one girl said, 'If I get a mark that I'm not too happy with, my parents won't put me down for it.' The second approach directly hammers the student's worth. Remember, young people will get their sense of worth some-where, and if they're not getting it at home or school, they're likely to find it in ways that may be more damaging than a failed maths test.

Another way to reduce the link between your child's worth and his or her achievement is to again focus on parts of the process and not so much on the outcome. The process involves things like study skills, preparation, organisation and hard work.

When students broaden their view of success to include these things suddenly the result in the test or assignment won't impact so much on their sense of self-worth. These students begin to get their sense of worth from things that they have a lot of control over – how much schoolwork they do and the way they do that schoolwork.

Reducing the link between your worth and your child's achievement

It can get worse. Not only can a child's worth be wrapped up in how he or she achieves at school, I've found that their parents' worth can also be wrapped up in the child's achievements. This can put enormous pressure on children. And don't think they're not aware of this pressure. Kids are very quick to pick up on the fact that Mum or Dad gets a lot of kudos out of their marks at school.

So, building on our previous example, the child can walk into the maths test seeing it more as a test of their own and their parents' worth than a test of maths. If the fear of failure wasn't running on overdrive already, it certainly is now.

You must be very careful not to live your life through your child's, and not to invest your own feelings of worth in your child's achievement.

If you find yourself pinning a lot on your child's achievement, keep it to yourself. If your child studies to satisfy your needs, it isn't the best foundation for their ongoing motivation. I've found that type of motivation can run out – and sometimes at the worst times. I once counselled a young man who in the fifth year of medicine dropped out because, 'I never wanted to do it anyway.' Rather, it was his parents who wanted him to do medicine.

I want to make it clear that this doesn't mean you can't be proud of your child's achievements. Of course you can, and you should let your child know this. Nor does it mean that you can't be disappointed with poor results. Of course you can be disappointed, and you can let your child know this too.

The trick is to celebrate and take pride in the behaviours that got the great marks – like persistence, effective study, hard work and good preparation. Don't carry on as though your child is a fundamentally better person because of the achievement – the underlying message you're giving your child is that they are only as worthwhile as their accomplishment. This raises the stakes for the next exam and sows the seeds for a fear of failure.

For poorer results, the trick is to be disappointed in the behaviours that led to that performance, like lack of study or preparation. Don't carry on as though your child is somehow less of a person because of the poor performance. If you tackle the behaviour and not the person, you aren't putting the person on the line in the next exam. This reduces the fear of failure leading up to the exam.

Fear of failure amongst peers

Before leaving the topic of fear of failure, I should mention another form of failure that can terrify students. This occurs when success and trying hard are seen as failure in the eyes of their peers. (Fear of success is dealt with in detail in chapter 14 on gifted and talented students.) In talking to many students and teachers it has become clear that one of the barriers to students' motivation is their fear of standing out from the pack in terms of effort and achievement. Students don't want to be seen to be trying too hard because it makes them look like crawlers, and they risk social rejection as a result.

This means many students have to play a delicate balancing act between putting in enough effort to get through but not putting in so much that they're seen to be a 'try hard'. One girl told me, 'You don't want to be seen as a bookworm, but you also have to do the work. You have to be able to do your work and also listen to your friends in class – otherwise you'll be left out.' Unfortunately not all students get the balance right.

In more extreme cases, fear of peer disapproval leads to the 'cool to be a fool' problem where, particularly amongst boys, it is a status symbol to underachieve. My analysis of the cool to be a fool problem suggests there is a little more to it than this. I've found for many students it's cool to be a fool provided that he or she has an alibi so their intelligence or ability can't be questioned – the classic self-saboteur scenario.

The cool to be a fool syndrome kills two birds with the one

stone. First, it is a way of gaining peer approval. Secondly, it is a way of not trying hard so that if or when the student screws up, it is their lack of effort that is to blame and not their lack of ability or intelligence. So you'll find these students being very public about being a fool (say, by clowning around or disrupting others), and what they manage to do is appear foolish but not necessarily dumb. What's the difference between being a fool and being dumb? A very important one.

A fool is simply ignorant and with appropriate effort can achieve if they want to. Someone who is dumb is, in many students' eyes, not capable of achieving no matter how hard they try. So, by appearing the fool no one can say that the foolish student is dumb – all they can say is that they were foolish to have mucked around as they did. Because of this, the student manages to protect his or her sense of dignity and worth – it is far less threatening to one's fundamental feelings of worth to appear the fool than to be seen as dumb or unintelligent.

Because this type of failure fearing can be linked to the same factors underpinning the other forms of failure fearing described above (especially self-sabotage), similar strategies will be effective, particularly:

- taking a fresh look at mistakes
- improving the reasons students learn
- taking a healthy view of effort
- more effectively dealing with fear
- reducing the link between your child's worth and his or her achievement.

I'll add one more to this list:

- reducing the link between your child's worth and the approval he or she gets from friends.

The more your child pins their feelings of worth to the approval of their friends, the more that will affect their willingness to try hard at school. Now, this doesn't pose too much of a problem if your child's friends are motivated – they all seem to motivate each other. However, I should add that it is a problem if your child starts falling behind these friends and begins to feel worthless as a result.

Brian, junior high

Brian grew up in a family of high achievers whose academic success was valued and prized. However, he never dealt with performance pressure very well. In fact, he seemed to deal with it by disengaging from his schoolwork. He tended not to make the work important to him and made sure that others saw that he didn't think it was important. He rarely took schoolwork entirely seriously and rarely put in 100 per cent – that way he could not be accused outright of lacking ability. He hardly ever handed anything in on time and was at the mercy of his teachers' goodwill when his work was graded. The teachers would often get the blame for his poor marks after he handed in late work.

Although I didn't follow Brian through to the completion of his studies, I did note just before I left him that a story his dad had told had made quite an impact on him. He told Brian that when he was a boy he was terrified of screwing up because his parents would give him a hard time. He learnt that to stay in good with his parents he had to achieve, and so he did everything he could to perform highly. His brother (Brian's uncle) dealt with his parents' pressure in almost the reverse way by becoming a bit of a rebel and barely scraping through school. Brian's dad told him about a time he'd failed an exam, how ashamed and terrified he'd been to tell his parents, and how it didn't go down well with them. Brian's dad told him he knew what it was like to stuff up and that it was not the end of the world.

The 'stop-the-press' message Brian got from this was that his father had failed an exam. He never knew this. He thought (and everyone continually told him) that his father had led a consistently successful life. Clearly, screwing up was not the end of the world and even the best of them did it. I don't know how Brian fared in the end, but I do know that an essential ingredient for effectively tackling his self-sabotage was for him to view mistakes and poor performance quite differently to how he had viewed them thus far in his life. His dad's story was a very important first step in that direction.

This link is more of a problem if your child's friends are unmotivated or even anti-school. This can lead to your child behaving in similar ways, particularly if schoolwork isn't interesting to them. According to one boy, 'If I have a friend in class and he doesn't really like that subject and I don't really like it either, we usually end up mucking around.'

This is a tough situation, particularly during adolescence when your child is developing his or her identity as a young man or woman and strongly relates to his or her friends. How can you possibly compete with this?

Recently I worked on a research project that involved in-depth interviews and discussion groups with students aged between thirteen and sixteen – the age group in which friends have a very strong influence. At the end of the interviews and discussions I asked students who had a bigger impact on their motivation: their friends or their parents. I was surprised to find that almost half said their parents had the biggest impact, one quarter said their parents and friends had an equal impact, and only one quarter said their friends had the biggest impact. So, three out of every four adolescents I spoke to reported that their parents had an impact on their motivation.

This means that parents who apply strategies suggested in this book can have an effect on their child's motivation over and above the effect of their child's friends. I talk more about this in chapter 11 which discusses building a good relationship with your child.

Motivation by success, not failure

I've spent most of this chapter in fairly unhappy territory. Fear of failure and students' responses to it is not a happy topic. But it's a topic that needs significant attention. This is because it can have some very negative effects and also because in our competitive school system, fear of failure is rife.

So what's the alternative? At the start of this book I described another approach: the approach taken by success strivers. Success strivers:

- are optimistic and confident
- are high in self-esteem

- are focused on success and how to achieve it
- don't dwell on their shortcomings
- don't dwell on mistakes – instead, they take what they need to improve
- aren't frightened of challenge – in fact, they enjoy challenge
- aren't debilitated by setback or pressure.

When I refer to success strivers, I'm not necessarily talking about students at the top of the class. I'm really talking about students who are working to their potential and doing the best they can at that time. There are success strivers in all ability groupings: so-called 'smart kids' have absolutely no monopoly on success striving.

Given this, it is clear that any child can be a success striver. How do you get them there? Well, the past nine chapters have discussed at length how this is done. Building success strivers is about:

- enhancing students' belief in themselves
- building students' sense of control
- instilling in students a belief in the value of school
- developing students' learning focus
- supporting students' study management and planning
- enhancing students' persistence
- reducing students' anxiety
- reducing students' fear of failure

As you can now see, there is no single magic pill or magic answer. But there are some clear pathways to motivation that are accessed by increasing the motivation boosters in your child's life and reducing the motivation mufflers and guzzlers. Part Two of this book has addressed each of these boosters, mufflers and guzzlers.

In Part Three to follow I deal with four other issues central to motivation. These are about building a good relationship with your child, re-engaging the disengaged child, motivating gifted and talented children and enhancing the motivation of boys.

Living in the real world

In the real world not everything happens like they say in the books. Here are a few things for you to think about when digesting this chapter.

- Don't expect to completely eliminate fear of failure from your child's life. To be frightened is human. Instead, aim to reduce their fear of failure and you'll have done a good job.
- Some students seem to need a bit of fear to get them working. My emphasis is on 'a bit' and while it stays 'a bit' it probably won't have devastating or damaging effects. Just make sure you work on reducing it if it starts becoming more prominent in your child's life.
- Some perfectionists manage to get everything done. If perfectionism is working for your child, good luck to you and them. Just make sure it's not interfering with functioning in other parts of life or making your child unhappy.
- Not all procrastination or time wasting is self-sabotage. For example, sometimes there are other reasons for procrastinating – usually when we don't like doing some-thing or we've got something better to do. But when time wasting becomes habitual and seems to arise out of a fear of failure, you might start thinking about the possibility it's self-sabotage.
- You probably won't eliminate the link between your child's worth and his or her achievement, but you can and you should aim to reduce it.
- It can be really hard for a parent to reduce the link between their own worth and their child's achievement. It's hard not to get kudos out of your child's achievements. The main thing is that you don't let your child know that you have more than their school fees invested in their achievement.
- It can be really hard not to be disappointed in your child if they screw up at school. Just do your best to focus on the behaviours that led to the poor result and try to avoid labels or accusations that get at the person (such as, 'You're lazy' or, 'You're hopeless').

- Don't expect your child not to seek their friends' approval. Friends are a big part of anyone's life and we often bounce ideas and aspects of ourselves off them to more clearly define who we are. You really only need to look at ways of reducing your child's reliance on their friends' approval if they are affecting your child's health, well-being or achievement in ways that worry you. I say 'reduce' because trying to eliminate the influence of friends risks alienation from you and increased identification with the friends. I talk more about this in chapter 11 which discusses building a good relationship with your child.

- Sometimes 'what if' brainstorming can lead to a conclusion that is not pleasant or attractive to your child. At this point you may have to fall back on the old 'You'll deal with that when you come to it' line and talk with your child about how things seem to be easier to deal with when they arrive and are scarier when you look into the future at them.

Chapter summary

Fear of failure is rife in our competitive school system. Students respond to their fear of failure in many different ways. Some deal with it by working themselves to the bone so that they don't fail. That is, they avoid failure by succeeding. Others set unrealistically low expectations leading up to an exam or assignment. This is called defensive pessimism and is a way of lowering the bar so it is easier to jump over, and also reduces the student's disappointment if they do fail. There are others who seem to sabotage their chances of doing well so that they have an alibi or excuse if they fail. At the end of the line are the students who have repeatedly and unsuccessfully tried to avoid failure and have simply given up and disengaged from their schoolwork.

Strategies to reduce students' fear of failure include changing the way students see mistakes and deal with their fears, developing better reasons for learning, developing a healthier view of effort, distinguishing excellence from perfection and reducing the link between the child's worth and his or her achievement.

CHAPTER TEN TOP 5

1. Students tend to respond to their fear of failure through overstriving, perfectionism, defensive pessimism, self-sabotage or failure acceptance.

2. Seeing mistakes as important information about how to improve can be a very effective way to reduce fear of failure.

3. Fear of failure can be reduced when students switch from learning for the purposes of avoiding bad marks or not disappointing teachers or parents to learning in order to improve, reach personal bests and develop new skills and understanding. Your child should be encouraged to see hard work as an indication of success and not something to hold back so they have an excuse in case they fail.

4. Teaching your child to deal more effectively with fear involves identifying a current worry or concern, developing new ways to think about that worry, identifying something that can be done to address it, developing your child's belief in his or her ability to deal with it and setting a goal to work towards to reduce it. It can also involve engaging in some 'what if' brainstorming with your child.

5. Reducing the link between your child's worth and his or her achievement is important. The less students believe their worth as a person depends on how well they do at school, the less failure is something to fear.

Part Three

SPECIAL ISSUES IN MOTIVATION

CHAPTER 11

BUILDING A GOOD RELATIONSHIP WITH YOUR CHILD

I'm going to stick my neck out here and propose that one of the most important parts of motivating your child is to build a good relationship with him or her. When the relationship is a good one, you'll find applying the strategies in this book so much easier.

What if your relationship with your child isn't such a great one? Don't worry; even slight improvements in the relationship can have some great effects on your child's willingness to get into the schoolwork a bit more. Also, when the relationship improves, you'll find your ability to apply the strategies improves as well. Remember, we're not after perfection – we just want some positive shifts, some improvements.

I should say it straight up: there's no such thing as the perfect parent. We're all human. So, if you achieve a positive shift in your relationship, that's great. Sure, some relationships may improve

HOW WAS SCHOOL TODAY?

TODAY'S SATURDAY. SCHOOL WAS YESTERDAY

more than others, but no matter how small the shift, that is progress. If it keeps your child just hanging in there (when previously they'd have dropped out), then you've done a good job. Perhaps your child will be receptive to some significant other who comes along later and can make even greater gains.

What's the secret behind a good relationship? Well, there is no secret. Research has shown that there are particular characteristics and attributes of good relationships that separate them from relationships that aren't so good. These characteristics involve specific behaviours and attitudes, and as I've argued many times before, behaviours and attitudes can be changed.

A good relationship is the foundation of motivation

You may be thinking, who's this guy telling me how to improve my relationship with my kid? Well, I am a parent – but I'm not going to speak as a parent. Speaking as a parent I'd probably lose objectivity. Furthermore, because no parent is perfect, I'd probably pass on some of my own ineffective practices, which will be of no help to you.

Instead, I'm going to base this chapter on research – my own and that of others.

Over the past few years I've worked on a few parenting research projects for government and non-government organisations. These projects have examined parenting styles, parents' confidence, parents' knowledge about child rearing, children's behaviour and how parents deal with it, and parenting programs provided by community and welfare organisations.

It may comfort you to learn that this research (and loads of other research before it) found that parenting is not necessarily an intuitive thing, parenting is tough and demanding for most people, that every now and then most parents need support and information to help them do a better job, parents have strengths that can be built on to improve their parenting, and people can learn more effective parenting styles and strategies.

I've also conducted a lot of research amongst school students. When I ask them to tell me why a particular teacher brings out their best work, they say this teacher likes and respects them and they like and respect this teacher in return. These students talk in a similar way about their parents.

I've also spent a fair bit of time researching the ways teachers develop good relationships with their students. We can learn a lot from teachers – they are experts at handling kids, motivating them and getting them to do things they're reluctant to do at first. I've paid particular attention to teachers who do a good job of hooking students into schoolwork. When I look closely at what they do, I find they have taken the time to first build a good relationship with the student.

Finally, I've done a fair bit of social research that looks at young people's transition through school and into further education and training or employment. I've paid particular attention to the 'at-risk' students or the students who have dropped out of school and the welfare agencies that seem to get them back into the system and on the straight and narrow. Talking to youth workers I've found that underpinning their successes with difficult young people is their focus on developing a good relationship with that person.

My conclusion from the data I've collected from hundreds of teachers and parents, youth workers, parenting project workers, psychologists and counsellors is: **If you build a good relationship with your child, up to half the work is done.**

This is supported by research showing that students' motivation and achievement is affected by their parents' attitudes and expectations and their relationship with their parents. Parents who are less controlling and more supportive have children with greater self-motivation at school and who are rated by teachers as less troubled academically. In fact, research shows that the quality of your relationship with your child predicts a good relationship between your child and their teacher.

Again I remind you that even slight positive shifts in the relationship is reason to feel pleased with yourself and your child. This may be all it takes to keep them hanging in there until they find more direction, encounter a significant other who really enthuses them, stumble onto a subject that really gets them in or enables them to complete school when they wouldn't have otherwise. Or it may be the beginning of a solid upward climb to much stronger motivation and achievement.

In this chapter I'm going to present three parenting styles: authoritative, authoritarian and permissive – and suggest that it is the authoritative parenting style we need to aim for. Following this I present what I consider to be the top five characteristics, attributes and behaviours that reflect a good relationship between an adult/parent and child, though they probably number in the hundreds.

One of my research projects looked at what parents identified as the most difficult thing about parenting. There were two consistent responses. The first was parents' lack of knowledge about child rearing. The second, which flowed directly from the first, was parents' lack of confidence in child rearing. In another research project I found that parents who were confident in their child rearing were more effective as parents and had better relationships with their children. This chapter, then, aims to increase both your knowledge and your confidence.

Parenting styles

A lot of research has looked at parenting styles. Parenting style refers to the way you behave with your child, the way both of you interact, the way you communicate and the attitudes you have towards your child and about parenting.

As I mentioned above, parenting style can be divided into three types: authoritative, authoritarian and permissive.

Authoritative parents

These parents are assertive and strong in a supportive and fair way, not in a punishing way; they are flexible when there is a need to be and will adjust rules if the situation demands it; they will explain rules and the reasons behind them; they make sure their child is responsible for his or her own behaviour, but provide the support their child needs to do this; they are confident and provide their children with positive feedback that makes the child confident also; they are focused on doing a good job and on their strengths and not on their shortcomings; however, they recognise their shortcomings and make changes when they are needed; they love their child unconditionally, but are clear about behaviours they do not approve of; they look for opportunities to affirm their child, not for opportunities to identify weaknesses or problems in their child.

Authoritarian parents

These parents are assertive and strong, but in a punishing and restrictive way; they are not flexible and rigidly stick to rules even if the situation suggests the rules should be relaxed; they do not explain rules nor why they are made; they make sure their child is responsible for his or her own behaviour, but expect their child to do this with little or no support from them; their confidence is shaky and they tend not to give their child the supportive feedback their child needs to develop their own confidence; they are unwilling to recognise their shortcomings and they don't make changes in their parenting when changes are needed; they love their child conditionally – on the basis that their child does what they want them to; they tend not to affirm their child and tend to focus on their child's weaknesses or problems.

Permissive parents

These parents are not assertive; they are so flexible that there is little consistency in their parenting; they tend not to set or enforce many rules; they don't pay much attention to whether their child is responsible for his or her own behaviour, and don't provide much support for their child to become responsible; they are not very confident and don't provide the feedback that their child needs to develop confidence; they don't think about their parenting too much and so aren't aware of changes needed; they love their child but don't look for many opportunities to develop their child further.

You've probably guessed by now that the authoritative parent is the one research has linked to the most positive outcomes for the child and the parent–child relationship.

This isn't to say that the other two styles unquestionably damage your child. Different children respond to parenting styles in different ways. For example, children of permissive parents can learn how to bring themselves up and become very motivated and responsible for themselves. However, there are others who are directionless and don't know whether they're Arthur or Martha. Children of authoritarian parents can grow up with a strong sense of responsibility, law abidance and respect for the system – there are many high achievers who cope quite well with this parenting style. However, there are others who develop an intense fear of authority and failure, and in chapter 10 on fear of failure we saw how this can adversely affect children.

You may find that you slip in and out of different styles and that your style depends on the situation and the child you're dealing with. This is to be expected. Sometimes we can't explain the rationale for every rule. Sometimes 'No means no, and now isn't the time and place to discuss it!' Sometimes we're just too stressed and hassled to take the time to be the authoritative parent. The vital question is which style you adopt most of the time. Then it's a matter of looking for more opportunities to move your style into the authoritative pattern and out of the other two.

How do you do this? My reading of the research and my own research suggests the following top five factors in building an authoritative parenting style and a strong parent–child relationship:

- mutual respect
- stepping into your child's shoes
- balance
- drawing more than driving
- being a lifelong learner.

Mutual respect

Kids know it when you don't respect their opinions, attitudes, beliefs or behaviour. And they don't like it. Talking with adolescents I've found respect is one of the most important things about relationships that motivate them. They have all the time in the world for an adult whom they believe respects what they think, say and do.

I've headed this section with the word 'mutual' because when an adult genuinely respects a child, they tend to respect the adult in return. This leads me to a very important point about respect from young people. *You must earn a child's respect*. Like it or not, for many young people gone are the days when you could say, 'I'm an adult and you'll respect me!' For better or worse, that doesn't work for many young people. I could fill a thousand-page book with the names of teachers and parents who have crashed and burnt by this approach. I could also fill a thousand-page book with the names of teachers and parents who have earned young people's respect and reaped the many rewards and satisfactions that follow directly from it. The classic example is the student you'd swear should be expelled in one class, yet is a willing and co-operative participant in another. The difference you'll find is in how the teacher treats the student. I've met some rough, wild, and tough kids who would walk through jungles and over mountains for the teacher or youth worker who treated them with respect.

There's no magic about earning a young person's respect. It certainly does not mean you have to pander to everything they think or do. Students have told me they don't mind if their teacher or parent disagrees with them or forbids them doing something – so long as they had a good, fair and genuine hearing for their side of the story.

Here are a few ways that teachers tell me they earn respect from young people:

- don't assume you've got it before earning it
- take the time to get to know the child – really know how they see the world and what they think
- really value their interests and what they do for recreation
- look for opportunities to have one-on-one time with the child
- actively listen to the child's perspectives – this requires the adult to take in and understand all the detail of what the child is saying
- look for opportunities to take the child's side of things (but not so much that you are significantly compromised)
- affirm the child as often as possible, not with fake praise, but with genuine and heartfelt praise
- catch them doing good as much as you can
- give the child more responsibility (within appropriate boundaries).

Respecting your child also means that sometimes you'll need to go in on an angle. What does this mean? It means you try not to tackle some things head on. You try to avoid full-on confrontation. You try not to back your child into a corner. You try not to put them in a situation where they may lose face.

In potentially dangerous situations I've seen youth workers

handle extremely aggressive young people with gentle and subtle expertise. They tackle the situation in a non-threatening way, recognising that the young person is really angry, and letting them know that they are trying to understand why. But they also assure them that together they can find a way through this problem other than aggression and violence. They go in on an angle, not head on.

A similar approach could probably save a few heated situations in your home. Go in on an angle in the same way the youth worker did. Don't scare your child off, don't put them in a situation where they may lose face, and don't back them into a corner because that's when they turn off or get really unreasonable – and that's no way for solution-focused negotiation to take place.

Stepping into your child's shoes

Through my research with young people, I've found that a major reason they identify so much with their friends is because their friends understand what it's like to be an adolescent and understand their perspective on life. Young people place a high value on being understood, and if their parents don't understand them they'll find someone who does. One girl told me, 'My friends have a bigger influence because I agree with their point of view more than with my mother's. I listen to them more because I think they're right.'

Also through my research with young people, I've found that a common complaint of theirs is that parents and teachers don't know what it's like to be a teenager today. One boy told me, 'My friends know my point of view because they've been there and they know what's going on. My parents just assume they know, but they've never been there, they don't know what's going on.' Does this mean you're locked out of your teenager's life simply because of your age? Not at all. Talking with young people, I've found they are readily able to name adults they believe remember what it was like to be young. It is these adults with whom they have a good relationship.

Let's get something straight. Stepping into your child's shoes does not mean you have to act like a child and try to be cool or whatever. The adults who remember what it was like to be young keep their authority intact but recognise that young people don't always see the world in the way they do. They recognise that young people don't have the same attitudes as them and that young people don't behave in the same way they do. Having recognised this, they accept the differences. Having accepted the differences, they affirm the differences.

Motivating parents and teachers recognise and accept the fact that young people are energetic, that young people push boundaries to learn more about themselves, that young people will muck up on them every now and then, that young people will be moody, and that young people are challenging and difficult. They also recognise that when the young person knows they accept these things, the relationship can be a joy to experience.

It's important to recognise that life at this age can be tough. As one adolescent girl said, 'There are so many things that go on at this age. This is the prime age that teenagers kill themselves and start going on drugs. A lot of this is because of the way people make them feel.' Stepping into your child's shoes means recognising the tough times and your role in helping them through. If you asked me if I'd like my teenage days back, I'd say that although I'd like most of them back, there were many I'd quite happily leave behind – those days were straight out tough and unpleasant.

My advice is to carefully listen to your child, step out of your shoes and into theirs, and try to remember what it was like to be young. Remember to accept your child's point of view – even if it's different from yours and challenges your comfort zone. Affirm your child's view as worthwhile and valid – even if you think it's only going to last for a week or until the next fad or whatever. It goes without saying that if your child's behaviour is harming themselves or others then all bets are off and you need to deal with the situation differently.

In some cases you won't understand your child's priorities. But I'm not asking you to understand them – just recognise, accept and affirm them. Speaking from my point in life now, I can't for the life of me understand why particular things were important to me at the age of 15 or 17 or whatever. Yet, at the time, I'd have sworn black and blue that it was the most important and significant thing in the world. An adult telling me that those things weren't important would simply have alienated me.

At all costs parents must stay in the loop – even if it means they have to cop some things about their child that they might not like. While they are in the loop, they can still have influence. One way to tell whether you are starting to be kept out of the loop is if you find your child is keeping important things from you because they feel they function better without your involvement or knowledge. As one girl told me, 'I had two exams and I passed them because I didn't tell my parents. I passed because I didn't have their pressure on me.'

Stepping into your child's shoes means you need to be aware of difficulties they experience in their schoolwork, but it also means you don't automatically assume the worst about them if they're not doing well. Let me explain.

In my ongoing research into student motivation I administer the Student Motivation Scale to students. This measures each of the boosters, mufflers and guzzlers. I also give parents a survey that asks them about their child's motivation. I've been stunned at the discrepancy between the two and this highlights the fact that even on motivation issues there can be a big gap between parent and child. Where there's a gap, young people will feel their parents won't understand where they're coming from.

In the table on page 220 I present some results of how students rate themselves and how parents rate students. The score is out of 100, so a high score on a booster is good and a high score on a muffler or guzzler is not so good.

In a number of cases, there are some pretty big differences between how the students rate themselves and how parents rate their children. Let's take the example of students' learning focus. There's a massive 18-point difference between what students say about themselves and what parents say about students. Students report that they are quite interested in learning new things, solving problems and developing skills. On the other hand, parents say that their children aren't very interested in these things. Who's right? The truth probably lies somewhere in the middle. However, in terms of a good connection between parent and child, if parents treat their children as though they have a low learning focus but the children think they have a good learning focus, there's a problem.

Motivation ratings

	Students' rating of their own motivation /100	Parents' rating of their child's motivation /100
Boosters		
Self-belief	80	76
Value of schooling	81	69
Learning focus	81	63
Planning	58	51
Study management	69	57
Persistence	70	65
Mufflers		
Anxiety	60	58
Failure avoidance	49	58
Guzzlers		
Low control	52	51
Self-sabotage	41	63

Let's take another example – value of schooling. Here there's a big 12-point difference between students and parents. Students believe that school is relevant, important and useful. On the other hand, parents report that students don't value school so highly. I can just picture a parent standing over their child accusing them of not taking school seriously enough while the child feels hard done by and misunderstood because they don't think school is as bad as all that. In fact, talking with students over the course of my research I've found that most of them believe school is a place where they learn important things for life. Who's right? Again, the truth probably lies somewhere in the middle. Nevertheless, the difference between the two is so large that unless the parent recognises some middle ground, the child may decide that the distance to travel is too great and they won't even try.

The message is clear. Your child probably doesn't see their own motivation in the same way you do. To keep your child receptive to what you're asking or telling them, you need to know where they're coming from. How do they see their own learning focus or how much value do they place on school and schoolwork? Showing them that you recognise where they're at keeps you in the loop.

There is perhaps a more unsettling feature of these results. On every booster, parents rate students lower than students rate themselves. This is a pretty depressing view from where parents stand. The risk of this view is that in some direct and indirect ways the child picks up on their parents' depressing opinion of their motivation. Educational research has shown that this can have a self-fulfilling effect: students come to behave and achieve in ways consistent with their parents' and teachers' expectations. How do parents head this off at the pass? One important way is by taking the time to step into their child's shoes.

Balance is important

Talking with young people, I've been struck by how some parents push so hard that the kids kick back or feel dreadful about themselves. As one girl said, 'My mum tries to make me do extra credit stuff so I get straight As. Last year I got an A and a B and she freaked out and grounded me. It made me feel really bad. Sometimes it increases my motivation but most of the time I just rebel.'

Other parents don't push at all and leave their child totally directionless and unmotivated.

However, there are some parents who seem to do enough pushing to get their child moving, yet pull back at the right time so that their child can take over and do the rest. They get the balance just right. One girl said, 'I think we compromise. They see that I know where I want to be and how I'm going to get there. They let me do my own work if they see results. If I'm flunking I'll do it their way.'

Balance seems to be the key to a lot of successful parenting. Effective parents seem to get the right balance in terms of:

- discipline and tolerance
- authority and friendship
- fun and serious application
- pushing the child and letting go
- applying rules and being flexible
- taking a stand and easing off.

When you aim for balance in your relationship with your child, in house rules and in expected behaviour, you're not pushing your child into a corner. When you aim for balance your child is more likely to forgive the tough stands and decisions you make. One boy told me, 'Sometimes my parents can be pretty tough, but other times they say do it at your own pace, just as long as it gets done.'

I suppose another way of looking at balance is to see it as fairness. Young people highly value fair rules, decisions and consequences. When the rules are fair, your child is more likely to forgive the tough consequences if they step over the line.

How do you achieve balance? It's probably first important to recognise when things are not in balance. A good clue is when there are extremes of any kind such as too much sport, too much free time, too much study (yes, I believe students can do too much study!), too many hours in the part-time job, too many phone calls at night or too many study breaks. Another clue is if your child's grades or study time are sliding – it's likely to be because they're doing too much or not enough of something. Another clue is if other aspects of behaviour become problematic. For example, if they're putting on excessive weight or are generally unhealthy, they could probably do with some exercise and a more balanced diet.

When you suspect there is imbalance in your child's life, it's important to talk with your child – not in an accusing or confrontational way, but so they won't feel threatened listening to you. You can then say you're not wanting them to stop Behaviour X altogether, but would like them to do a bit less of it. Tell them that you understand Behaviour X is important to them – and because of this it's important to you. You could then ask (don't tell) them how much they'd like to do or how much they think they need to do of Behaviour X, how much they think is fair. Ask them what you can do to help or how you can make it easier for them to do less of Behaviour X.

If they want to do more of Behaviour X than you'd like and you can't seem to budge them, ask yourself, 'Can I live with it?' If you can live with it (even if you don't like the arrangement), then let it go. You've made two gains: you talked a young person closer to your position (many parents would kill for that!) and you built a nice little platform of balance and respect – a very strong position for your next negotiation. If you can't live with it, you may need to be more creative about how to resolve this issue. What other things can you both agree on that makes this situation more acceptable to you? What else have you both got to trade? Remember, be focused on the solution and not the problem – this keeps you in safer territory when dealing with a headstrong child or a stormy adolescent.

Balance means you fully recognise and accept that being young is about having friends, having lots of fun and making lots of mistakes. It's not only about study. When I conduct staff development in schools and I've got a spare moment, I like to wander around and read the honour boards. What has struck me is that the dux is also often the swimming captain, or in the debating team, or on the student representative council. These students are great ambassadors for balance.

Drawing more than driving

Some parents and teachers draw young people to be the best they can be. They are supportive, have positive expectations for the child, help the child learn from their mistakes, are encouragement-focused, allow the young person to explore their talents and strengths and believe that every young person has the capacity to reach their potential.

Some parents and teachers drive young people so they don't make mistakes, punish or reprimand them when they don't do so well, are overly disappointed about the mistakes the child makes, believe that unless young people are pushed they won't do any good and push the child in directions they think are best for them.

It probably goes without saying that the parent who draws their child has a better, more trusting and open relationship than the parent who drives their child. The first relationship is one based on support, encouragement and optimism. The second relationship is based on fear and coercion.

Building a relationship that draws your child means:

- focusing on your child's strengths
- recognising your child's weaknesses, but focusing on solutions that make full use of their strengths
- being optimistic that your child can succeed and providing the support they need to do this

- allowing your child to make and learn from mistakes
- affirming your child's worth as a person no matter how they achieve at school.

Does this mean you never drive your child? Of course it doesn't. Let's be realistic, sometimes you have to push your child to do things they might not like. Sometimes your child will need to be pushed in a direction that you think is best for them. That's what being a parent is about. As one boy told me, 'Sometimes they won't ask me if I have any homework, they just leave it up to me to do it. And that makes it harder because then I won't do it if they don't tell me to.' One girl told me straight out that she wanted her parents to push her: 'I always need someone there pushing me and saying that I have to do it.'

But being an effective parent is about having the wisdom to know when to draw and when to drive. My advice is to make sure you draw more than drive. The more you can draw your child, the more affirming and enjoyable your relationship with him or her will be.

Consider yourself a lifelong learner

If I've heard it once, I've heard it a thousand times, 'You never stop being a parent.' Older parents are the ones who usually tell me this; often in response to me (naively) informing them that I can relax once my kids hit twenty-one. If it's true that you never stop being a parent, then to cope with your children's changes, your changes and changes in the world, your best defence is to consider yourself a lifelong learner.

Lifelong learning has become very popular in recent years. It's mostly talked about in vocational research largely because the world of work is changing so rapidly that anyone wanting to stay employable must continually upgrade their skills and knowledge.

The same applies to parenting. To keep up with your kids and the world in which they live, you're going to have to upgrade your skills and your knowledge every now and then. You know full well that each year your child develops requires you to build different strategies to deal effectively with their growth and maturity. If you relied on the same strategies you used five years ago when they were ten, you're not going to keep up with them. Instead, they'll be so disgusted that you treat them like a child that your relationship will suffer. Don't let this happen.

Being a lifelong learner means you need to regularly look at yourself and your parenting practices. Are they working as well as they could? Are they working for your child? Are they working for you? Are they fair to your child? Will they help your child be a better person tomorrow and then a better parent in twenty years time?

It also means taking an interest in developing your skills as a parent. Read a parenting book every now and then, see a movie that brings you in touch with your child's interests, talk to other parents about how they handle their challenges. It means listening to your child when they disagree with your point of view – what are they telling you and does it suggest you need a skill or knowledge upgrade?

Lifelong learning means you accept you're going to make mistakes and when you make them you need to learn from them. It also means your child seeing you make mistakes – and seeing you learn from them. There's no greater way to reduce your child's fear of failure than to deal with your own failures honestly, proactively and without shame. Talking with young people, I've found they respect teachers who are able to laugh at themselves when they stuff up, and then correct their own mistakes. These teachers teach them a very important lesson in life. You can teach them similar lessons.

Living in the real world
In the real world not everything happens like they say in the books. Here are a few things for you to think about when digesting this chapter.

- There is no such thing as the perfect parent, so don't beat yourself up if you think you're not perfect. On the other hand, it doesn't mean you can't aim to develop more effective parenting skills – remember, as a parent you need to be a lifelong learner.

- Don't expect yourself to totally understand your child's priorities and preferences. As long as they are not harmful to themselves or others, learn to accept and affirm these priorities and preferences.
- You may not love or even like some of the things your child does, and if they won't budge ask yourself if you can live with it. Even though you don't like it, and as long as it doesn't harm them or others, if you can live with it, let it go. To win the war you may need to lose a battle or two.
- Sometimes you won't approve of what your child does and there will be many occasions when they need to know this. Maintaining a good relationship with your child does not mean you never disapprove of their behaviour or lose your authority. Remember, focusing on the behaviour and situation and not the person will keep your child's worth and self-respect intact.
- Don't expect yourself to be an authoritative parent all the time. Sometimes we just blow a fuse and deal with things in a more authoritarian way, and sometimes we're just so damned tired that we may border on the permissive. Aim to be authoritative as much as you can and perhaps focus on particular situations in which you tend to drop your bundle – target these as risky situations where you need to be especially careful.
- Sometimes going in on an angle may not be appropriate in your view. Sometimes you'll feel you have to hash it out, head on. That's fine. Just try to reduce the number of head-on collisions in the home. Research has shown that numerous head-on collisions in the home run the risk of establishing what is called a 'coercive cycle of relations', in which you and your child get stuck in a downward spiral of confrontation.
- Don't freak out if your child's life is a bit unbalanced in some way. Teenagers in particular can get pretty obsessed with some things. I remember my own obsession with a couple of rock bands during adolescence. As long as they aren't hurting themselves or others, you may sometimes have to ride it through until your child bobs up again for air.

- It's important that your child experiences all the joys of youth: friends, sport, fun and mistakes. But school years are also about study and you need to negotiate with your child how to balance study with other aspects of their life. I've found that students will often forgive their parent or teacher for their tough demands regarding study if they're given a bit of rope for fun and friends at other times.

- You won't always draw your child. Sometimes you won't have the time, energy or patience and you'll drive them to do something you think they should be doing. This is fine so long as at the final wash-up there's more drawing than driving, and that you aim to increase the amount you draw your child over the medium to longer term.

- Don't feel you have to read every book on parenting or enrol in every short course or seminar to be a lifelong learner. As long as you upgrade some key skills every year to keep up with your child's development, then you can be pleased with yourself. Understand that the strategy you used successfully last year may not be so effective this year. When you read a parenting book (including this one), don't feel you have to accept everything they're saying. You know yourself and your child better than anyone. Balance this knowledge with what the book is telling you to do. Take what you think is achievable and workable and do a good job of applying that. Remember, doing fewer things better is preferable to doing a greater number of things not very well.

The ideas presented in this chapter revolve around some core principles that underpin good relationships. However, there are some relationships that require professional assistance or intervention and so need advice that is beyond what this chapter is about. These difficult relationships may involve two otherwise properly functioning individuals who just don't function well together. Or, they may involve issues such as conduct disorder, attention- or hyperactivity-related disorders, substance abuse, mental illness, and the like. Don't be frightened to get assistance and don't be frightened to shop around to get the help most useful to you and your child.

Chapter summary

Building a good relationship with your child can make the world of difference to your ability to support and develop their motivation. The most effective relationships are those in which the parent holds a position of authority but does so in a supportive, encouraging and loving way. These parents apply established house rules but can be flexible, adjusting rules in special situations and circumstances. They create a climate in which making mistakes is not the end of the world and in which the child is willing to try to learn from mistakes. Five core foundations of a good relationship between parent and child are mutual respect, understanding where your child is coming from, striving for balance, drawing more than driving, and a willingness to be a lifelong learner.

CHAPTER ELEVEN TOP 5

1. Mutual respect is a key to a good relationship. Mutual respect is gained through recognising that one earns respect, taking the time to understand your child's perspective, valuing your child's priorities and preferences, one-on-one time, active listening, giving your child more responsibility, and affirming your child whenever possible.

2. One of young people's greatest frustrations is that their parents and teachers don't understand them or take the time to see their point of view. Stepping into your child's shoes is an important foundation to building a good relationship with them.

3. Young people recognise when their parents get the right balance between pushing them and letting go. When they are pushed too hard or are not pushed at all, they have more difficult relationships and their motivation suffers. In this and other ways, look for opportunities to inject balance at home, in your child's life, and in the way you treat them.

4. The difference between drawing and driving your child may seem subtle, but in practice it is enormous. Drawing your child requires you to be optimistic for them, supporting and encouraging more than coercing or punishing them, and accepting mistakes or failure by focusing on how they help your child improve. It means encouraging your child to want to be a better student.

5. Being an effective parent is also about being a lifelong learner. You change, your child changes, and the world changes. To stay relevant to and influential in your child's life, you need to be prepared to reflect on your parenting and parenting skills. Your parenting may need an annual service – or at least a tune-up.

CHAPTER 12

RE-ENGAGING THE DISENGAGED CHILD

Okay, we're at the tough end of town. In chapter 4, I described how students can slide through a cycle of fear of failure into failure acceptance (also referred to as learned helplessness or disengagement). This slide began with overstriving and progressed through defensive pessimism, and then into self-sabotage. I also described how self-sabotage may lose its appeal and it is at this point that the student is at risk of disengaging from his or her schoolwork. This chapter looks at strategies you can use to begin to engage the child again.

I should warn you that these students are the hardest to shift. These are the students who have little or no interest in school or schoolwork, don't care if they fail, don't care if they drop out of school (or get booted out), have a strong belief that there's nothing they can do to avoid failure or attain success and firmly believe that any-thing they try turns out badly. They fully accept they are going to fail and have become helpless in the face of this.

Disengagement often results from a run of poor performances or un-pleasant experiences and is coupled with a very pessimistic and hopeless outlook. Because of this, it's important not only to try to change the student's experiences in some way so that the cycle of unpleasantness is cut (at least for a while), but also to try to shift their extreme negativity and hopelessness.

Many of the strategies I've discussed so far in this book are also helpful for the disengaged child. I draw your attention particularly to chapter 4 on control. This is because the consistently defining feature of disengaged students is a rock bottom sense of control. Following this, you might like to have another look at chapter 3 on self-belief – particularly the chunking section. In addition to this, in this chapter I'm going to discuss some other things that you might like to consider. These are:

- protecting your child's mental health
- digging deeper into control and your child's 'explanatory style'
- getting back to basics
- chunking the chunks
- linking with the school
- breaking the cycle of failure
- building better strategies and skills
- being innovative
- getting some support for yourself.

Protecting your child's mental health

I want to discuss mental health first because disengagement is often correlated with anxiety and depression. Research seems to suggest that the disengaged person can pass through intense anger and anxiety in the early stages of helplessness and that after a time this can lead to depression. Their absolute conviction that there is nothing they can do to affect outcomes in their lives (for example, to avoid failure or to attain success) can lead them to feel pretty miserable and abandon their sense of hope. The cycle of poor performance often feeds directly into extreme negativity, and the joint operation of hopelessness and negativity can give rise to depression.

It is at this point that a child's mental health becomes more important than anything else – even their grades. I stress to you that if your child is depressed or is experiencing anxiety that is interfering with their functioning, you must get help. You can ring a national mental health professional association (for example, the national psychology society or association) for a referral to a mental health professional. Psychology and psychiatry departments at universities sometimes run their own clinics. Alternatively, your nearby hospital might have a psychology or psychiatry unit. Your GP may also be able to refer you to someone. If you can see someone who specialises in child or adolescent mental health, that's even better.

Protecting mental health also means staying in touch with your child and not disaffecting them. You may have to put your judgments, disappointment, resentment and anger on hold. This may be an opportunity for you to show your child that their worth as a person has priority over their pretty unremarkable track record at school. I don't say this lightly because often disengagement has a history of hurt and unpleasantness for both the child and the parents and it's a big ask to put this aside while the all-important mental health issue is addressed.

The reason I suggest you develop an embracing rather than disaffecting approach is because as long as the child is mentally healthy, there's a better chance that they can engage again with the system. There's also a better chance they will be receptive to some significant other (either a mentor at school, a coach, a boss, a girlfriend or boyfriend, a youth worker, a teacher) who may wield the positive influence they seem to need.

Starting off the chapter in this way isn't intended to frighten you. There are many disengaged students who are mentally healthy. If your child is such a student, good luck to you (though I'm aware this is cold comfort because they are, nevertheless, disengaged). However, as I said earlier, there is a correlation between helplessness and depression and anxiety and getting professional help is important if this is relevant to your child.

I should also mention a couple of other reasons students may disengage from school and which can also be related to mental health issues. The first is because they may be experiencing social problems at school. They may be feeling lonely or disconnected from others at school and this is not going to make them feel too great about other aspects of school, such as schoolwork and study. Another reason is that they may be being bullied at school. For a victim, bullying can turn school into a very scary place where there is not much room for effective engagement with schoolwork and study. Because this book is about academically oriented approaches to enhancing motivation, dealing with these two phenomena is beyond its scope. However, it is important to mention that these two problems can affect disengagement. Be prepared to talk with your child very honestly and sensitively about these issues. Raise your concerns about bullying with the school (either your child's teacher, the year co-ordinator or the counsellor in the first instance) and ask about the school's policy and practice for dealing with bullying. Find out what you can do to support your child during this difficult time. In the reference list at the back of this book, I've included a couple of books on bullying that you might find helpful.

Digging deeper into control and your child's 'explanatory style'

As I noted above, a low sense of control is one of the most consistently identified predictors of helplessness. When individuals believe they cannot influence outcomes in their lives they start to feel helpless. When this is backed up by a run of poor performance, the rot can set in and they may give up.

You'll recall that chapter 4 on control discussed a few things that can lead to a child's loss of control. One was the feedback you provide to your child and the importance of that feedback being consistent and based more on the task or activity than on the mark allocated for that task. I raise the issue of your feedback again because helplessness in children has been associated with the type of feedback they receive from teachers and parents. In particular, inconsistent feedback that is focused on the outcome rather than the process has been linked to helplessness in students.

In chapter 4, I also discussed how the way a student sees the cause of an event influences his or her sense of control. That is, the way a student explains why something happened can affect their sense of control. This is referred to as a student's *explanatory style*. Explanatory style is the student's typical way of

Ingrid, final year of school and beyond

Ingrid was an intelligent final-year school student. Although she had done okay in middle high school, in senior high she had been performing lower than she and her family expected and this hit her pretty hard. In middle high, not much work was needed to succeed. But in senior high, it took more work to succeed and work was something Ingrid didn't have much experience with. After a while, she consistently performed at levels lower than her potential. This, in her mind, was equivalent to a run of failures. The result of this poor run was a fragile self-esteem (she was only as good or bad as her last performance) and a steady decline in her belief in her ability to turn around her bad trot (that is, low control). Essentially, she was steadily losing touch with success and also losing her sense of hope.

To make matters worse, when her father found out about each successive poor performance, he crashed down on her like a tonne of bricks. Perhaps worse still, not only did he focus mercilessly on her failures with little recognition for her successes, he also gave her the distinct message that he believed she no longer had the ability to turn things around. This shattered her self-esteem and it was at this point that she abandoned all sense of hope for success. She decided that she couldn't tolerate one more poor performance, and without consulting anyone, in the final month of her final year of school, she dropped out. Despite the best efforts of her teachers, she could not be convinced to return. Ten years on she has no intention of ever completing her schooling.

After leaving school Ingrid got a clerical job to support her move away from home. She did good work, and through small successes she started to salvage her sense of worth. It was a brave move when she joined a weekend amateur acting group, something she'd always wanted to do and privately thought she mightn't be too bad at. Now she was succeeding at work and receiving a great deal of support from her troupe to develop skills in a new domain. She was rebuilding her sense of efficacy and control.

→

Ten years on from school, she's leading a productive and happy existence. However, things could have gone horribly wrong at the point she left school. I know that she contemplated taking her own life and if it weren't for some very strong friendships with her girlfriends, things might have ended tragically.

Ingrid's pathway to disengagement could be summed up by a series of poor grades, her father's excessive focus on failure and neglect of success, and his belief that she didn't have what it took to succeed. Her sense of hope was rescued through breaking the cycle of failure, experiencing some small successes, and immersing herself in a supportive group that built her sense of worth and control by believing in her ability to develop skills in a new area.

I believe, however, that the cycle could have been broken while Ingrid was at school. Her father could have taken a more supportive approach that would have made it easier for her to complete school, and she need not have sunk so low that she contemplated taking her own life. Through addressing the cornerstones of control, things could have been different and it was a testament to Ingrid and her friends that things turned out as well as they did.

explaining events and outcomes in their life. In chapter 4, I discussed one aspect of a student's explanatory style: that relating to the controllability of an event. Examples of controllable factors include how much work students do, how they do that work, where they do that work, the presentation of their work and so on. Examples of uncontrollable factors include the test questions, good or bad luck, the teacher's marking and so on. The more students focus on the controllable factors in their life, the more control they will feel.

In this chapter, I'm going to look at two other aspects of a student's explanatory style: the extent to which the cause of an event is seen as sweeping or specific and the extent to which the cause of an event is changeable or unchangeable. For most people, just focusing on the control side of things is sufficient. But for the disengaged students you may need to bring out the big guns and look at more specific aspects of their explanatory style.

Sweeping versus specific causes

When students give reasons for failing a test they may opt for a focused and targeted explanation (that is, identify specific causes) or may make more generalised and sweeping explanations (that is, identify sweeping causes). Here is an example of each:

> Specific explanation: 'I didn't study very well for that test.'
> Sweeping explanation: 'I don't study very well.'

As you can see, one explanation is targeted, focused and confined to that particular test. The other is global and sweeping and applies to all aspects of the student's study. It probably goes without saying that the sweeping explanation is going to make a child feel more helpless than the specific explanation. This is because the sweeping explanation pretty much dismisses the person as a hopeless studier. On the other hand, the specific explanation identifies that study for that particular test could have been better, but does not contaminate the students' sense of hope for the next test. Obviously, we need to try to gently direct our children's explanations towards more specific ones. You need to try to put a fence around their explanations so they don't interfere with other aspects of their school and study life. Helpless students routinely make sweeping explanations about their poor performances – watch out for these explanations and gently rein them in to focus on the particular event or situation.

Changeable versus unchangeable causes

Another aspect of students' explanatory styles concerns the extent to which they make explanations that refer to changeable or unchangeable factors. When students give reasons for failing a test they can either focus on factors that can be changed next time (that is, identify changeable causes) or on factors that can't be changed next time (that is, identify unchangeable causes). Examples of the two types of explanations are as follows:

> Changeable explanation: 'I didn't study very well for that test.'
> Unchangeable explanation: 'I've got a hopeless teacher.'

The first explanation is one that leaves the door open for the next test – this student can change his or her study next time and so is focusing on a changeable cause of failure. Even though they probably don't feel too good about failing, they certainly will be less inclined to feel helpless because they have some control over changing the outcome next time. The second explanation can shut the door on hope. This is because the student will probably have this teacher for the rest of the year and the teacher is unlikely to teach any better (in the student's eyes), and so the factor that led to the failure in this test will probably be present for the next test. That is, in the student's eyes it is an unchangeable cause of their poor performance. This is fertile terrain for loss of hope and descent into helplessness.

The perfect cocktail: a controllable, specific, changeable outlook
Now comes the tricky bit. We need to identify the factors in students' lives that reflect all three of the vital ingredients for hope and optimism: factors that are controllable, specific and changeable. I've done the hard work for you. In the table on page 240 I've listed a number of explanations students use when they don't do well and I've also indicated how they meet our three criteria for greater empowerment. I've focused on poor performance because the disengaged students are usually at this point because of a run of poor performances.

Looking at this table, you'll probably clue in to the fact that controllability and changeability can be rubbery things, and so what is controllable and changeable for one student may be seen by another as less controllable or changeable. I'll take each statement one at a time and describe why I categorised them the way I did.

I didn't study hard enough for it. This is controllable, specific and changeable – this is the type of explanatory style that empowers.

I'm hopeless at maths. This may or may not be controllable depending on whether the student believes they can improve their maths ability, and, relative to effort and study strategy, it is unclear whether it is changeable. It is also not very specific because it makes a sweeping statement about being hopeless at maths and does not say, for example, that further work in calculus is needed.

Towards empowering explanations

I failed the maths test because	Controllable	Specific	Changeable
I didn't study hard enough for it.	✓	✓	✓
I'm hopeless at maths.	?	✗	?
The test was too hard.	✗	✗	✓
The teacher hates me.	?	✗	✓
The teacher is a mean marker.	✗	✗	✗
It was just bad luck.	✗	✗	✓
I didn't read the instructions carefully.	✓	✓	✓
I misread the question.	✓	✓	✓
I didn't concentrate much while I was studying.	✓	✓	✓
I'm not smart enough.	?	✗	?

The test was too hard. This is not controllable because the ease and difficulty of test questions is beyond the student's control. It is not very specific because it doesn't identify what parts were difficult.

The teacher hates me. This may or may not be controllable and changeable depending on whether the student can behave and apply himself or herself more to win the teacher's favour; it is not really specific because it is a sweeping statement about his or her whole self. If the student had said, 'The teacher doesn't like my behaviour,' that would be more specific.

The teacher is a mean marker. This is not controllable because the student has little to do with the marking standards; it is not really specific because it is a statement about the teacher's marking as a whole and not restricted to that particular test; as far as the student is concerned, it's also not very changeable.

It was just bad luck. This is not controllable because good and bad luck is generally beyond one's control; is not specific because luck is more of a sweeping and vague thing than something easily identified or defined.

I didn't read the instructions carefully. This is controllable, specific and changeable – the type of explanatory style that empowers.

I misread the question. This is controllable, specific and changeable – the type of explanatory style that empowers.

I didn't concentrate much while I was studying. This is controllable, specific and changeable – the type of explanatory style that empowers.

I'm not smart enough. This may or may not be controllable depending on whether the student believes they can improve their intelligence, and, relative to effort and study strategy, is less changeable; it is not specific because the student has made a sweeping statement about their smartness and not confined it to maths or particular skills in maths.

Actually, I want to spend a touch more time on this last explanation. Helpless students often use this explanation ('I'm not smart enough') for failure. This is dangerous because the students are rating themselves low on the very attribute they usually think it takes to do well, and this low rating can lead to a loss of hope. In fact, research has found that these students can actually distort the past to their disadvantage. They do this in two ways. The first is by revising the explanations they gave for previous success. Whereas they previously said they did well because they tried hard or worked effectively (a great explanatory style), when helplessness takes hold they say they failed because they weren't smart enough to succeed (a less helpful explanatory style). The second way they distort the past is by selectively forgetting successes and remembering more failures than actually occurred. That is, not only do they not take credit for all the successes they achieved but they also beat themselves up with more failures than actually took place.

So what's their alternative? You need to gently encourage explanations similar to those in the table that have a tick in all three columns. These explanations are the perfect explanatory style in that they involve factors that are within the student's control, they are focused on the specific behaviour or situation and they are changeable from situation to situation. These are the cornerstones of hope and empowerment.

Before concluding this section on control, I should also say that it may be that a sense of control can be just as effective as actual control. This means that even if the student isn't in control of things now, if he or she believes that by trying hard and working effectively he or she can seize control then that's good enough. Research suggests that those who haven't yet got control, but believe they can get it through effort and strategy, perform as though they have got it. This is a very empowering notion and where there's empowerment there's very little helplessness.

Getting back to basics

When a child is disengaged or at the point of giving up you may need to temporarily let go of some of your more stringent or ambitious expectations of him or her – but do not give up hope or communicate that you have given up hope. For a while, you may need a new set of goals to aim for. For example, that A– grade may not be the most realistic ambition to hold for your child right now. Instead, getting him or her to go to school may be a triumph or getting him or her to turn one page for the test is an achievement. What I'm saying is that for a time, it'll be back to basics.

The first basic principle is to sustain a good relationship with your child. While you do this, you'll always have a hearing from them and your influence can still factor into their life. This is a good thing. Chapter 11 provided details on how to build and sustain a good relationship with your child.

The second is to really focus on process and temporarily put outcomes on the backburner. This involves focusing on effort (how hard your child works) or, even better, strategy (the quality of that work) and not on marks or grades or comparisons with other students or siblings. It also means starting small – for example, 30 minutes study can be the start of a climb back.

The third principle to remember is to give credit where credit is due. For example, the fact that your child is disenchanted with school and schoolwork, yet still turns up to school is to be recognised. This is a glimmer of persistence that has enormous potential when the student once again engages with school. Or, if following three hard hits in history they're still doing some history homework, that shows some tenacity. I know it's a crying shame that you have to be thankful for things that other parents take for granted, but we're in basic survival mode here and need to look for small mercies wherever they can be found.

The fourth basic rule is to do what in other circumstances you possibly shouldn't do: provide some 'extrinsic reward' for some of the good (or even marginally okay) things your child does. Extrinsic rewards include some special TV time, an outing, some tasty food or some other thing that is attractive to your child. I should say that in general terms it is far better that students develop intrinsic or inner reasons for doing their schoolwork – such as the satisfaction of good effort, doing a good job, feeling yourself improve or learning new things and so on. However, the helpless or disengaged student has little or no intrinsic motivation and so waiting for them to develop some may be a long wait indeed. Having said this, the purpose of extrinsic reward is to kick-start the process that can't be initiated otherwise. You should aim to phase out your administration of extrinsic reward as the desired behaviour gets going. When it comes to the disengaged student I can be quite utilitarian – I'll do whatever it takes to get them back in the loop.

The fifth principle is to start small – really small. Be aware that most disengaged students are very hard to shift and so expectations should not be unrealistically high. Unrealistic expectations may paralyse the disengaged student even further. How do I reconcile this with the need for parents to hold positive and challenging expectations for their children? My answer is that expectations need to be challenging relative to where your child is now. Moreover, for the disengaged student they need to be attainable in the near future. Distant goals and expectations (such as getting into university) may be too overwhelming. Put these on hold for the moment – once your child is back in the loop you can dust off these distant expectations and subtly present them to your child once more. Depending on the nature and degree of your child's disengagement, examples of starting small include:

- turning up to school
- staying at school for the whole day
- doing a bit of homework
- attempting an assignment
- starting to read a novel
- asking a teacher for help
- taking a few notes in class
- listening during a lesson.

Make no mistake. For the disengaged student, these are essential milestones on the journey to engaging again. For the disengaged student they are not trivial. You need to recognise this. Again, I know it probably breaks your heart that your gratitude has come to rely on things that most other parents take for granted. But this is the reality and, if only for your own sanity, you need to recognise small successes.

Chunking the chunks

Picking up on the previous point of starting small, I want to return to the chunking idea. You'll recall that chunking comprises two steps: breaking tasks into bite-size chunks and recognising the completion of each chunk as a success. The first step is vital because it makes work more manageable for students. The second is vital because it builds more opportunities for success into students' lives and this is motivating.

For the disengaged student who sees even the easily achievable tasks as daunting and overwhelming, chunking is absolutely critical. However, when approaching chunking with your disengaged child, you'll need to remember that what is a bite-size chunk for most children may be too big a mouthful for your own child. Have a good look at components of tasks and schoolwork and make sure that your child won't choke on them. I'll give an example.

In chapter 8, I presented the chunks needed to do an essay. One chunk involved doing a search for information for the essay. For many students, this sort of search is a chunk they can bite off and handle with no problems. However, for the disengaged student this may be daunting, so it needs to be chunked even further. These chunks might include:

- asking the teacher for some key words to use in a search
- asking the teacher for some good references
- deciding which library or libraries to go to
- asking a librarian for help to run a search on the library catalogue
- understanding how to find books using the catalogue numbers
- understanding how to borrow a book from the library
- what to do if a book isn't on the shelf
- understanding how to reserve a book
- doing a secondary search for information on the internet
- deciding which internet information is useful and accurate
- saving or printing information off the internet.

Now, formally presenting all these steps to some children will also be daunting, so you may need to informally talk about these so that they're not frightened off. For other children, this could be a great list they can take to school or the library and enjoy ticking off each chunk as they do them. Play it by ear – you know your child best.

Linking with the school and identifying a mentor at school

I'm all for parents making good strong links with school and their child's teachers. Not only does it provide students with a greater sense of connectedness between school and home but it can also be great support for teachers who sometimes feel a bit isolated in the education of students. It also means that consistent messages can be communicated to students – a united strategy (that is, between school and home) will be most effective.

For the disengaged student, strong and positive links between parent and school are even more important. Let the school know that your child is disengaging or disengaged (if they haven't told you already) and ask what you can do to help support the school or the strategy in place to engage your child again. The school will probably be more expert at re-engaging students than you are, so be prepared to take its advice very seriously. Having said this, you probably know your child best and so you need to have the confidence to put in your two-cents' worth – but do so with respect for the teachers' professionalism and breadth of experience.

When talking with the school, find out about school-based re-engagement programs your child might become a part of. Ask if any programs are on the back-burner that could be brought forward. Remember that your child will probably not be the only one disengaged at the school, so the school may be happy to put something in place for this group of students. Let the school know of anything in your child's life outside school that may be affecting his or her engagement.

Because relationships lie at the core of any capacity to motivate someone else, I also suggest discussing with the school the possibility of someone taking your child under their wing. The school may assign a teacher or counsellor they know is good at re-engaging students. Or your child may request a particular teacher's or counsellor's help. In some schools, re-engaging students is such a priority that the principal personally takes these students under their wing or provides special recognition to those in the process of re-engaging. The function of the mentor is to develop an affirming relationship within the school and for the teacher or counsellor to advocate for your child in some areas of their life that are troubling them most. In the first instance, it may be more of a pastoral care role. When the relationship develops, academic engagement can be tabled as the primary issue to deal with.

Breaking the cycle of failure and trouble

I've said on numerous occasions that a lack of control underpins helplessness. I should also say that it often follows a run of poor performances or failures. Usually students can withstand isolated failure (although students low in academic resilience can have trouble with even this). One failure is seen by most students as a challenge. But a run of failures is hard for even the most resilient students to cope with. I therefore suggest that in addition to developing a greater sense of control, the cycle of failure needs to be broken – at least for a while.

Obviously, one way to cut the cycle of failure is to build more opportunities for success into your child's life. Chapter 8 dealt with this in some detail through its discussion of chunking and the importance of broadening your view of success. I want to discuss a couple of other ways teachers and parents manage to maximise opportunities for success.

The first is through a strategy called 'scaffolding'. This involves developing very clear and progressive links from one part of a task to another. It involves providing a very firm platform from which students can move to the next platform. In practical terms it means:

- parents and teachers reviewing what the disengaged child knows before presenting new information
- not moving ahead too quickly when teaching the child new things
- ensuring the child understands the present bit of work before moving on to the next bit
- giving the student detailed but straightforward instructions
- getting the student to demonstrate their understanding before moving on
- monitoring the student when they start applying the new information or skills
- giving the student enough time to complete work.

Another strategy some teachers use is to allow students to present their schoolwork or assignments in whatever form they wish. Some students will prefer to present their answer in a multi-media form, others in an essay form, others as a role-play, others as a website, others as a debate and so on. Teachers do this so that every now and then students put their best foot forward and maximise their chances of succeeding. A similar strategy is to assign a few tasks (say, a series of short answer questions, an essay question and a practical exercise) and allow students to select one of these as their assignment. More often than not, students select the task that provides them with a greater chance of succeeding. Again, using this strategy every now and then can break a cycle of relatively poor performance for some students.

Parents can use some strategies in the home as well. Particularly for disengaged students, the home can be a place where a negative cycle of relationships exists between them and their parents. Usually this cycle is a downward one, and the further it spirals the harder it is to break and the more unpleasant it becomes. In fact, the cycle itself can become the feeding force, not the original disengagement – and so after a while the cycle becomes more of a problem than the disengagement. It is very important to cut these cycles. Some parents recognise when the cycle is starting to spiral downward and aim for a 'trouble-free day'.

A trouble-free day is one in which the parents, to the best of their ability:

- do not feed the cycle
- temporarily turn a blind eye to smaller or more trivial things that would normally feed the cycle (and which are not illegal, harmful to the child or someone else, or blatantly or provocatively disregard house rules)
- try to do something with the child that is unconnected to the problem and which is enjoyable
- jolly the child along more than forcing or coercing them
- talk about 'safe' topics and issues (such as band practice) and avoid talking about issues that are known to feed the cycle (such as progress in the social science essay)
- do things with the child that are known to be relatively free from conflict.

Every now and then you and your child need a day off. A day off cools heads, calms nerves, recharges batteries and provides a bit of perspective. I'm not suggesting you ignore problems and I'm not suggesting that you turn a blind eye to everything all the time. But I am suggesting that a circuit-breaker is needed at critical times. It is important to know when these times are upon you and for a short time to strategically manoeuvre so you can avoid the usual trouble spots.

Building better strategies and skills

In broad terms, there are two types of disengaged students. There are those who have effective skills and strategies (for example, they can manage their time, prioritise, chunk and set goals), but who for one reason or another have given up. That is, there is more a motivation deficit than a skill or strategy deficit. Then there are those who do not have the skills and strategies needed nor do they have the motivation or will to apply themselves. The kids in this second group are tougher to shift because they have a skill deficit and a motivation deficit. If your child is one of these, then not only are the chapters on self-belief and control important, so too is the chapter on developing better schoolwork and study (chapter 7).

Research has looked at effective ways to build skills in students and identified four key steps (although, as I said earlier, you may need to chunk each of these steps even further). These steps are:

1. Observation
2. Imitation
3. Exploratory application
4. Full transferal.

The table on page 248 provides an explanation and example for each step.

Being innovative

The reality may be that mainstream, 'bread and butter' approaches to your disengaged child have not been entirely effective. Approaches that engage most students may not be reaching your child. Reminding students to start study early will reach a good proportion of students. Telling students to take detailed notes in certain parts of the lesson will also reach a good proportion of students. Insisting on a particular due date for the assignment will work for most students. Requiring all students to sit a weekly class quiz will result in the majority of the class participating. However, in all of these situations there can be a few who do not engage with the request or expectation. For these students, something more or something different is needed, possibly something innovative.

Four key steps to building skill

Step	Description	Example
1. Observation	Students need to see the skill in action: what it looks like and how it's done. It may be important to demonstrate the skill in a couple of contexts or situations. It may also be important for the student to see a couple of ways to apply the skill. They must also see positive consequences for having applied the skill.	Dad sits down with his daughter, Fiona, and talks about the steps involved in doing a social science project. After they talk, he writes out a list of these steps. They then talk about how this list might be useful in doing a better project.
2. Imitation	Students need to imitate the skill in a fairly similar and controlled situation in which mastery and success are likely. The parent or teacher needs to monitor and provide task-based feedback on areas of strength, which areas to improve, and how to improve them. To make the point, the teacher or parent might demonstrate the skill again.	After they discuss the list, the ordering of the items and which other items should be included, Dad asks Fiona to think about her geography project. They talk about the steps involved in successfully completing the project. As they talk, Dad asks Fiona to list the steps on a sheet of paper.
3. Exploratory application	Students practise and apply the skill away from the teacher or parent but in similar situations to the one in which they first learnt the skill. This is where they begin to attain a sense of independence and control.	Dad encourages Fiona to think about how this chunking skill can be used for an upcoming class test. He encourages her to independently develop a study strategy using the chunking strategy.
4. Full transferral	Students practise or apply the skill away from the teacher or parent and in quite different settings and situations from the one in which they first learnt the skill. This is where they attain a sense of independence and control in their ability to effectively deal with new and challenging situations.	Fiona starts seeing other tasks in her life in terms of smaller components. One example was her preparation for the school play and setting up a website to promote the play.

Examples of innovative approaches include:

- a contract system (a formal or semi-formal agreement between you and your child)
- special exemptions for the child in order to get them to start some schoolwork (for example, relaxing some of the marking criteria)
- special incentives for the child to study for an exam
- choices in how to present schoolwork
- extracurricular activities (for example, sport, a hobby or a club) that might enhance the child's energy levels
- a part-time job that might create some added interest in the child's life
- enrolment in a course of interest (for example, vocational education)
- some community work to hook them into the world a bit
- some peer tutoring to relieve some of the pressures the child might see in the authority of teachers and parents.

These are just a few ideas; the list is by no means exhaustive. Talk with your child's teachers about some innovative ideas you might use to more effectively engage him or her. I realise that some of these suggestions do not directly lead to improved academic performance, but for some helpless students sparking any interest in productive activity can be an important start.

Getting some support for yourself

I don't need to tell any parent that parenting is tough. But I should make the point that it's particularly tough for parents of disengaged, failure accepting or helpless students. It is important that these parents receive some sort of support and cut themselves some slack at critical times.

Support can either be formal or informal. Formal support might include professional help (for example, from a psychologist, psychiatrist, counsellor, or social worker), a support group or a help line. Informal support can be from a relative, a friend, a book or a chat group on the internet. Whatever the support base you use, it needs to be non-judgmental, give you some sense of emotional support and hope, be constructive and make you feel okay about being a parent.

You also need to cut yourself some slack. Some messages in this book suggest that every now and then you need to cut your child a bit of slack. You must also do the same for yourself. There is no such thing as the perfect parent, so don't expect yourself to be one. This isn't to say that you should stop trying to develop yourself as a parent, but it does mean you accept some of the things you can't change. Sure, some parents seem to have it easier, but focusing on how these parents manage things will not make you feel any better. Their ability to cope is none of your business, unless of course they are able to provide some good guidance for you. But even then, don't assume that what works for their kids should work for yours (avoid those 'shoulds' in your life!). Cutting yourself some slack also means going for a trouble-free day every now and then, having some time off or time out, and doing things with your child that both of you enjoy and which are relatively free of conflict.

Some other aspects of helplessness

Up to this point I've talked about helplessness in students and how that helplessness results from that student's personal experience of failure or their own experience of things being beyond their control. I also want to talk briefly about a couple of other aspects of helplessness.

Research has found that some children can actually learn to be helpless simply by seeing someone else fail repeatedly or by seeing events in someone else's life being beyond their control. For example, some students can see things go badly for other students and personalise this to their own lives. That is, they can feel helpless simply by seeing how another student's poor marks were due to the teacher being in a bad mood or fail because of sheer bad luck. This finding is also relevant to the home environment because children can see how their parents react to setback or challenge and learn their own responses to setback or challenge from what they observe. So, if a parent responds to setback as though there's nothing they can do about it or act somewhat helpless in the face of challenge, children can learn to react in a similar way.

The good news is that if children can learn unhelpful ways of responding to setback and challenge, then they can also learn very empowering responses. For example, if parents respond to setback and challenge by being solution focused (not problem focused), exploring options to overcome the setback, and being confident in the face of adversity, then children can learn to respond in a similar way. That is, by parents showing their children that they focus on the controllable things in their life, children can learn that this is how to deal with the world. Does this mean you should hide your fears from your child or hide the fact that you find some things difficult to deal with? Not at all. In fact, one of the most powerful lessons you teach your child may be showing them that sometimes you're scared and yet you still face these situations with courage and with a focus on what's controllable. You've shown them that being scared or finding things tough does not mean you've failed in some way.

Living in the real world

In the real world not everything happens like they say in the books. Here are a few things for you to think about when digesting this chapter.

- Not for a moment is this chapter meant to imply that shifting helpless students is an easy thing to do. How much effort does it take to shift them? I don't know. I'm aware of some business research showing that five times as many resources are needed to get a dissatisfied customer back as to keep a satisfied customer. I don't doubt that it may well take at least five-fold as much time, energy and commitment to re-engage a helpless student as to increase the motivation of the 'average' student. But I also argue that the potential pay-offs are worth it.

- Not all disengaged students will re-engage. This is a pretty depressing statement, but it's the truth. Having said this, although total re-engagement is the desired outcome, it is not the only positive outcome. For example, keeping your child in the system and mentally healthy is a good outcome for students who would otherwise have fallen through the cracks or become depressed. Look for small mercies where they can be found.

- A number of students will disengage from only one or two school subjects. Although they can't be said to be totally helpless, they certainly act like it in some subjects. The up side with this type of student is that your support can be targeted. Research shows that the more your approach is targeted, the more effective it is likely to be. What's more, these students have areas of strength and skill that can be harnessed for those one or two subjects where they have disengaged.

- As I've said before, don't expect your child to pick up the chunking skill immediately (or other skills for that matter). It may take some time. Even if he or she only does a half decent job, this may be good going.
- You may not always see eye to eye with your child's school, but it's important you work together as much as possible. Your child's interests need to be at the forefront of any dealings with the school and teachers.
- Don't overdo the trouble-free days. They are intended to be a special circuit-breaker. There are important house rules and expectations that need to be upheld most of the time. This doesn't mean you rule with an iron fist, but clear and consistent boundaries are important.
- Being innovative does not mean taking unnecessary or excessive risks. You need to be sure that your innovation serves the higher good and does not put in place short-term strategies that end up disaffecting or disengaging your child in the medium to longer term.

Chapter summary

Although disengagement and helplessness apply to a relative minority of students, there are few things more frustrating (or even soul-destroying) to parents than a child who has disengaged from school. Research shows that the main reason students disengage from school and schoolwork is because of their rock-bottom sense of control. Increasing this sense of control is achieved through tackling students' explanatory styles. Other important strategies to address disengagement include effective links with the school, breaking the cycle of failure and being somewhat innovative in your approach. Accompanying these strategies is the need to ensure your child stays mentally healthy, the need for you to maintain a good (or reasonable) relationship with him or her, and also the need to cut yourself some slack during this tough time.

CHAPTER TWELVE TOP 5

1. A great deal of helplessness arises from a low sense of control. Control is enhanced when students make links between their actions and outcomes. This involves developing explanations for outcomes that involve factors that are controllable, specific and changeable.

2. Getting back to basics is important. This includes attending to your relationship with your child, starting small, recognising small successes, taking some of the focus off grades and placing more focus on effort and strategy, and chunking in even greater detail.

3. Effective links with school can be very important. Don't be frightened to talk with your child's teachers or the school counsellor. But remember to stay solution-focused, not problem-focused.

4. A run of poor performances can sometimes fast-track helplessness, particularly if your child feels little or no control over those poor performances. Breaking this cycle – at least temporarily – is important. This can involve maximising opportunities for success through chunking, scaffolding and broadening your own and your child's view of success. It may involve providing clear instructions on how to develop skills such as chunking through encouraging your child to observe the skill, imitate it, apply it and then transfer it to new situations. It can also involve aiming for trouble-free days at critical times.

5. Don't underestimate the role of mental health in all of this – your child's mental health and your own. You may need to draw on some professional support or some informal support from family and friends.

CHAPTER 13

MOTIVATING BOYS

Y ou may have groaned as you turned the page to find this chapter about motivating boys. Not another expert on boys!

The reason I've included this chapter is because over the last couple of years I've conducted a fair bit of research into boys' education. I've collected motivation data from thousands of school students, interviewed many teachers and principals, consulted with many respected academics and conducted a major review of previous research into the education of boys. I've learnt a few things about motivating boys and I'd like to share them here. It's also a chance to see how boys fare on the boosters, mufflers and guzzlers.

Before I kick off I want to emphasise that although I focus on boys as a group distinct from girls, individual boys are very different from each other. Some like practical, hands-on activities; some don't. Some like physical activities such as sport; some don't. Some are loud and impulsive; some aren't. Some need more male role models in their lives; some don't. Some hate reading and writing; some don't. Some love gadgets and technology; some don't.

I'M TOO BUSY SAVING THE WORLD FROM MUTANT ANDROIDS

What's more, it's my view that there are more similarities than differences between boys and girls. I'll go even further and say that the differences from boy to boy can often be larger than the differences between boys and girls. So, although I'll generalise in this chapter about boys, your job is to tailor the message to your son and his strengths, weaknesses, likes and dislikes.

You may ask: if boys and girls are so similar, why spend a chapter on motivating boys? The reason is that my research has found some significant differences between boys and girls in motivation, and it's important to know what they are and what to do about them. Even though there are many similarities, this doesn't mean there are no differences between boys and girls when it comes to school.

Differences in motivation between boys and girls

I've found that there are statistically significant differences between boys and girls on the following boosters:

- Study management – girls manage their study more effectively than boys
- Learning focus – girls are more focused than boys on developing skills, understanding new things, personal bests and solving problems
- Persistence – girls are more persistent than boys when it comes to difficult or challenging schoolwork
- Planning – girls are more inclined than boys to plan their schoolwork and check their progress as they are doing it.
- Value of school – girls are more likely than boys to believe in the value of school.

There is also a statistically significant difference between boys and girls on the following guzzler:

- *Self-sabotage* – boys are more inclined than girls to put obstacles in their path to success (e.g. they procrastinate, waste time, clown around).

Does your son reflect any of these results? If he does, you might like to revisit the chapters in this book that deal with the relevant boosters and guzzlers in detail. However, when measuring your son against these results, remember that they don't apply to every boy. These results are based on averages across thousands of students. Your son may well be different from the average.

What about the girls?

Although the focus of this chapter is on boys, parents ignore the motivation of girls at their peril. You'll see from the above results that girls score significantly higher than boys on study management, planning, learning focus, persistence and value of school. These are girls' strengths and they need to be sustained. The very strategies that increase these boosters are the strategies parents need to use to sustain their child's strengths. I should also say that not all girls are stronger on these boosters and to the extent that this is the case for your daughter, there is some work to do to increase these boosters in her life.

Furthermore, girls are significantly higher than boys in anxiety, and many would benefit from a reduction in this muffler.

Let's also not forget that girls' post-school pathways are still not on par with boys'. Later in life, men still get better paying jobs, get better pay in the same job, and tend to be promoted ahead of women. So working on your daughter's self-belief, persistence and sense of control now will stand her in good stead in her adult years.

What do boys need?

There are literally hundreds of experts telling parents what boys need. My analysis indicates that boys do have particular needs. However, I've also found that many of these needs are more relevant to students generally than to boys exclusively.

In my research with students, I certainly have found that many boys express a strong preference for practical, hands-on learning at school. But many girls tell me they'd like that too. I've found many boys love getting outside doing some physical stuff. But many girls tell me that's great as well. Heaps of boys tell me school isn't relevant to their lives. Many girls tell me that also. Boys tell me group work in class is what they enjoy most. Many girls enjoy working in groups too.

So what's the difference between boys and girls? I've found the main difference is *how much* boys like physical, hands-on activities, working in groups, doing stuff outside and so on. They seem to like it more than girls. When we understand this, we understand that boys' and girls' interests aren't competing interests. If there's a bit more hands-on work in class, good luck to both girls and boys. Sure, it may not suit some girls as much as others, but education is about breadth of experience and developing diverse skills. A bit of hands-on work will probably do them the world of good – just as there is no getting around the fact that many boys must develop a stronger capacity to sit on a chair in class and get some theory under their belts.

There are lots of parts to the boys' education debate. I'm going to focus on those things that are directly related to boys' motivation. I'm not going to focus on things like conceptions of masculinity, literacy, bullying, or male role models. I recognise that they are related to motivation, but I feel they are more than adequately addressed elsewhere and there are more central issues to address in this book which is primarily concerned with motivation. Having said this, however, I do touch on the issue of single-sex versus co-educational schooling later in this chapter.

My reading of previous research and my own research have led me to believe there are eight critical factors that underpin boys' motivation:

- good relationships
- respect
- a sense of humour
- relevance and usefulness
- ensuring mastery
- experiences of success and reward
- control and responsibility
- low fear of failure.

Although I'm sure you'd be able to identify many more, these are the top eight as I see them.

Good relationships
Chapter 11 discussed the importance of a good relationship between parent and child and how to achieve it. Just to recap, it was suggested there that good relationships are developed through:

- mutual respect
- stepping into your child's shoes
- aiming for balance whenever possible

- drawing your child more than driving him or her
- being committed to lifelong learning to bring out the best in your child.

These are all central to building a good relationship with your son and I urge you to have another look at chapter 11 which explained these in detail.

In my research, I've been particularly interested in the characteristics of adults who bring out the best in boys. When I ask successful teachers how they build a good relationship with boys, these are the factors they mention:

- building trust with them
- getting to know them
- talking about their interests
- taking opportunities for one-on-one work with them
- actively listening to their perspectives
- finding things in common with them
- sharing a joke with them
- affirming them as often as possible
- giving them responsibility.

Teachers and parents who build these components into their relationships with boys tend to have better relationships with them.

Respect

Respect means a lot to boys, and as I said in chapter 11, respect must be earned. The teachers or parents who have the child's respect are in the strongest position to motivate them. Talking with boys, I've found the following attitudes and behaviours show them that you respect them:

- listening to what they are saying and taking time to understand them
- affirming them for who they are and not wishing they were someone different (this is different from wanting to change some behaviours)
- taking time to explain schoolwork – a number of times if necessary
- showing an interest in their lives

- accepting and affirming things that are important to them
- not showing favouritism (even if privately you find your daughters easier to motivate)
- giving them a say in things that affect them
- clearly explaining rules and why you have made them, but at appropriate times negotiating rules or changes in rules
- not treating them like children but providing space and freedom for them to explore who they are.

Adults who respect the boy and who in return earn his respect get a fair hearing. These adults are then in a position to have an influence on him. Adults who don't respect the boy and in return don't earn his respect won't get a hearing – they are shut out. Don't let yourself be shut out of your son's circle of influence.

Also remember our earlier discussion about going in on an angle. Avoid situations in which you put your son in a position where he loses face, particularly in front of his friends. I've seen many a teacher and parent crash and burn doing this. You may have found that you can't force your son to do something he really doesn't want to do. If he really chooses to dig his heels in, then you're in a corner. Going in on an angle means first trying to avoid confrontation in front of others and then tackling things one-on-one, slowly, sensitively and perhaps indirectly. Let him see that you're trying to see his side. Give him options, let him direct some of the negotiation, keep his dignity intact and you won't evoke that fight or flight response we so often see in students.

A sense of humour

I've been amazed how much mileage some teachers and parents get out of a bit of humour. A lot of learning and motivation can be inspired by humour. Boys have frequently told me how much they like teachers who can share a joke with them. As one boy said, 'They joke around with you and pay out on you. If you pay them out, they'll pay out back. That's good.' I should make the point, however, that this is quite different from verbal abuse or sledging.

I've found the really effective teachers who hook in even the most difficult boys are experts at keeping the mood light. This way they almost trick boys into learning. When there's a need to pull a kid up for misbehaving there's less of a threat to that boy's dignity if the mood's kept light. One teacher told me, 'I jolly them along.' Some boys can become quite aggressive and it's humour that can effectively defuse this.

Humour is a great leveller. It's a great connector. It's a great hook for interest. It's a great defuser. It's a great energiser. It's a great humaniser and so much about motivating boys begins with the human relationship.

It's also important to boys that adults accept their own mistakes. They particularly appreciate it when adults laugh at their own mistakes. There's nothing more humanising in a boy's eyes than for the teacher to roll his eyes, smack his forehead and say what a dummy he is after screwing up a calculation on the board. A humorous spin on mistakes made by an adult does two things: it reduces the boy's own fears about failing or screwing up and it humanises that adult – a fundamental element of a good relationship.

I ask boys about the adults whom they have fun with and whether these adults keep control and authority. My data suggests an adult's ability to have fun and share a joke enhances their control. It seems that with a bit of fun and a shared joke boys will forgive half an hour of theory and will even knuckle down to it.

Relevance and usefulness

I've lost count of the number of boys who bitterly complain about how schoolwork is not relevant to their lives, is not useful or meaningful to them. Schoolwork that motivates boys tends to be work that they believe has a purpose, is useful now or will be later, and is connected to their lives and other school subjects.

In chapter 5 on the value of school, I discussed ways to increase your child's belief in the value of school. These included hooking their subjects into their interests, their part-time work and what they want to do in the future. They also included developing thinking skills and social skills that are important later in life.

There are some other ways to build relevance and usefulness into boys' lives. Teachers and parents should look for opportunities to:

- allow boys to apply what they learn
- provide boys with hands-on learning tasks

- allow boys to work with other students when and where appropriate
- get boys outside for some contextualised learning
- get boys involved in workplace learning or work experience
- get boys to do some community work
- organise some vocational education and training for boys
- involve technology in boys' lessons where appropriate.

These types of activities tend to engage boys, and when they are used appropriately boys become more motivated. When they have opportunities to do some of these things they are more likely to forgive some of the hard work they have to do in between. Teachers often tell me that they mix some of the more tedious work with more novel and interesting ways to learn. Look at ways you can mix things up for your son. If you manage to mix some sugar in along the way, he'll be more likely to forgive you when you ask him to do some hard yards as exams approach.

Ensuring mastery

Boys often lose interest in their schoolwork because they fall behind, they don't understand it or they're not good at it. Boys tell me that teachers who keep them interested in schoolwork take the time to explain work to them. These teachers are happy to explain things more than twice if necessary and in different ways to make sure they are understood. They slow down the lesson when they can to make sure everyone keeps up. They ask questions to make sure everyone's hanging in there. They make sure the boys demonstrate that they understand what they've been taught. That is, these teachers ensure their students master the work they are required to do. As one boy said, 'They get you into the work. They help you out. They explain it to you before you do it. They give you a bit more attention.'

As a parent you can do these things also. In fact, you're better placed than teachers to do this because you have more one-on-one opportunities with your son. You might consider some tutoring for your son if he seems not to understand his homework, or ask your son's teacher how you can more effectively help him.

This leads to my next point, building more success into your son's life.

Experiences of success and reward

My research amongst teachers who engage boys has shown that they are very good at maximising opportunities for boys to succeed. Research has also shown that there are some steps parents and teachers can take to help students succeed. When helping your son with schoolwork, try applying these steps:

1. Begin with a quick review of what your son knows.
2. Talk about what you aim to do.
3. Go through the schoolwork in small steps.
4. Get your son to apply what he has learnt at each step.
5. Be clear and detailed in your explanations.
6. Ask your son questions to check he understands.
7. Guide your son's work at first.
8. Give your son clear feedback that is focused on what he's doing right and what he can do to improve.
9. Keep checking his progress for a while.
10. Give your boy sufficient time to complete the work.
11. Do a bit of troubleshooting; try to spot the potholes before your son hits them and figure out how to get over them.

Don't forget the other ways to build more success into your son's life: chunking, broadening the definition of success to include things like personal bests, and effective goal setting.

Boys appreciate recognition of their success and mastery through reward and praise. If you are going to provide rewards make sure you tie them directly to the process of learning, so the reward recognises study skills, trying hard and personal bests. Aim to phase out material rewards as your son experiences more success and that success becomes motivating for him.

I don't recommend giving big rewards and I don't recommend tying them to marks. I remember one parent who did both. In desperation, she promised her son a brand new sports car if he got 85 per cent in his finals. There were two problems with this. First, she promised such a massive reward that anything else became trivial. Praise no longer rated, nor did free time after a study session, nor did a trip to the beach. The sports car swamped all the things that could motivate this student on a day-to-day basis. The second problem was that the parent tied the reward to a mark. What's the problem with this? It's too hit or miss: by the middle of the year the son decided that 85 per cent was not achievable and simply gave up.

What should the mother have done? First, she should have used rewards that were sustainable on a day-to-day basis. Secondly, she should have tied them to things that were achievable or could be worked towards at any time, such as improving, developing better study skills, trying hard and personal bests.

Success and rewards are very powerful. Building more success into your son's life and using rewards carefully and effectively can increase your son's motivation.

In providing more opportunities for success, don't be frightened to give your son challenging schoolwork, goals or tasks. Research into effective teaching has found that learning is enhanced when students are given work that challenges them. Boys don't mind challenges. One boy said, 'If it's not a challenge it's not really learning.' In presenting your son with challenges try to make sure they are given in a way that doesn't evoke a high fear of failure and that the focus is on giving things a really good try and not on getting everything perfect.

More on rewards

I should say a bit more about rewards. Rewards are something that most parents and teachers provide but which get a lot of bad press amongst educational researchers. Why do rewards get such bad press? Five reasons. First, research suggests that 'paying' children to do what they'd otherwise do quite freely can turn what is enjoyable into drudgery – as some researchers argue, nothing has the capacity to turn play into work as much as pay. Second, when 'pay' is not forthcoming or is insufficient kids no longer work. Third, reward takes the focus away from the task and the more satisfying aspects of learning and places it on the reward. Fourth, reward can give children the feeling that they are being controlled by others or the sense that they are not determining or controlling their own lives. Finally, reward can reduce the value of a task – children think that if they have to get 'paid' to do it then it mustn't be worth doing.

It's a pretty grim picture the researchers paint and in all fairness there is merit in a good deal of what they say. Surely rewards can't be as bad as all this. Well, in my opinion they're not. Moreover, many parents and teachers swear by the benefits of reward. As with most other things, we shouldn't throw the baby out with the bathwater. Rewards can be quite effective for young children. Rewards can be quite effective in kick starting the learning process for children who aren't engaged in school-work. Rewards can be useful to sustain kids' interest in school-work until the work becomes more personally interesting or enjoyable. Rewards can be useful in keeping some kids engaged with uninteresting work. As you can see, rewards can have their place. Where I'd probably ease off rewards is when a child finds the task interesting and is doing it in a motivated and happy way. In this case, encouragement is more effective than reward.

Control and responsibility

Boys highly value having a say in the topics they study and the ways they study. They highly value having choices in their life. The more input they have into the decisions that affect them, the greater their sense of control. You'll recall that a sense of control is fundamental to students' motivation. Chapter 4 on control identified many ways to enhance students' control, including providing more choices, focusing on controllable factors in their students' lives, providing them with clear feedback and boundaries, and encouraging an improvement view of intelligence.

Boys also appreciate being given responsibility. Teachers often tell me that they hook hard-to-reach boys in by getting them to do something important or something the other students haven't been selected to do. Many parents also capitalise on opportunities to give their son more responsibility. The son recognises he is being treated more like an adult and rises to the occasion. Even if he makes the wrong choice or decision, he should be given an opportunity to learn from that so he can make more effective decisions next time.

Fear of failure

Research amongst boys has shown that boys don't like to stand out from the pack and don't like to be seen to be different. One reason for this is that they are scared of screwing up. To be male means you need to achieve – if you don't achieve you're seen as less of a person. This puts pressure on boys, and if they can't handle it they react in one of a few ways.

They may sabotage their chances of success so they have an alibi in case they don't do so well. Examples of this are clowning around, procrastinating and wasting time. You'll recall from the start of this chapter that boys are significantly more likely than girls to self-sabotage.

Another way boys deal with their fear of failure is by disengaging from school and simply giving up. Too many boys do this.

Others might try to 'achieve' in anti-academic ways. Boys in these situations think it's cool to be a fool. This gives students an alibi if they don't do so well. However, most importantly, it's not cool to be dumb. Being a fool means you didn't try hard enough; it does not mean you're dumb. Being the fool may protect boys' self-esteem – provided they are seen to be clowning around, not trying, not studying, they can't be accused of being dumb and so do not lose self-regard.

Chapter 10 discussed a number of ways to reduce students' fear of failure. These include encouraging your son to take a fresh look at mistakes, improving the reasons your son learns, teaching your son to more effectively deal with fear, reducing the link between your son's worth and his achievement and reducing the link between your own worth and your son's achievement.

More about the girls

How much of this chapter applies to girls? Absolutely all of it. I don't need to tell you that girls will greatly benefit from:

- good relationships with their parents
- their parents having respect for them, their priorities and preferences
- a sense of fun and humour in their learning experience
- relevance and usefulness in what they learn
- attaining mastery in their schoolwork
- experiencing more opportunities for success
- gaining a greater sense of control and more responsibility
- a reduced fear of failure and a greater success orientation.

These are all strategies you can use to sustain your daughter's strengths and tackle areas of concern.

Single-sex or co-educational schools?

I haven't given any attention to the issue of single-sex versus co-educational schooling. Some research has suggested that in *terms of achievement* there are differences between the two, with students in single-sex schools performing a little higher than students in co-educational schools. My analysis of this research tells me that there isn't a big enough difference between the two types of schools for me to unreservedly recommend one over the other in terms of achievement. In fact, differences between single-sex and co-educational schools pale into insignificance when you look at the effect of the teacher on students' achievement. It is the teacher that has a massive impact on students' achievement – far more than whether the school is single-sex or co-educational.

Instead, you might like to give more thought to the many other factors that are relevant to your child's education. Factors such as the importance you place on having girls in your son's school life (or boys in your daughter's school life), the pastoral care at the school, the religious or spiritual focus there, hearing that other students are happy at the school, hearing that the teachers really enjoy teaching there, hearing that relationships between teachers and students are highly valued, the links with parents and parent involvement, the links with the wider community, the reputation the school has for developing young adults with integrity, the way the school prepares its students for life after school, links the school might have with a university or an active research program, or the value-added things the school offers such as vocational education or small pastoral care groups or small class sizes or a good anti-bullying strategy or a peer support program or vocational testing and so on – you get the picture. School is so much more than just achievement. This is not to diminish achievement in any way because schools are very much about achievement too – but don't lose sight of the fact that school also offers your child a pathway to adulthood; a pathway that encompasses much more than the school's gender composition.

Living in the real world

In the real world not everything happens like they say in the books. Here are a few things for you to think about when digesting this chapter.

- Not all boys are the same. I've had to generalise in this chapter to a level that almost hurts me. Your job is to tailor my message to your son and his individual strengths, weaknesses, likes and dislikes.

- Your daughter can easily benefit from everything discussed in this chapter. The principles and messages are applicable to any student, but they are especially relevant to many boys.

- Is there a problem with boys? No way. Boys are great and we should be careful not to convince them that they are academically or motivationally flawed. Sure, they're lower on a few boosters than girls, but building their skills on these boosters is perfectly achievable and for this reason we should be optimistic about our boys.

- Can mothers have a significant and beneficial impact on their boys? Absolutely. You don't have to be Einstein to see that all the strategies presented in this chapter can be applied just as effectively by mums (or female teachers, female youth workers etc) as by dads. As a number of boys have told me, it comes down to the person and the relationship they have with that person. One boy said, 'Whether they are male or female doesn't matter. I don't mind as long as that person is trying to help me learn. That's all that really matters.'

- Respecting your son does not mean you have to agree with everything he says or does. You can be very respectful of him as a person yet not be happy about some of the things he does. Moreover, telling him you don't like his behaviour does not undermine your respect for him or his respect for you.

- You can't have a sense of humour all the time. Sometimes things just aren't funny and you and your son need to take them seriously. Sometimes things are funny but you just don't have a sense of humour at that time. That's okay, don't force it.

- There are some parts of schoolwork that are just plain boring and hard to connect to your son's world in a meaningful way. I've talked to a lot of teachers about this and they tell me that if there are other parts of schoolwork that can be made interesting or relevant, boys will forgive you for the bits that are outright dull. They've also told me that mixing the schoolwork up a bit can be a good way to deal with boring work: for example, doing 15 minutes of practical work and then 30 minutes of theory.

- Most kids don't understand everything they do at school. I certainly didn't, but I became good at mastering the stuff that was important to know for an assignment, an exam or future understanding of other stuff. Expecting or aiming for your son to master everything might not be realistic. Don't push your son to master everything but aim for mastery on the things that really count.

- You don't want to be required to reward your son for everything he does. Pick your moments, such as when his interest is sinking, when he has to do really important tasks, after he tries really hard, or after he reaches an important milestone. Teach him to build his own rewards into his learning process. For example, he might play a computer game or surf the internet at the end of a good study session, or listen to a CD halfway through a Saturday afternoon of essay writing.

- You probably can't give your son choices in everything he does, and sometimes you really have to limit his choice. Having said this, he's more likely to go along with you at these times if he can see you've made a real effort to give him a say at other times.

- Don't assume that just because he's a boy your son thinks it's cool to be a fool, or he fits the stereotype of popular culture's portrayal of boys. Some girls think it's cool to be a fool and many boys don't.

- Don't expect to totally eliminate fear of failure from your son's life. As I suggested in chapter 10 on fear of failure, make it your aim to reduce it. Also, don't expect that your boy will no longer try to assert his masculinity (whatever he thinks that is) or no longer want to appear to be tough, and so on. Accept the fact that there are many pressures being exerted on boys (and girls) to act in ways popular culture says boys (and girls) should behave. If you can lighten your son's load in a way that assists his motivation, you can be pleased.

- I haven't said much about your son's friends. Don't forget that whether you like them or not they are important to your son. Talking with boys, I've been struck by how much they enjoy having their mates in the class and how this can make them feel okay about being at school. One boy told me, 'When you're in a class with your friends, you socialise and also get work done most of the time. But in a class where there's no one around, you just sit there alone and scribble on your book and it's just not that interesting.'

- Having said this, don't forget that your son may have trouble balancing the pressures his friends place on him with the pressures of schoolwork. One boy summed it up as follows: 'My mate's the sort of friend who talks all the time and gets into trouble all the time. I can't concentrate. I can't do my work properly. I could move desks if I wanted to but then I'd be next to someone I don't really want to be next to. I want to be next to my friend, but I don't want him to talk all the time.' Try to encourage your son to balance the two pressures in appropriate ways. Another boy provided some advice on this: 'You've got to have two sides to yourself. You've got to have a good side of learning and also have a muck around side of yourself. You can do really well at school and then muck around after school with your friends.'

Chapter summary

I have paid particular attention to boys' motivation in this chapter. Although I believe there are more similarities than differences between boys and girls, it is important to recognise that there are some parts of boys' motivation that are different from girls' motivation. In my research, boys score significantly lower than girls in planning, study management, persistence, value of schooling and learning focus. Boys also score significantly higher than girls in self-sabotage.

Through my review of previous research into boys' education and my own research amongst thousands of students and their teachers, I suggest the following are the most effective strategies to enhance boys' motivation: building good relationships with them, respecting their priorities and preferences, maintaining a sense of humour, identifying the relevance and usefulness of schoolwork where possible, ensuring mastery of schoolwork, building more opportunities for success and reward, enhancing boys' control and responsibility, and tackling boys' fear of failure.

CHAPTER THIRTEEN TOP 5

1. Aim to build a good relationship with your son by respecting his priorities, preferences, choices and interests, and developing a sense of humour and fun in the relationship.

2. Take the time to ensure your son understands important aspects of his schoolwork and experiences success as often as possible. This involves clear explanations, a slower pace, asking him questions to check for understanding, and allowing your son to apply what he has learnt.

3. Where possible, link what your son learns to other aspects of his life, the world more generally, and what he might do in the future. Show your son how the thinking skills he develops along the way can be useful in many situations now and in the future. When the schoolwork is a bit dull, try to mix it up with schoolwork your son enjoys.

4. Give your son responsibility, within sensible parameters. Give him input into decisions that affect him and the family. Give him choice in what he studies and the way he studies. Be patient when standing on the sidelines, but provide adequate support and direction when appropriate.

5. To reduce your son's fear of failure, his inclination towards thinking it's cool to be a fool and his fear of standing out from the pack, try: encouraging your son to take a fresh look at mistakes; improving the reasons your son learns; teaching your son to more effectively deal with fear; reducing the link between your son's worth and his achievement; and reducing the link between your own worth and your son's achievement.

CHAPTER 14

MOTIVATING THE GIFTED AND TALENTED

Before I get started on this chapter, I want to invite *all* parents to stick around and read it. I extend this invitation for the following reasons:

- Issues that are really important in motivating gifted and talented kids are also important to all kids.
- I cover a few things, like fear of success, in detail in this chapter that were not dealt with in so much detail in earlier chapters.
- Many students have strengths in one or two subject areas and so although they are not labelled 'gifted or talented', they are close enough that the same strategies apply.
- You may not think your child is gifted or talented when in fact they are – so play it safe and read on.
- Irrespective of whether your child is gifted or talented, your child may be an under-achiever. Underachievement will be dealt with in detail in this chapter too.

I FEEL IT'S A WASTE OF MY GENIUS TO RESORT TO MENIAL LABOUR

I've included a separate chapter on gifted and talented

students because I have been struck by the number of schools, teachers and parents that raise this as an issue central to motivation. Indeed, I've never seen such depths of frustration as those revolving around underachieving and unmotivated students who are gifted or talented. Again, however, I stress that although this chapter deals with motivation and underachievement in the gifted and talented, there are some very important and powerful lessons for all students.

How do I know if my child is gifted or talented?

As with most classifications, there is no single and totally agreed upon definition of giftedness. Some define it simply in terms of an IQ score (say, 140+). Some see it in terms of ability in multiple areas (often called multiple intelligences). Some define it in terms of the age/grade-level at which the child is performing (say, two years ahead of peers). Some say that gifted students are those who are highly capable and that talented students are those gifted students who are performing to their highest capabilities.

Which definition am I comfortable with? I suppose I'm not 100 per cent comfortable with any one definition. Rather, I think a well-rounded assessment needs to be considered from a couple of perspectives, such as an IQ test and a close look at performance in a few school subjects or talent areas such as art or music. I also suggest you draw on fully qualified and accredited professionals who are highly experienced in testing and assessing children.

If your child is considered borderline this immediately places them in a high-ability category and so most of this chapter is relevant to them too. Also don't forget that many gifted and talented or highly able children are exceptional in one or two areas and may be considered mainstream in most other areas.

What are the motivation issues relevant to gifted and talented students?

In many cases the same motivation issues apply to gifted and talented students as to mainstream students. The difference often lies in the extent to which they apply or the particular ways they are played out in gifted and talented students' lives.

This chapter covers the following areas of motivation relevant to gifted and talented students:

- their view of what 'being smart' means
- the dangers of effort and trying hard
- their view of intelligence
- their low sense of control
- fear of failure
- fear of success and the impostor syndrome
- perfectionism
- balancing challenge and skill
- their view of competition.

In addition to these, I'll again look at the importance of the relationship you have with your child and at some of the characteristics of relationships to which gifted and talented students respond best.

Students' views about 'being smart'

Gifted and talented students have often experienced a great deal of success without trying too hard, without a great deal of study or practice, and without a great deal of preparation or organisation. In itself, this is not such a bad thing.

The problem with effortless success begins when students draw the conclusion that being smart means doing things easily and without effort, practice, preparation or organisation. This conclusion is often exacerbated by parents and teachers marvelling at the fact that these students succeed with so little effort. Indeed, saying, 'Aren't you clever!' can be a direct message to the student that succeeding with little effort means they are smarter than if they succeeded through trying. This can be dangerous for a number of reasons.

First, if students believe that being smart means succeeding without effort they often get quite unsettled if they need to do something that is challenging or requires a bit of a struggle.

Secondly, they may come to avoid taking risks or taking on challenges – because it means they will probably need to try – and trying means they are not so smart.

Thirdly, when parents and teachers marvel at a student's cleverness when they succeed with little effort, there is the risk that the student gets a sense that they are somehow more worthwhile and valued more highly when they achieve and when they demonstrate their competence. If they come to this belief, then every test, assignment and project becomes a test of their worth as much as a test of their history or maths or whatever. This is not so much of a problem while the child keeps succeeding, but it can become a real problem if there is a risk or fear of failure.

There are a number of ways you can foster a more helpful view of 'smartness'.

One way is to genuinely put the focus on skill development, improvement and personal bests and a little less focus on marks or grades. Doing this communicates to children that the journey is as important as the destination, promotes an improvement view of intelligence or smartness (thus giving a reason for students to keep trying), and puts more of the focus on effort (which is controllable by students) and takes it away from intelligence (which many students see as not so controllable).

It is also important to put a good focus on improvement, skill development and personal bests because for gifted and talented students who generally receive straight As, this is the only indication that they are moving forward. The problem with straight As is that the child has hit the ceiling of grading and doesn't really get a sense of improvement. This is not an argument for grading them harder. Rather, it may be important to give them an additional index of performance, such as a personal best score, that tells them how much they've matched or exceeded a previous performance.

Another strategy is to provide clear task-based feedback to your child and reduce the amount of feedback directed at the person or their ability. So, instead of saying, 'You're really clever' or 'What a good boy!' which focus on the person and their ability, say 'That's a really good way of writing about that event' or 'Your presentation of that science prac is well organised and clearly detailed', or 'That was good spelling'. Task-based feedback puts the focus on effort and not on the person. The problem with putting feedback on the person is that when new schoolwork is assigned, the person is on the line and this can be very threatening in situations where there is any risk of poor performance.

But before you unquestioningly focus on your child's effort as the way out of their problematic view of smartness, it is important to first understand that some students (but not all) see effort as a dangerous commodity. If this is the case you will need to position effort very carefully.

The dangers of effort

Effort – encompassing working hard, trying, studying hard, practising etc – can be seen as a dangerous thing by some students, particularly underachieving gifted and talented students in high school (but younger children not so much). The previous section on smartness showed that the amount of effort students put in can be seen by them as an indication of how smart they are – or are not. Research has shown that people who succeed without trying are seen by others as smarter or more competent than people who succeed by working hard. The same applies to students. The smartest students are often viewed as the ones who succeed without much effort or study.

This holds some very significant implications for parents telling their child to try harder. First, the child may come to the conclusion that the parents are implying they aren't smart. Secondly, the child may be frightened to put in much effort because any success will be seen as second-rate if they had to try hard to get it. Thirdly, if they fail after trying hard it is even more damning of their ability or smartness. Fourthly, if they succeed after not trying they look even smarter. As one boy exclaimed to me after doing well in a test after not studying, 'Man, how smart am I!'

What can you do as a parent? You certainly should continue to value effort because it is one of the main aspects of schoolwork over which students have control, and control is important. Effort is also a very strong predictor of achievement.

Having said this, you must also send a clear message that how hard your child tries does not necessarily reflect on their ability or smartness. All duxes and distinguished thinkers need to work hard to get where they are. Elite athletes must train really hard to succeed. Top business people need to spend many years developing skills to be successful. Rock stars need to spend a lot of time practising and recording in studios to knock out great albums. There is simply no evidence that people at the top get there without trying hard.

It might also be a good idea not to go over the top praising your child for succeeding with little effort. Sure, you need to acknowledge their success, but don't focus the praise on the fact that they succeeded with little effort. Instead, praise the success and perhaps look at ways they can extend themselves next time. Where do they go from here and how can they improve on what they've done? This will require them to put in a bit more effort. However, when doing this, make sure you don't diminish your child's achievement.

Another way around this potential problem with effort is to focus on the quality of the effort more than the quantity of effort. Although students see *how much* they try as an indication of how smart they are, they don't see *the way* they try as saying something about their smartness. Here's a great clue. It means that encouraging students to study more effectively, to manage their time better, to prioritise, plan, monitor and prepare does not threaten their smartness. These elements of study all refer to the quality of effort rather than the quantity. Of course, in a perfect world we'd increase both quality and quantity of effort, but if your child links the amount of study with his or her smartness, then focus more on the quality of study and schoolwork. This gives your child a way out of the effort–smartness dilemma.

Students' views of intelligence

Gifted and talented students have a tendency to define themselves in terms of their intelligence and their ability to succeed without effort. They learn that their natural ability gets them through and that there is little need to spend extra time and effort developing more effective skills because they already have what it takes. This way of thinking lays the foundation for a fixed view of intelligence. You'll recall that a fixed view of intelligence is one which holds that you can't improve or increase your intelligence. This fixed view is further entrenched when they never really get a chance to extend themselves or to overcome something that is difficult or challenging. Mainstream students, on the other hand, have more opportunities to develop an improvement view of intelligence because they often experience difficulty and challenge that require them to develop new skills – instant proof that intelligence can be developed and improved. Gifted and talented students don't get enough opportunities to witness evidence of skill development.

It is therefore important to first be very clear that intelligence can be improved and developed. But to learn this, your child needs to test out this theory. They can only really do this by seeking challenges that are a touch beyond them and developing skills or extending themselves to meet these challenges. To do this they need to have a helpful view of effort (described above) and a low fear of failure (described below). Once they rise to the challenge or overcome the difficulty, it is important they reflect on the lesson to be learnt – namely, that they aren't stuck with their level of ability or intelligence.

This is particularly important in later years of education, when even gifted and talented students' ability alone may not get them through. Many come unstuck when they get their first B in senior high or at university or college – because their fixed view of intelligence implies they can't extend themselves to meet new challenges or overcome difficulties. These students are not very academically resilient. On the other hand, students with an improvement view of intelligence aren't unsettled as much – they have a sense of optimism and control because they know that their ability can be extended with quality study and preparation.

Students' low sense of control

Another reason gifted and talented students have a low sense of control is because of the way they view their successes and failures. In chapter 4 on control I showed that the way students see the causes of their successes and failures affects how much control they have over future schoolwork.

Gifted and talented students who underachieve often make a fatal mistake: they attribute the causes of their success to factors outside their control (such as luck, an easy test, easy marking or the teacher liking them) and the causes of failure to their lack of ability. This is a lethal pattern of thinking. Basically, they take no credit for their success and blame their poor performance on the fact that they are 'dumb'. They give themselves no reason to feel good or proud and every reason to beat themselves up and feel hopeless.

Not only does this way of thinking make students feel rotten, but it also strips their sense of control. They don't feel they have

Monique, school and university

Monique came from a poor family and had received a scholarship to attend one of the top private schools. She was a prized and celebrated member of the family, mainly because of her exceptional ability. Blessed with a photographic memory, she could succeed in exams simply by listening in class and scribbling down a few notes. In fact, she prided herself on never having read an entire book in her life. However, although she sailed through high school, she hit the wall at university.

She'd enrolled in a very demanding university course and there was no getting around the fact that only about 20 per cent of the course assessment was based on lectures and tutorials – the rest required intensive independent study. This was a shock to Monique for a number of reasons. First, study was something that the 'dumb' kids had to do – not her! Secondly, would she be valued so highly if she had to work hard to succeed? And thirdly, how in the world did you study anyway? She found that turning around study habits at university was not as easy as it might have been at school.

Monique muddled through university and performed okay, but not brilliantly. She would have done better if she'd learnt some important lessons along the way. These lessons revolved around developing a healthier view of effort, taking a new view of smartness, reducing the link between her worth and her ability to perform (or perform without effort), and seeing mistakes in a less threatening way. Through support from their parents and teachers, other gifted students learn these lessons and so are able to break out of some of the classic gifted and talented motivation traps described in this chapter.

control over their ability to repeat success because their previous success was beyond their control. They don't feel much control over their ability to avoid failure because their previous failure was due to a lack of ability and they tend to have a fixed view of ability which means they can't improve to avoid failure next time. Quite a bind!

As I discussed in chapter 4, it is important to guide your child's focus onto controllable factors in their life and to develop more of an improvement view of intelligence. Factors in their control include, to name a few:

- the amount of study or practice
- the quality of study
- preparation of schoolwork
- presentation of schoolwork
- time management
- organisation of the study environment
- prioritising of work and deadlines.

You also need to reduce the focus on factors outside your child's control, including:

- luck
- test questions
- marking or grading of work
- teachers' attitudes towards your child
- environmental difficulties (such as the bus breaking down, the weather, the test conditions).

Another way to enhance your child's sense of control is to give them a greater say in decisions that affect them. This was discussed in detail in chapter 4. This not only increases their sense of control but also develops their decision-making skills, which will be of value for life.

Finally, some parents and teachers enhance children's sense of control by encouraging them to evaluate their own work. They teach the child how to step aside and view their work objectively and analytically. This is a very important skill because it develops the child's ability to monitor progress and to make appropriate adjustments and changes if needed. Educational psychologists call this self-regulation. Self-regulation is increasingly being seen as a vital ingredient in student motivation. You may then evaluate the child's work and you can compare notes and discuss any discrepancies. This provides children with even more insight into how to evaluate and refine their schoolwork. Most importantly, this should be undertaken in an improvement-focused context in which the student does not feel threatened or judged as a person. Make it clear that the work is being evaluated, not the child.

Fear of failure

Although fear of failure was dealt with in detail in chapter 10, it deserves another mention here. This is because fear of failure is rife amongst underachieving gifted and talented students. Many of these children have built their identity on their ability. Many of these children believe they are valued only to the extent that they achieve. Is it any wonder they fear failure? Bob Dylan once wrote, 'When you've got nothing, you've got nothing to lose.' The opposite is the case for gifted and talented students: when you've got everything, you've got everything to lose, hence an excessive fear of failure. Charlie Brown said it all when he commented to Linus, 'There is no heavier burden than a great potential.'

There are two main ways to deal with students' fear of failure.

First, gifted and talented students need to see that mistakes provide important information about how to improve next time and do not mean they are hopeless or useless or that there's no point trying again. By taking the sting out of failure, students do not live in fear of failure. This does not mean students should not care about mistakes. They certainly should care, but in the sense that they can be the launchpad to future success. Indeed, every now and then, encourage your child to sacrifice accuracy for a bit of risk taking. For example, in developing a new study technique, your child may not perform as highly as he or she likes as they refine this new technique – but that these teething problems are worth it to develop a more effective study technique.

The second way to reduce students' fear of failure is to reduce the link between students' achievement and their worth as a person. If students only feel okay when they achieve, it drastically raises the stakes of every test, assignment and exam. Thus the maths test is not only a test of their maths, but also a test of their worth. Is it any reason they fear failure when failure can mean they fail as a person? Parents and teachers must clearly communicate to children that their worth as a person is a given and must not be confused with their achievement. This does not mean you can't be disappointed if they don't do so well – but be disappointed in their lack of study or effort, not disappointed in them as a person.

Fear of success and the impostor syndrome

Just as gifted and talented students can underachieve due to their fear of failure, a fear of success can also get in their way. Much of this book has looked at how the threat of failure can be a great pressure on students. However, success also carries its own pressures.

Success means that there is something to lose next time and some students curse the minute they get a great mark because in their mind the only place to go from there is down. Thus, a great mark or score is seen as an instant pressure to perform next time.

Success can mean students are seen as different from their friends or peers. The need to conform is very important to adolescents, and if a good mark makes them stand out from the pack it can be something to fear. Boys in particular have this fear.

Success can also mean that the student has outperformed others in the class and some students worry that this will upset or hurt their friends or make them unpopular in some way. Girls in particular have this fear.

To some students success means that one day they will be found out and their lack of ability will be exposed. Every time they succeed, they feel the fraud of their success is one step closer to being revealed. Essentially, they feel like an impostor masquerading as a capable student. This is commonly called the impostor syndrome, a characteristic more typical of girls (but boys can fall victim to the syndrome as well).

Perhaps the most common factor that underpins fear of success is low self-belief. These students feel they do not deserve whatever success they gain, they lack the confidence that they will be liked if they outperform other students, and think so poorly of themselves that they do not take credit for their success, instead seeing it as just another instance of managing to fool everyone around them.

In chapter 3 I presented a number of ways to enhance students' self-belief. However, for the success fearer only one is particularly relevant – tackling negative thinking. As we have already seen, this involves:

- identifying negative thinking traps
- developing more positive self-talk
- developing realistic optimism.

To recap, there are some very common *negative thinking traps* students fall into including:

- black and white thinking (things are either easy or impossible)
- biased thinking (taking a negative interpretation of things that happen)
- end-of-the-worlding (thinking it's the end of the world if they fail a test)
- turning positives into negatives (if they succeed in an exam they only see it as more pressure to succeed next time)
- mega-generalising (if something unpleasant happens in one subject, it's going to happen in other subjects).

I explained in chapter 3 that developing more *positive self-talk* requires students to challenge the negative thinking traps with positive thinking. Usually this involves nothing more than some commonsense thinking. Commonsense tells students that if they take their study a step at a time, if they put in some hard work, if they improve the quality of their study and schoolwork, if they take more notice of teachers' feedback on their work, and if they get more organised and plan ahead, they increase their chances of doing well at school.

There are three areas of your gifted or talented child's thinking in which *realistic optimism* can be developed:

- the way he or she views past events (not dwelling on poor performance or mistakes but taking the lesson to be learnt and then moving on)
- the way he or she views current events (being happy with where they are in the moment and not dwelling on what's happened in the past or worrying about what might happen in the future)
- the way he or she views the future (thinking that whatever comes up in the future, he or she has the ability to deal with it).

Students who fear success spend too much time thinking that past successes were lucky, that present success puts more pressure on them for the future, and that future success will meet with their friends' disapproval or that they will be found out as an impostor.

Perfectionism

Perfectionism is a common problem for gifted and talented students. Because their ability to excel can be such a part of their identity or because their worth is so heavily based on their academic excellence, they feel very much at risk if they turn in work that falls short of excellence. Unfortunately, they see perfection as the only guarantee that they will excel. Moreover, because they get so much praise and approval for doing well and perhaps perfecting some tasks, they come to believe that anything short of perfection risks a reduction in praise and approval.

Importantly, for gifted and talented students perfectionism can also be a way that they avoid failure. In striving for perfection they can fall back on their excessively high goal as the excuse for their relatively poor performance: anyone would have fallen short of the high standard they had set leading up to the test or assignment.

Striving for perfection can also be a way that students justify their procrastination or their lack of effort. How could anyone be blamed for putting off working towards such a high standard?

The problem with aiming for perfection is that it's pretty hard to reach – even for gifted or talented kids – and if your child is to reach perfection it can often be at the expense of lots of other things. Often these include assignments or projects in other subjects.

Of particular relevance to the perfectionists is the important difference between excellence and perfection. Motivated students recognise this difference and are satisfied with excellence. This means that they can get on with other assignments and study and do their best across all subjects. You might like to revisit chapter 10 which discussed in some detail the difference between excellence and perfection. A second way to reduce perfectionism is get your child to set strict time limits – reading limits, writing limits, or double-checking limits – for themselves. This is where they might say, for example, 'At 9pm tonight I will stop working on my project, I'll reread it once, I'll staple it together and put it in my bag to hand in tomorrow.' A third way to tackle perfectionism is to aim to be more of an all-rounder: that is, getting good at lots of things rather than being perfect in one or two things. However, your should recognise that for students who are talented in only one or two subjects, performing highly across the board may be too demanding. Finally, you can help reduce your child's perfectionism by insisting that they get more balance in their life. This means they must see that life is more than a perfect score in maths, for example. One thing perfectionists are short on is balance.

Balancing challenge and skill

Educational and sport psychology research has shown that people are most engaged in what they do when their level of skill matches the level of challenge – or even better, when the challenge is a touch ahead of the level of skill. Some psychologists call this the 'zone of proximal development'. Other psychologists call it 'flow'.

When students are in the 'zone' or in 'flow' they are completely absorbed by their schoolwork, aren't worrying about how they compare with others or how they will be evaluated, work really effectively and are totally learning focused.

This has direct implications for gifted and talented students who are often not engaged or absorbed by the task and are constantly worrying about how they compare and how they will be evaluated. The answer in this case is to carefully select a level and type of work that gets the balance between challenge and skill just right.

In the diagram on page 286 you can see the consequences of getting this balance right – and the consequences of getting it wrong.

As you can see, students are in the 'zone' or in 'flow' and totally absorbed and interested when the level of challenge matches or slightly exceeds their level of skill. When the level of challenge exceeds their level of skill by too great a margin, they feel anxious. They fear they are not up to the job of meeting this challenge. When their level of skill is low and the challenge is low, they are apathetic. There's no real challenge, and even if there was they're not up to the job.

When the level of skill exceeds the level of challenge, highly skilled students are at first relaxed but soon this turns to boredom. It is this category that gifted and talented students often fall into. It is fundamental that these students are presented with challenges that are appropriately matched to their skill. You will understand that accompanying this challenge, students must also have a reasonable self-belief and sense of control. When there is

MATCHING CHALLENGE TO SKILL

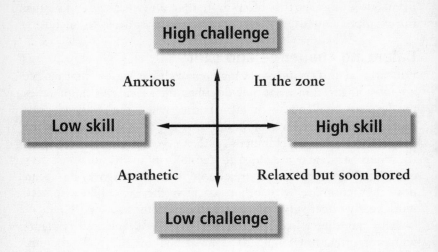

Adapted with permission from Jackson and Csikszentmihalyi (1999), *Flow in sports: The keys to optimal experiences and perfomance*. Champaign, IL: Human Kinetics.

the belief in one's ability to succeed, the sense of control over how to attain that success and the presence of a challenge that is worth wrestling with, the gifted and talented student is in an ideal position to really engage with the task.

Research has identified a number of ways that students can be extended so that the level of challenge is regularly matched to their skill. I want to talk about one that I believe is particularly effective for extending students' thinking skills and developing challenging activities for them. It involves what's called Bloom's Taxonomy. In the 1950s Benjamin Bloom, an educationalist, identified six levels of thinking, with each successive level being a little more challenging and complex than the previous level. The six levels and a brief description are shown in the table on page 288.

As you can see in this table, Bloom's Taxonomy is a great way of knowing where your child is at and where they go from there. The strength of this taxonomy is that it is transferable to many aspects of your child's schoolwork – and to many other aspects of their life for that matter. The example of the Peloponnesian War in the table is just one way of showing how a child's thinking can unfold, always with a view to moving them to the next level. It is also a great way of knowing whether you are presenting challenges that are beyond your child. For example, if your child does not have the facts under his or her belt, then expecting them to analyse or synthesise is not fair. Instead, you need to ensure they are in possession of all the facts and knowledge they need, then work on their understanding of these facts or events, then get them to apply their understanding. Once you are sure they can do these three things they are ready for analysis and synthesis. Many teachers have made really effective use of this taxonomy to develop their teaching programs, not only for gifted and talented students, but also for mainstream students and those who experience learning difficulties.

Students' view of competition

Underachieving gifted and talented students can have an intense fear of competition. This is because in competition there are winners and losers and underachieving gifted and talented students fear losing because it reflects poorly on their identity and sense of worth.

However, competition is here to stay and it is therefore important to help these students deal with competition more effectively. Dealing with competition was tackled in detail in chapter 6. In that chapter I discussed the following strategies for developing less of a competitive focus and more of a learning focus:

- increasing the emphasis on personal bests
- reducing comparisons with other students
- arousing curiosity whenever possible
- encouraging active learning
- recognising the journey as much as the destination
- focusing on effort and strategy more than ability or intelligence.

In addition to these strategies, I suggested the following ways to help your child better deal with competition:

Bloom's Taxonomy, an example

Thinking level	Description	Example
1. Knowledge	Knowing and remembering facts and events	Remembering that the Peloponnesian War* started in 431 BC
2. Comprehension	Understanding facts and events	Being able to describe major events of the war in your own words
3. Application	Being able to apply understanding from one context to another	Recognising that an imbalance of power between two states – one of the main causes of the Peloponnesian War – has also been the cause of some twentieth-century wars
4. Analysis	Understanding something in sufficient depth so it can be compared or contrasted with something else or enable an opinion on something else	Understanding the Peloponnesian War in sufficient depth that you are able to assess and analyse twentieth-century wars in detail
5. Synthesis	Creating new ideas or new understandings or interpretations from the previous four levels of thinking	Using the idea of an imbalance in power as reflected in ancient history and refining it to propose alternative courses of action for current situations such as possible solutions for peace in the Middle East
6. Evaluation	Reflecting on, evaluating and judging one's previous five levels of thinking	Having proposed alternative courses of action for peace in the Middle East, you are able to critically assess your proposal, identify possibilities for further development of your thinking, and suggest future thinking and analysis that need to happen to make your ideas more applicable and feasible

* The Peloponnesian War was fought between Athens and Sparta from 431 BC to 404 BC.

- In competition, encourage your child to compete with their own previous performance or strive to reach personal bests – this keeps them energised but also keeps the focus on their own standards by seeing themselves as their own benchmark.
- In competition, encourage your child to see others as an inspiration to bring out their best rather than seeing others as people to beat – this creates friendly competition and reduces dog-eat-dog competition which can arouse an intense fear of failure.
- If your child doesn't compete successfully, encourage them to see their effort (how hard they work) and strategy (their study skills, preparation, planning, and so on) rather than their ability or intelligence as the means to do better next time – this keeps them in control and increases optimism.
- Make it clear to your child that if they don't compete successfully, this doesn't mean they are less of a person or you think they are less worthwhile – this will reduce their fear of failure in competition.
- If your child doesn't do so well in competition, show them how to look for lessons or clues in the competition to use to improve next time – this too will reduce their fear of failure in competition.

I recognise that this material has been presented elsewhere but research has shown that underachieving gifted students can have an intense fear of competition in which they believe they might fail. They would rather not compete and risk failure through a lack of effort than compete and risk failure after having tried hard. For this reason the issue of competition is particularly pertinent to underachieving gifted students.

Characteristics of adults with whom gifted and talented children respond well

In this book, I've put a lot of emphasis on the importance of relationships. I said earlier that in developing a good relationship with your child, up to half the job can be done in getting them more motivated. Relationships for gifted and talented children are no exception.

Research into the education of gifted and talented students suggests that the following are the characteristics of adults with whom gifted and talented students respond well:

- a genuine respect for the child (respect keeps emerging as an important factor for all students)
- a real enthusiasm for the education and learning of the child
- a joy of lifelong learning themselves, acting as models for the child
- a flexible parenting style that is comfortable with the child doing different types of activities, learning different types of things and learning in different ways
- good active listening skills
- knowledge of the unique characteristics and needs of gifted and talented children and a willingness and ability to accommodate them
- a willingness to encourage risk taking and teach the child that making mistakes is okay and can be a launchpad for future success
- an ability to recognise the child's strengths and weaknesses and encourage the child to accept both without embarrassment
- a desire to expose the child to new ideas and encourage them to explore these ideas
- a sense of humour about themselves and about the child
- a willingness to advocate for the gifted and talented child but without undermining teachers' or other educators' authority or professionalism.

Living in the real world

In the real world not everything happens like they say in the books. Here are a few things for you to think about when digesting this chapter.

- Much of this chapter focused on underachieving gifted and talented students. It goes without saying that these are also important principles for sustaining gifted and talented students who are already motivated.
- Gifted and talented children are people too. Labelling

gifted and talented children as such tends to objectify them as something different from the rest of us. They aren't. They just happen to perform better in some areas. They still need love, approval, affirmation, friends and the opportunity to make mistakes and not feel rotten about them. In fact, we should be referring to 'children who are gifted and talented' and not 'gifted and talented children' – this would put them as children first and foremost.

- Including a chapter on children who are gifted and talented is in no way intended to diminish other aspects of exceptionality, such as children with learning difficulties, children who are hearing or sight impaired or children who are intellectually impaired. Nor is it intended to suggest that gifted and talented children are inherently better or in greater need than these other children or mainstream children. When I say that the principles in this chapter apply to all children I mean it. In some ways, gifted and talented children in this chapter could well be seen as proxies for all exceptional children.

- It can often be the case that one of your children is gifted and talented and the others are more mainstream or indeed have learning problems. It is critical that all children are valued equally, irrespective of how they achieve at school. It also goes without saying that comparing siblings can be lethal. Every child has some strengths as well as areas that could be developed further.

- I have deliberately avoided discussion of the practice of grade skipping, ability grouping, selective schools, and related issues. These are complex areas and ones on which I'm not sure I've made up my mind. Because of this, the information presented in this chapter is designed to be applicable to the gifted and talented child in any learning environment.

Chapter summary

In the research focusing on gifted and talented students, some core motivational factors consistently emerge. These suggest that there are clear motivational benefits for gifted and talented children (and their parents) by genuinely reworking their ideas of what it means to be smart, positioning effort in a much healthier and more positive way, reworking their view of intelligence, addressing their fear of failure and fear of success, and gaining a good balance between challenge and skill. Addressing some, most or all of these factors places your gifted and talented child in a much stronger position to achieve to their potential. They need not view their potential as a burden. Rather, their potential should be seen as something exciting and energising.

CHAPTER FOURTEEN TOP 5

1. Gifted and talented students' views on effort and intelligence can cause problems for them. Developing a healthy view of effort and intelligence requires them to see that trying hard does not reflect poorly on their smartness, that even the most brilliant students and academics need to try hard (as do elite athletes, top business people etc), that intelligence is something that can be improved, and that the quality of their effort is just as important as the amount of effort.

2. Fear of failure is a common problem amongst gifted and talented students. The two most effective ways to deal with this are to show them that mistakes provide important information for future improvement, and that their worth as a person is a given and not dependent on how they achieve at school.

3. Fear of success is a problem often arising out of a low self-belief and feelings of being a fraud or impostor whose lack of ability will be 'found out' one day. The main way to reduce a fear of success is to identify negative thinking traps, develop more positive self-talk and challenge the negative thinking with some commonsense realistic optimism.

4. Getting the right balance between challenge and skill is vital to engaging the gifted and talented child. Failing to get this balance right can lead to anxiety, apathy or boredom. Bloom's Taxonomy provides a useful way of determining how to present challenges that are a touch ahead of your child's skill.

5. As with all students, the relationship the gifted and talented child has with their parents and teachers is important. Good relationships with gifted and talented children are developed through respect, flexibility, active listening, genuine interest in the child and a sense of humour, to name a few.

CHAPTER 15

THE BOTTOM LINE

You'll remember that at the start of this book I suggested that you do fewer things better rather than more things not so well. The question now is how do you select which boosters, mufflers and guzzlers to focus on, and within the selected boosters, mufflers or guzzlers which particular strategies should you use?

In terms of the boosters, mufflers and guzzlers, my first suggestion is to have another look at the quick test of your child's motivation in chapter 2. This will give you an idea of one or two strengths and one or two weaknesses to focus on. My second suggestion is to follow your gut feeling. If there were a couple of boosters, mufflers and guzzlers that really jumped out at you as being particularly relevant or potentially useful, this is a good clue as to what to focus on. My third suggestion is to show your child the model of boosters, mufflers and guzzlers (the student motivation wheel in chapter 2), talk about each one and maybe work together to select a couple to focus on.

This leads to the next question. When you've identified a couple of boosters, mufflers or guzzlers, which particular strategies should you use to address them? My first suggestion is to again follow your

PLEASE GOD... I'LL DO ANYTHING TO HAVE A SUCCESSFUL CHILD!

gut feeling. If there were a couple of strategies that really appealed to you, this is a good clue as to what to focus on. My second suggestion is to talk with your child about possible strategies and perhaps work together to identify which ones might be most effective.

To give you a bit more help with which strategies to use, I'm going to present what I consider to be the top two strategies for each booster, muffler and guzzler and also two important strategies for enhancing your relationship with your child. Before you read them, though, I should point out that my selection of the top two strategies is very much based on *my* gut feeling – so if you're in any doubt I suggest you go with *your* gut feeling because you know your child and I don't.

In terms of *self-belief*, I suggest a focus on chunking – breaking schoolwork into bite-size parts and seeing the completion of each part as a success. I also suggest tackling your child's negative thinking through identifying negative thinking traps he or she may fall into, challenging negative thinking with more positive self-talk, and developing a sense of realistic optimism.

To enhance your child's sense of *control*, I suggest encouraging a greater focus on factors within their control – including effort (how much work they do) and strategy (the quality of that work). My second suggestion is to provide very clear, task-based feedback on what they do that also includes information about how to improve.

In terms of students' belief in the *value of school*, it is important to connect what they learn at school to their life, the world more generally, and the things they might do after they complete school. I also suggest regularly drawing their attention to the skills they develop at school that are useful in many parts of their life. Three very important skills they develop at school are social skills, thinking skills and decision-making skills.

To enhance students' *learning focus*, it is important to emphasise the process as much as or more than the outcome. This means recognising the significance of skill development, personal bests, learning new things and solving problems, and reducing comparisons with others. My second suggestion is to arouse your child's curiosity as much as possible. Curiosity is the best way to fast-track a learning focus.

Building your child's *persistence* requires effective goal setting. Effective goals are achievable, believable, clear and desirable. I also suggest enhancing your child's persistence by drawing on previous challenges they have faced and examining exactly how those challenges were overcome and how the lessons learnt can be used to help your child now or in their next challenge.

Effective *planning* is best achieved by chunking schoolwork and then monitoring progress against the identified chunks. Monitoring is enhanced by encouraging checking strategies such as rereading the question before jumping in and answering, regularly looking back at the test or exam question while writing the answer, and perhaps double-checking answers before moving on to another question.

Your child's *study management* is enhanced by developing an effective and realistic study timetable and working to this timetable in conditions that allow him or her to concentrate best. A second way to enhance study management is through effective general management skills such as prioritising, managing time, multi-tasking, preparation and organisation.

Anxiety is reduced by developing an effective relaxation technique (this can range from meditation through to exercise) that also assists your child to deal with his or her worry thinking. Your child can also deal more effectively with anxiety by developing test-taking skills through practice tests, reading instructions carefully, understanding test questions better, staying on track when answering questions, checking answers and sketching essay plans quickly.

To deal with *failure avoidance* and *self-sabotage* I first suggest you clearly show your child that mistakes provide important information about how to improve and do not mean they are hopeless or useless or that there's no point trying next time. Secondly, I suggest you reduce the link between your child's achievement and their worth as a person. You must clearly communicate to your child that their worth as a person is a given and must not be confused with their achievement.

Finally, your ability to help motivate your child will very much depend on the *relationship* you have with him or her. If I were to select two factors that seem to underpin every healthy and happy relationship, the first I would emphasise is the importance of respecting your child, their preferences and their priorities in school and life more generally. The second I would emphasise is your ability to step into your child's shoes and understand where they are coming from. Both these encompass genuinely valuing your child's interests, actively listening to your child and regularly affirming your child for who he or she is.

A journalist once asked me when it was too late to try to help a child, at what point was it not worth trying to motivate them. This question caught me by surprise, although I guess it was a reasonable one. I answered the question by telling him a story about a youth centre I once visited as part of my research. This centre was identified to me as one that was doing good work with homeless young people. It not only offered these young people accommodation but also managed to hook them into some sort of education or training. I interviewed the director of the centre who was telling me all the great things they were doing and how much the young people benefited from the program. As he was talking, an ambulance pulled up outside and paramedics were soon carting away a young boy on a stretcher. A girl came into the office and told the director that he'd overdosed. After the director checked with the paramedics that the boy would be okay, he returned to our interview. I clearly looked uncomfortable, quite obviously not knowing how to proceed from that point (do I pretend it didn't happen? do I talk about it straight up?). Perhaps to help me out, he asked me, 'Where's he going to go if we don't keep him?' The answer was obvious: back on the street and then perhaps the cemetery if he was somewhere that nobody could or would call an ambulance if he overdosed again.

Now, I'm not for a moment suggesting your child is a tough case like this kid, but I can be pretty confident that they are going to push you sometimes to a point where you think you're having no impact on them or you may even feel like giving up. I told the journalist that the lesson I learnt from my experience at the youth centre is that even if we're not having the big, direct and immediate impact we'd like to have, we still have a very vital role in keeping our children engaged, mentally healthy and receptive to opportunities and supportive significant others (such as a youth worker, teacher, boss, coach, boyfriend or girlfriend) as they present themselves to our children at various points in their lives. I also told the journalist that I'd seen enough tough cases turned around through the presence or development of affirming and honest relationships to come to the conclusion that it's unsafe to give up on any kid.

You have very good reasons to be optimistic for your child. This is because motivation is learnable and the strategies presented in this book show many ways in which this can be achieved. Through greater opportunities for success, a focus on more controllable factors in your child's life, an enhanced learning focus, a reduced fear of failure, the development of more effective learning skills, lower levels of anxiety, a belief in the value of school and a positive and supportive parent–child relationship, your child will be more motivated and in a stronger position to achieve to his or her potential.

Students can learn to think differently about themselves and their abilities. Students can develop more positive attitudes towards school and schoolwork. Students can develop more effective behaviours and strategies when going about their studies. Parents do play a part in their child's thinking, attitudes and behaviours. If all this is true – and research clearly shows that it is – then your child's motivation can be improved and sustained and you have a part in this.

I wish you and your child every success.

NOTES

Chapter 1
Three parents sat on a park bench . . . joke thanks to Andrew Fuller in his Keynote Address at the 2001 Australian Guidance and Counselling Conference. Brisbane, Australia.

Failure acceptance, failure avoidance, and success striving drawn from research by Covington – see Bibliography.

Chapter 2
Further details on the *boosters, mufflers,* and *guzzlers* can be found in papers by Martin – see Bibliography.

Further details on *transition through school* can be found in the edited volume by Pajares and Urdan – see Bibliography.

Concepts relating to *our child's strengths are our windows* are adapted from the Positive Psychology literature – see Fredrickson in Bibliography.

Further analysis of *people's ability to change* is presented in a paper by Polivy and Herman – see Bibliography.

Chapter 3
Negative thinking trap concepts adapted from Tanner and Ball – see Reading for Parents.

Quote from *Mark Twain* from Pudd'nhead Wilson's Calendar.

Realistic optimism concepts adapted from Schneider – see Bibliography.

Chapter 4
Further detail on *learned helplessness* can be found in work by Peterson, Maier, and Seligman – see Bibliography.

More detailed discussion on the causes of success and failure and their relationship to motivation is in research by Weiner – see Bibliography.

Children's views on intelligence are discussed more fully in work by Dweck and work by Stipek and Gralinski – see Bibliography.

Smart environments are discussed in a paper by Barab and Plucker – see Bibliography.

Chapter 5
Different types of valuing is detailed in work by Eccles and Wigfield – see Bibliography.

Chapter 6
The concepts and discussion of *learning focus* and *performance focus* are drawn from work by researchers such as Duda, Dweck, Elliot, Harackiewicz, Kaplan, Maehr, Meece, Midgley, Nicholls, Pintrich, and Urdan – see Bibliography.

The *origins of the word 'competition'* drawn from Jackson and Csikszentmihalyi – see Bibliography.

Social and avoidance reasons for learning are drawn from research by Elliot, by Maehr, by Urdan, and by Dowson and McInerney – see Bibliography.

Research on *multiple goals* is described by Elliot and by Harackiewicz – see Bibliography.

Chapter 7
Planning an assignment table adapted from Orr – see Reading for Students.

Part of the *study timetable* structure adapted from Lewers – see Reading for Students.

Study conditions table adapted in part from Fry – see Reading for Students.

Concept of *'in-between time'* adapted from Fry – see Reading for Students.

Chapter 8
A full discussion of *goal setting* can be found in research by Locke and Latham – see Bibliography.

Chapter 9
Relaxation exercise adapted in part from Orr – see Reading for Students.

Some concepts in *preparing for tests* and *the day of the test* adapted from Orr – see Bibliography.

Chapter 10
Overstriving concept discussed more fully in work by Covington and by Martin – see Bibliography.

Detailed discussion of *perfectionism* is in research by Hewitt and Flett – see Bibliography.

Defensive pessimism discussed in more detail in research by Norem and Cantor and also in work by Martin – see Bibliography.

Self-sabotage (also called self-handicapping) is detailed by researchers such as Berglas, Covington, Harris, Martin, Midgley, Snyder, Rhodewalt, Thompson, and Tice – see Bibliography.

Failure acceptance and *learned helplessness* are described in detail by

Dweck, by Covington, by Weiner and also by Peterson, Maier, and Seligman – see Bibliography.

Avoidance goals (eg. working hard to avoid looking dumb or disappointing parents) are discussed in detail by Elliot and by Midgley – see Bibliography.

Table on *dealing with fears more effectively* is adapted from Lewers – see Reading for Students.

Students' *problematic views of effort* is discussed in early work by Covington and Omelich and later work by Covington – see Bibliography.

Research into the *link between a child's worth and his or her achievement* is detailed in research by Covington and by Martin – see Bibliography.

Success striving is described in detail by Covington – see Bibliography.

Chapter 11
Failure acceptance and *learned helplessness* are described in detail by Dweck, by Covington, by Weiner and also by Peterson, Maier, and Seligman – see Bibliography.

Work on *bullying* has been conducted by Field and by Sullivan – see Reading for Parents.

Explanatory style is discussed in detail by Weiner and by Peterson, Maier, and Seligman – see Bibliography.

Steps in building students' skills is described in detail by Zimmerman – see Bibliography.

Chapter 12
Parenting styles are described more fully in Baumrind – see Bibliography.

Chapter 13
Steps in *maximising opportunities to succeed* are adapted from McInerney – see Reading for Parents.

A discussion of *single-sex and co-educational schooling* is provided in Martin's report on boys' education and in Rowe – see Bibliography.

A detailed discussion of rewards is provided by Cameron, by Covington, and by Deci, Koestner, and Ryan – see Bibliography.

Chapter 14
More detailed *explanations and definitions of giftedness and talent* are presented in work by Gagné, Gross, McNabb, Renzulli, Rimm, and Winebrenner – see Bibliography.

Gifted and talented students' *views about being smart* is discussed in work by McNabb and by Winebrenner – see Bibliography.

More detailed discussion of the *dangers of effort* is in work by Covington and by Nicholls – see Bibliography.

Discussion of the *quality and quantity of effort* is presented in Covington – see Bibliography.

Students' views of intelligence is discussed more fully in reports by Dweck, by McNabb, and by Stipek and Gralinski – see Bibliography.

Discussion of gifted and talented students' *sense of control* is described in work by Rimm – see Bibliography.

Quote by Charlie Brown from Charles M. Schulz.

A discussion of the *Impostor Syndrome* is presented by Fried-Buchalter and by Winebrenner – see Bibliography.

Negative thinking trap concepts are adapted from Tanner and Ball – see Bibliography.

A detailed discussion of *perfectionism* is in research by Hewitt and Flett – see Bibliography.

Research into *flow* and *balancing challenge with skill* is presented by Jackson and Csikszentmihalyi – see Bibliography.

A discussion of the *zone of proximal development* is in Vygotsky – see Bibliography.

Figure representing the *balance between challenge and skill* is adapted with permission from Jackson and Csikszentmihalyi – see Bibliography.

A detailed account of Bloom's Taxonomy is presented in Bloom and also in Winebrenner – see Bibliography.

An account of the Peloponnesian war is provided by Thucydides in *The Peloponnesian War* (Penguin Classics).

The discussion of *characteristics of adults to whom gifted children students respond well* is adapted from Winebrenner – see Bibliography.

BIBLIOGRAPHY AND FURTHER READING

Chapters 1 and 2: Introduction; Boosters, Mufflers and Guzzlers

Bandura, A. (1997). *Self-efficacy: The exercise of control.* New York: Freeman & Co.

Covington, M.V. (1992). *Making the grade: A self-worth perspective on motivation and school reform.* Cambridge: Cambridge University Press.

Garvin, M., & Martin, A.J. (1999). High school students' part-time employment and its relationship to academic engagement and psychological well-being. *Australian Journal of Guidance and Counselling, 9,* 1–14.

Martin, A.J. (2001). The Student Motivation Scale: A tool for measuring and enhancing motivation. *Australian Journal of Guidance and Counselling, 11,* 1–20.

Martin, A.J. (2002). Boost your child's motivation. *Choosing a School For Your Child.* Sydney: Universal Press.

Martin, A.J. (2002). Motivation and academic resilience: Developing a model of student enhancement. *Australian Journal of Education. 14,* 34–49.

Martin, A.J. (forthcoming). The Student Motivation Scale: Further testing of an instrument that measures school students' motivation. *Australian Journal of Education.*

Martin, A.J. & Tracey, D. (2002). Motivating students to learn. *Learning Links, 3,* 1–5.

Pajares, F., & Urdan, T. (2002) (Eds). *Academic motivation of adolescents.* Connecticut: Information Age Publishing

Polivy, J., & Herman, C.P. (2002). If at first you don't succeed: False hopes of self-change. *American Psychologist, 57,* 677–689.

Chapter 3: Increasing Your Child's Self-belief

Bandura, A. (1997). *Self-efficacy: The exercise of control.* New York: Freeman & Co.

Eccles, J.S., Wigfield, A., & Schiefele, U. (1998). Motivation to succeed. In N. Eisenberg (Ed). *Handbook of child psychology: Social, emotional and personality development.* (pp. 1018–1095). New York: Wiley.

Fredrickson, B.L. (2001). The role of positive emotions in positive psychology. *American Psychologist, 56,* 218–226.

Harter, S. (1996). Teacher and classmate influences on scholastic motivation, self-esteem, and level of voice in adolescents. In J. Juvenen & K.R. Wentzel (Eds). *Social motivation: Understanding children's school adjustment.* (pp. 11–42). Cambridge, UK: Cambridge University Press.

Hattie, J. (1992). *Self-concept.* Hillsdale, NJ: Erlbaum.

Kernis, M.H., Cornell, D.P., Sun, C.R., Berry, A., & Harlow, T. (1993). There's more to self-esteem than whether it is high or low: The importance of stability of self-esteem. *Journal of Personality and Social Psychology, 65,* 1190–1204.

Marsh, H.W. (1990). A multidimensional, hierarchical model of self-concept: Theoretical and empirical justification. *Educational Psychology Review, 2,* 77–172.

Marsh, H.W., Martin, A.J., & Debus, R. (2002). Individual differences in verbal and math self-perceptions: One factor, two factors, or does it depend on the construct? In R. Riding & S. Rayner (Eds.). *International perspectives on individual differences.* London: Greenwood Publishing.

Martin, A.J. (2002). The lethal cocktail: Low self-belief, low control, and high fear of failure. *Australian Journal of Guidance and Counselling, 12,* 74–85.

Martin, A.J., & Debus, R.L. (1998). Self-reports of mathematics self-concept and educational outcomes: The roles of ego-dimensions and self-consciousness. *British Journal of Educational Psychology, 68,* 517–535.

Schneider, S.L. (2001). In search of realistic optimism: Meaning, knowledge, and warm fuzziness. *American Psychologist, 56,* 250–263.

Schunk, D.H., & Miller, S.D. (2002). Self-efficacy and adolescents' motivation. In F. Pajares & T. Urdan (Eds). *Academic motivation of adolescents.* Connecticut: Information Age Publishing.

Wigfield, A., & Tonks, S. (2002). Adolescents' expectancies for success and achievement task values during the middle and high school years. In F. Pajares & T. Urdan (Eds). *Academic motivation of adolescents.* Connecticut: Information Age Publishing.

Chapter 4: Building Your Child's Sense of Control

Barab, S.A., & Plucker, J.A. (2002). Smart people or smart contexts? Cognition, ability, and talent development in an age of situated approaches to knowing and learning. *Educational Psychologist, 37,* 165–182.

Connell, J.P. (1985). A new multidimensional measure of children's perceptions of control. *Child Development, 56,* 1018–1041.

Deci, E.L., & Ryan, R.M. (1980). The empirical exploration of intrinsic motivational processes. In L. Berkowitz (Ed). *Advances in experimental social psychology.* (pp. 39–80). New York: Academic Press.

Dweck, C.S. (1999). *Self-theories: Their role in motivation, personality, and development.* Philadelphia: Psychology Press.

Martin, A.J. (2002). The lethal cocktail: Low self-belief, low control, and high fear of failure. *Australian Journal of Guidance and Counselling, 12,* 74–85.

Schunk, D.H. (1983). Ability versus effort attributional feedback: Differential effects on self-efficacy and achievement. *Journal of Educational Psychology, 75,* 848–856.

Skinner, E.A. (1996). A guide to constructs of control. *Journal of Personality and Social Psychology, 71,* 549–570.

Skinner, E.A., Wellborn, J.G., & Connell, J.P. (1990). What it takes to do well in school and whether I've got it: A process model of perceived control and children's engagement and achievement in school. *Journal of Educational Psychology, 82,* 22–32.

Speirs, T., & Martin, A.J. (1999). Depressed mood amongst adolescents: The roles of perceived control and coping style. *Australian Journal of Guidance and Counselling, 9,* 55–76.

Stipek, D., & Gralinski, J.H. (1996). Children's beliefs about intelligence and school performance. *Journal of Educational Psychology, 88,* 397–407.

Weiner, B. (1985). An attributional theory of achievement motivation and emotion. *Psychological Review, 92,* 548–573.

Chapter 5: Increasing Your Child's Belief in the Value of School

Eccles, J. (1983). Expectancies, values, and academic behaviors. In J. Spence (Ed). *Achievement and achievement motivation.* San Francisco: Freeman.

Wigfield, A. (1994). Expectancy-value theory of achievement motivation: A developmental perspective. *Educational Psychology Review, 6,* 49–78.

Wigfield, A., & Eccles, J.S. (1992). The development of achievement task values: A theoretical analysis. *Developmental Review, 12,* 265–310.

Wigfield, A., & Eccles, J.S. (2002). The development of competence beliefs, expectancies for success, and achievement value from childhood through adolescence. In A. Wigfield & J.S. Eccles (Ed). *The development of achievement motivation.* San Diego, CA: Academic Press.

Chapter 6: Increasing Your Child's Learning Focus

Bempechat, J., London, P., & Dweck, C.S. (1991). Children's conceptions of ability in major domains: An interview and experimental study. *Child Study Journal, 21,* 11–36.

Dowson, M., & McInerney, D.M. (2001). Psychological parameters of students' social and work avoidance goals: A qualitative investigation. *Journal of Educational Psychology, 93,* 35–42.

Duda, J.L., & Nicholls, J.G. (1992). Dimensions of achievement motivation in schoolwork and sport. *Journal of Educational Psychology, 84,* 290–299.

Dweck, C.S. (1986). Motivational processes affecting learning. *American Psychologist, 41,* 1040–1048.

Dweck, C.S. (1991). Self-theories and goals: Their role in motivation, personality, and development. In R.A. Dienstbier (Ed.). *Perceptions on motivation: Nebraska Symposium on Motivation.* Vol 38. Lincoln: University of Nebraska Press.

Elliot, A.J. (1999). Approach and avoidance motivation and achievement goals. *Educational Psychologist, 34*, 169–189.

Harackiewicz, J.M., Barron, K.E., & Elliot, A.J. (1998). Rethinking achievement goals: When are they adaptive for college students and why? *Educational Psychologist, 33*, 1–21.

Jagacinski, C.M., & Nicholls, J.G. (1984). Conceptions of ability and related effects in task involvement and ego involvement. *Journal of Educational Psychology, 76*, 909–919.

Kaplan, A., & Maehr, M.L. (2002). Adolescents' achievement goals: Situating motivation in sociocultural contexts. In F. Pajares & T. Urdan (Eds). *Academic motivation of adolescents.* Connecticut: Information Age Publishing.

Maehr, M.L., & Midgley, C. (1996). *Transforming school cultures.* Boulder, CO: Westview Press.

Martin, A.J., & Debus, R.L. (1998). Self-reports of mathematics self-concept and educational outcomes: The roles of ego-dimensions and self-consciousness. *British Journal of Educational Psychology, 68*, 517–535.

Martin, A.J., Marsh, H.W., Williamson, A., & Debus, R.L. (forthcoming). Self-handicapping, defensive pessimism, and goal orientation: Personal perspectives of university students. *Journal of Educational Psychology.*

Meece, J.L., & Holt, K. (1993). A pattern analysis of students' achievement goals. *Journal of Educational Psychology, 85*, 582–590.

Middleton, M.J., & Midgley, C. (1997). Avoiding the demonstration of lack of ability: An unexplored aspect of goal theory. *Journal of Educational Psychology, 89*, 710–718.

Nicholls, J.G. (1989). *The competitive ethos and democratic education.* Cambridge: Harvard University Press.

Pintrich, P.R. (2000). The role of goal orientation in self-regulated learning. In M. Boekaerts., P.R. Pintrich., & M Zeidner (Eds). *Handbook of self-regulation: Theory, research and applications.* San Diego, CA: Academic Press.

Urdan, T.C., & Maehr, M,L. (1995). Beyond a two-goal theory of motivation and achievement: A case for social goals. *Review of Educational Research, 65*, 213–243.

Chapters 7 and 8: Assisting Your Child's Schoolwork and Study; Enhancing Your Child's Persistence

Covington, M.V. (2002). Rewards and intrinsic motivation: A needs-based developmental perspective. In F. Pajares & T. Urdan (Eds). *Academic motivation of adolescents.* Connecticut: Information Age Publishing.

Killen, R. (1998). *Effective teaching strategies.* Katoomba: Social Science Press.

Lens, W., Simons, J., & Dewitte, S. (2002). From duty to desire: The role of students' future time perspective and instrumentality perceptions for study motivation and self-regulation. In F. Pajares & T. Urdan (Eds). *Academic motivation of adolescents*. Connecticut: Information Age Publishing.

Locke, E.A., & Latham, G.P. (2002). Building a practically useful theory of goal setting and task motivation. *American Psychologist, 57*, 705–717.

Martin, A.J. (2002). Boost your child's motivation. *Choosing a School For Your Child*. Sydney: Universal Press.

Martin, A.J. (2002). Motivation and academic resilience: Developing a model of student enhancement. *Australian Journal of Education. 14*, 34–49.

Martin, A.J. & Tracey, D. (2002). Motivating students to learn. *Learning Links, 3*, 1–5.

Newman, R. (1994). Academic help-seeking: A strategy of self-regulated learning. In D.H. Schunk & B.J. Zimmerman (Eds). *Self-regulation of learning and performance* (pp. 283–301). Hillsdale, NJ: Erlbaum.

Pintrich, P.R., & DeGroot, E. (1990). Motivational and self-regulated learning components of classroom academic performance. *Journal of Educational Psychology, 82*, 33–40.

Schunk, D.H. (2001). Social cognitive theory and self-regulated learning. In. B.J. Zimmerman (Ed). *Self-regulated learning and academic achievement: Theoretical perspectives*. (pp. 125–151). Mahwah, NJ: Erlbaum.

Schunk, D.H., & Swartz, C.W. (1993). Goals and progress feedback: Effects on self-efficacy and writing achievement. *Contemporary Educational Psychology, 18*, 337–354.

Zimmerman, B.J. (2002). Achieving self-regulation: The trial and triumph of adolescence. In F. Pajares & T. Urdan (Eds). *Academic motivation of adolescents*. Connecticut: Information Age Publishing.

Chapter 9: Reducing Your Child's Test Anxiety

Hancock, D.R. (2001). Effects of test anxiety and evaluative threat on students' achievement and motivation. *Journal of Educational Research, 94*, 284–290.

McInerney, V., McInerney, D.M., & Marsh, H.W. (1997). Effects of metacognitive strategy training within a cooperative group learning context on computer achievement and anxiety: An aptitude-treatment interaction study. *Journal of Educational Psychology, 89*, 686–695.

Newbegin, I., & Owens, A. (1996). Self-esteem and anxiety in secondary school achievement. *Journal of Social Behavior and Personality, 11*, 521–530.

Sarason, I.G., & Sarason, B.R. (1990). Test anxiety. In H. Leitenberg (Ed). *Handbook of social and evaluation anxiety*. (pp. 475–495). New York: Plenum Press.

Spielberger, C.D., & Vagg, P.R. (1995). Test anxiety: A transactional process model. In C.D. Spielberger & P.R. Vagg (Eds). *Test anxiety: Theory assessment, and treatment*. Philadelphia, PA: Taylor & Francis.

Tobias, S. (1992). The impact of test anxiety on cognition in school learning. In. A.K. Hagtvert., & T.B. Johnson. (Eds). *Advances in test anxiety research*. (pp. 18–31). Bristol: Swets & Zeitlinger Publishers.

Chapter 10: Reducing Your Child's Fear of Failure

Atkinson, J.W. (1957). Motivational determinants of risk-taking. *Psychological Review, 64*, 359–372.

Baumeister, R.F., & Scher, S.J. (1988). Self-defeating behavior patterns among normal individuals: Review and analysis of common self-destructive tendencies. *Psychological Bulletin, 104*, 3–22.

Berglas, S. (1990). Self-handicapping: Etiological and diagnostic considerations. In R.L. Higgins, C.R. Snyder., & S. Berglas (Eds.). *Self-handicapping: The paradox that isn't*. New York: Plenum Press.

Covington, M.V. (1992). *Making the grade: A self-worth perspective on motivation and school reform*. Cambridge: Cambridge University Press.

Covington, M.V., & Omelich, C.L. (1979). Effort: The double-edged sword in school achievement. *Journal of Educational Psychology, 71*, 169–182.

Deppe, R.K., & Harackiewicz, J.M. (1996). Self-handicapping and intrinsic motivation: Buffering intrinsic motivation from the threat of failure. *Journal of Personality and Social Psychology, 70*, 868–876.

Fried-Buchalter, S. (1992). Fear of success, fear of failure, and the impostor phenomenon: A factor analytic approach to convergent and discriminant validity. *Journal of Personality Assessment, 58*, 368–379.

Harris, R.N., & Snyder, C.R. (1986). The role of uncertain self-esteem in self-handicapping. *Journal of Personality and Social Psychology, 51*, 451–458.

Higgins, R.L., & Berglas, S. (1990). The maintenance and treatment of self-handicapping: From risk-taking to face-saving – and back. In R.L. Higgins, C.R. Snyder., & S. Berglas (Eds.). *Self-handicapping: The paradox that isn't*. New York: Plenum Press.

Hobden, K., & Pliner, P. (1995). Self-handicapping and dimensions of perfectionism: Self-presentation vs self-protection. *Journal of Research in Personality, 29*, 461–474.

Martin, A.J. (2002). The lethal cocktail: Low self-belief, low control, and high fear of failure. *Australian Journal of Guidance and Counselling, 12*, 74–85.

Martin, A.J. & Marsh, H.W. (2003). Fear of failure: Friend or foe? *Australian Psychologist, 38*, 31–38.

Martin, A.J., Marsh, H.W., & Debus, R. (2000), Self-handicapping and defensive pessimism: How students protect their self-worth. In R.G. Craven and H.W. Marsh (Eds.). *Self-concept theory, research and practice: Advances for the new millennium*. Sydney, Australia.

Martin, A.J. Marsh, H.W., & Debus, R.L. (2001). A quadripolar need achievement representation of self-handicapping and defensive pessimism. *American Educational Research Journal, 38*, 583–610.

Martin, A.J., Marsh, H.W., & Debus, R.L. (2001). Self-handicapping and defensive pessimism: Exploring a model of predictors and outcomes from a self-protection perspective. *Journal of Educational Psychology, 93*, 87–102.

Martin, A.J., Marsh, H.W., & Debus, R. (2002), Self-Handicapping and Defensive Pessimism: Students' responses to their fear of failure. Keynote paper published in R.G. Craven., H.W. Marsh., & Simpson, K. (Eds.). *Self-concept research: Driving international research agenda.* Sydney, Australia.

Martin, A.J. Marsh, H.W., & Debus, R.L. (2003). Self-handicapping and defensive pessimism: A model of self-protection from a longitudinal perspective. *Contemporary Educational Psychology, 28*, 1–36.

Martin, A.J., Marsh, H.W., Williamson, A., & Debus, R.L. (forthcoming). Self-handicapping, defensive pessimism, and goal orientation: Personal perspectives of university students. *Journal of Educational Psychology.*

McClelland, D.C. (1965). Toward a theory of motive acquisition. *American Psychologist, 20*, 321–333.

Midgley, C., Arunkumar, R., & Urdan, T.C. (1996). "If I don't do well tomorrow, there's a reason": Predictors of adolescent's use of academic self-handicapping strategies. *Journal of Educational Psychology, 88*, 423–434.

Norem, J.K., & Cantor, N. (1986). Defensive pessimism: Harnessing anxiety as motivation. *Journal of Personality and Social Psychology, 51*, 1208–1217.

Rhodewalt, F. (1990). Self-handicappers: Individual differences in the preference for anticipatory, self-protective acts. In R.L. Higgins, C.R. Snyder., & S. Berglas (Eds.). *Self-handicapping: The paradox that isn't.* New York: Plenum Press.

Riggs, J.M. (1992). Self-handicapping and achievement. In A.K. Boggiano & T.S. Pittman (Eds.). *Achievement and motivation: A social-developmental perspective.* Cambridge University Press.

Snyder, C.R. (1990). Self-handicapping: Processes and sequelae – On the taking of a psychological dive. In R.L. Higgins, C.R. Snyder., & S. Berglas (Eds.). *Self-handicapping: The paradox that isn't.* New York: Plenum Press.

Thompson, T. (1994). Self-worth protection: Review and implications for the classroom. *Educational Review, 46*, 259–274.

Tice, D.M. (1991). Esteem protection or enhancement? Self-handicapping motives and attribution differ by self-esteem. *Journal of Personality and Social Psychology, 60*, 711–725.

Chapter 11: Re-engaging the Disengaged Child

Abramson, L.Y., Seligman, M.E.P., & Teasdale, J. (1978). Learned helplessness in humans: Critique and reformulation. *Journal of Abnormal Psychology, 87*, 49–74.

Atkinson, D.W. (1964). *An introduction to motivation.* Princeton, NJ: Van Nostrand.

Covington, M.V. (1998). *The will to learn: A guide for motivating young people*. New York: Cambridge University Press.

Craven, R.G., Marsh, H.W., & Debus, R.L. (1991). Effects of internally focused feedback and attributional feedback on the enhancement of academic self-concept. *Journal of Educational Psychology, 83*, 17–26.

Diener, C.I., & Dweck, C.S. (1978). An analysis of learned helplessness: Continuous changes in performance, strategy, and achievement cognitions following failure. *Journal of Personality and Social Psychology, 36*, 451–462.

McClelland, D.C. (1965). Toward a theory of motive acquisition. *American Psychologist, 20*, 321–333.

Peterson, C., Maier, S.F., & Seligman, M.E.P. (1993). *Learned helplessness: A theory for the age of personal control*. New York: Oxford University Press.

Schwarzer, R., Jerusalem, M., & Striksund, A. (1984). The developmental relationship between test anxiety and helplessness. In H.M. van der Ploeg., R. Schwarzer & C.D. Spielberger (Eds) *Advances in text anxiety research* (pp. 73–79). Hillsdale, NJ: Erlbaum.

Vispoel, W.P.; & Austin, J.R. (1995). Success and failure in junior high school: A critical incident approach to understanding students' attributional beliefs. *American Educational Research Journal, 32*, 377–412.

Weiner, B. (1985). An attributional theory of achievement motivation and emotion. *Psychological Review, 92*, 548–573.

Young, L.D., & Allin, J.M. (1986). Persistence of learned helplessness in humans. *Journal of General Psychology, 113*, 81–88.

Chapter 12: Building a Good Relationship with Your Child

Baumrind, D. (1991). Parenting styles and adolescent development. In R.M. Lerner, A.C. Patersen, & J. Brooks-Gunn (Eds.). *Encyclopedia of adolescence* (pp. 746–758). New York: Garland.

Deci, E.L., & Ryan, R.M. (2000). The darker and brighter sides of human existence: Basic psychological needs as a unifying concept. *Psychological Inquiry, 11*, 319–338.

Dishion, T.J., Duncan, T.E., Eddy, J.M., & Fagot, B.I. (1994). The world of parents and peers: Coercive exchanges and children's social adaptation. *Social Development, 3*, 255–268.

Eron, L.D., Huesmann, L.R., & Zelli, A. (1991). The role of parental variables in the learning of aggression. In D.J. Pepler & K.H. Rubin (Eds). *The development and treatment of childhood aggression*. Hillsdale, NJ: Erlbaum.

Grolnick, W.S., Ryan, R.M., & Deci, E.L. (1991). The inner resources for school achievement: Motivational mediators of children's perceptions of their parents. *Journal of Educational Psychology, 83*, 508–517.

Hemphill, S.A. (1996). Characteristics of conduct-disordered children and their families: A review. *Australian Psychologist, 31*, 109–118.

La Guardia, J.G., & Ryan, R.M. (2002). What adolescents need: A self-determination theory perspective on development within families, school, and society. In F. Pajares & T. Urdan (Eds). *Academic motivation of adolescents*. Connecticut: Information Age Publishing.

Linfoot, K., Martin, A.J., & Stephenson, J. (1999). Preventing conduct disorder: A study of parental behaviour management and support needs with children aged 3–5 years. *International Journal of Disability, Development, and Education, 46*, 223–246.

Martin, A.J., Linfoot, K., & Stephenson, J. (1999). How teachers respond to concerns about misbehaviour in their classroom. *Psychology in the Schools, 36*, 347–358.

Martin, A.J., Linfoot, K., & Stephenson, J. (2000). Exploring the cycle of mother-child relations, maternal confidence, and children's aggression. *Australian Journal of Psychology, 52*, 34–40.

Martin, A.J., Linfoot, K., & Stephenson, J. (2001) with Royal Children's Hospital Melbourne and University of Western Sydney. *Parenting and community education*. Report to NSW Department of Community Services. Sydney.

Osofsky, J.D., & Thompson, M.D. (2000). Adaptive and maladaptive parenting: Perspectives on risk and protective factors. In J.P. Shonkoff & S.J. Meisels (Eds). *Handbook of early childhood intervention*. Cambridge, UK, Cambridge University Press.

Patterson, G.R. (1982). *Coercive family processes*. Eugene, OR: Castlia Press.

Pettit, G.S., Bates, J.E., & Dodge, K.A. (1997). Supportive parenting, ecological context, and children's adjustment: A seven-year longitudinal study. *Child Development, 68*, 908–923.

Rubin, K.H., & Mills, R.S.L. (1990). Maternal beliefs about adaptive and maladaptive social behaviors in normal, aggressive, and withdrawn preschoolers. *Journal of Abnormal Child Psychology, 18*, 419–435.

Ryan, R.M., Stiller, J., & Lynch, J.H. (1994). Representations of relationships to parents, teachers, and friends as predictors of academic motivation, and self-esteem. *Journal of Early Adolescence, 14*, 226–249.

Shonkoff, J.P., & Phillips, D.A. (2000). Nurturing relationships. In J.P. Shonkoff & D.A. Phillips (Eds). *From neurons to neighbourhoods: The science of early childhood development*. Washington DC: National Academic Press.

Wentzel, K.R. (1998). Social support and adjustment in middle school: The role of parents, teachers, and peers. *Journal of Educational Psychology, 90*, 202–209.

Chapter 13: Motivating Boys

Bleach, K. (Ed) (2000). *Raising boys' achievement in schools*. England: Trentham Books.

Browne, R., & Fletcher, R. (Eds) (1995). *Boys in schools: Addressing the real issues – behaviour, values and relationships*. Sydney: Finch Publishing.

Cameron, J. (2001). Negative effects of reward on intrinsic motivation – A limited phenomenon: Comment on Deci, Koestner, and Ryan. *Review of Educational Research, 71*, 29–42.

Collins, C., Batton, M., Ainley, J., & Getty, C. (1996). *Gender and school education*. Canberra: AGPS.

Connell, R.W. (1998). Teaching boys: New research on masculinity and gender strategies for schools. *Teachers College Record, 98*, 206–235.

Deci, E.L., Koestner, R., & Ryan, R.M. (1999). A meta-analytic review of experiments examining the effects of extrinsic rewards on intrinsic motivation. *Psychological Bulletin, 125*, 627–668.

Gilbert, R., & Gilbert, P. (1998). *Masculinity goes to school*. St Leonards: Allen & Unwin.

House of Representatives Standing Committee on Education and Training (2002). *Boys: Getting it right*. Canberra: Parliament of Australia.

Jackson, D. (1998). Breaking out of the binary trap: Boys under-achievement, schooling and gender relations. In D. Epstein, J. Elwood, W. Hey, & J. Maw (Eds). *Failing boys? Issues in gender and achievement*. Buckingham: Open University Press.

Kenway, J. (1995). Masculinities in schools: Under siege, on the defensive and under construction? *Discourse: Studies in the Cultural Politics of Education, 16*, 59–79.

Lingard, B., Martino, W., Mills, M., & Bahr, M. (2002). *Addressing the educational needs of boys*. Canberra, Australia.

MacDonald, A., Saunders, L., & Benfield, P. (1999). *Boys' achievement progress, motivation and participation: Issues raised by the recent literature*. Slough UK: National Foundation for Educational Research.

Martin, A.J. (2002). *Enhancing the educational outcomes of boys*. Report to the Australian Capital Territory Department of Education, Family and Youth Services, Canberra, Australia.

Martin, A.J. (forthcoming). Boys and motivation: Contrasts and comparisons with girls' approaches to schoolwork. *Australian Educational Researcher*.

Martino, W., & Meyenn, B. (2001). *What about the boys? Issues of masculinity in schools*. Buckingham: Open University Press.

Martino, W., & Pallotta-Chiarolli, M. (1997). *So what's a boy: Addressing the issues of masculinity and schooling*. Buckingham: Oxford University Press.

Millard, E. (1997). *Differently literate: Boys, girls and the schooling of literacy*. London: Falmer Press.

Mills, M. (2001). *Challenging violence in schools: An issue of masculinities*. Buckingham: Open University Press.

Noble, C., & Bradford, W. (2000). *Getting it right for boys . . . and girls*. London: Routledge.

Rowe, K.J., & Rowe, K.S. (2002). *What matters most: Evidence-based findings of key factors affecting the educational experiences and outcomes for girls and boys throughout their primary and secondary schooling*. Supplementary submission to House of Representatives Standing Committee on Education and Training: Inquiry into the Education of Boys.

Slade, M. (2001). Listening to boys. *Boys in Schools Bulletin, 4,* 10–18.

West, P. (2001). *Report on best practice in boys' education: A report for educators and parents.* Penrith: UWS Men's Health Information and Research Centre.

Chapter 14: Motivating the Gifted and Talented

Adderholdt-Elliot, M. (1989). Perfectionism and underachievement. *Gifted Child Today, 12,* 19–21

Bloom, B.S. (1956). *Taxonomy of educational objectives: The classification of educational goals.* New York: Longman, Green and Co.

Carrington, N. (1993). Australian adolescent attitudes towards academic brilliance. *Australasian Journal of Gifted Education, 2,* 10–15.

Csikszentmihalyi, M. (1990). *Flow: The psychology of optimal experience.* New York: Harper & Row.

Clinkenbeard, P.R. (1994). Motivation and highly able students: Resolving paradoxes. In J.B. Hansen & S.M. Hoover (Eds). *Talent development: Theories and practice.* Iowa: Kendall/Hunt Publishing Company.

Davis, G.A., & Rimm, S.B. (1998). *Education of the gifted and talented.* Sydney: Allyn & Bacon.

Dweck, C.S. (1999). *Self-theories: Their role in motivation, personality, and development.* Philadelphia: Psychology Press.

Fried-Buchalter, S. (1992). Fear of success, fear of failure, and the impostor phenomenon: A factor analytic approach to convergent and discriminant validity. *Journal of Personality Assessment, 58,* 368–379.

Gagné, F. (1995). From giftedness to talent: A developmental model and its impact on the language of the field. *Roeper Review, 18,* 103–111.

Greenspon, T.S. (2000). 'Healthy perfectionism' is an oxymoron! *The Journal of Secondary Gifted Education, 11,* 197–204.

Gross, M.U.M. (1993). *Exceptionally gifted children.* London: Routledge.

Hewitt, P.L., & Flett, G.L. (1991). Perfectionism in the self and social contexts: Conceptualization, assessment, and association with psychopathology. *Journal of Personality and Social Psychology, 60,* 456–470.

Jackson, S.A., & Csikszentmihalyi, M.C. (1999). *Flow in sports: The keys to optimal experiences and performances.* Champaign, IL: Human Kinetics.

Martin, A.J. (2002). Motivating the gifted and talented: Lessons from research and practice. *Australasian Journal of Gifted Education, 11,* 26–34.

McNabb, T. (1997). From potential to performance: Motivational issues for gifted students. In N. Colangelo & G.A. Davis (Eds). *Handbook of gifted education.* London: Allyn & Bacon.

Nicholls, J.G. (1989). *The competitive ethos and democratic education.* Cambridge: Harvard University Press.

Renzulli, J.S. (1978). What makes giftedness? Re-examining a definition. *Phi Delta Kapppan, 60,* 180–184, 261.

Rimm, S.B. (1997). Underachievement syndrome: A national epidemic. In N. Colangelo & G.A. Davis (Eds). *Handbook of gifted education*: London: Allyn & Bacon.

Vygotsky, L.S. (1978). *Mind in society: the development of higher psychological processes*. Cambridge MA: Harvard Uni Press.

Winebrenner, S. (2001). *Teaching gifted kids in the regular classroom*. MN: Free Spirit Publishing.

Further Reading for Parents

This list is designed to provide a sense of the breadth of books available to parents and does not necessarily represent an endorsement by the author.

Barton, S., & Ingram, K. (2001). *Build your teenager's self-esteem . . . and enjoy being a parent again*. Victoria: Anne O'Donovan.

Biddulph, S. (1997). *Raising boys*. Sydney: Finch Publishing.

Brooks, R., & Goldstein, S. (2001). *Raising resilient children*. Sydney: Contemporary Books.

Canter, L. (1993). *Homework without tears: A parent's guide for motivating children to do homework and to succeed in school*. HarperCollins.

Carr-Gregg, M., & Shale, E. (2002). *Adolescence: A survival guide*. Sydney: Finch Publishing.

Ceil, C. (1994). *Motivating underachievers: 172 strategies for success*. Australia: Hawker Brownlow Education.

Cholden, H., Friedman, J., & Tiersky, E. (1998). *The homework handbook: Practical advice you can use tonight to help your child succeed tomorrow*. Chicago: Contemporary Books.

Cloud, H., Townsend, J., & Guest, L. (1998). *Boundaries with kids*. Michigan: Zondervan Publishing House.

Covey, S.R., & Covey, S.M. (1998). *The 7 habits of highly effective families: Building a beautiful family culture in a turbulent world*. Golden Books Publishing Co.

Field, E.M. (1999). *Bully busting: How to help children deal with teasing and bullying*. NSW: Finch Publishing.

Figes, K. (2002). *The terrible teens: What every parent needs to know*. London: Viking.

Fuller, A. (1998). *From surviving to thriving: Promoting mental health in young people*. Melbourne: ACER Press.

Fuller, A. (2000). *Raising real people: A guide for parents of teenagers*. Melbourne: ACER Press.

Furedi, F. (2001). *Paranoid parenting: Abandon your anxieties and be a good parent*. London: Allen Lane.

Greene, L.J. (2002). *Roadblocks to learning: Understanding the obstacles that can sabotage your child's academic success*. New York: Warner Books.

Grose, M. (1999). *Raising happy kids*. Sydney: HarperCollins.

Hawkes, T. (2001). *Boy oh boy*. Frenchs Forest: Prentice Hall.

Heacox, D. (1991). *Up from underachievement: How teachers, students, and parents can work together to promote student success*. Minneapolis: Free Spirit Publications.

Irvine, J. (2000). *Thriving at school: A practical guide to help your child enjoy the crucial school years*. Sydney: Simon & Schuster.

Jensen, W.R., Rhode, G., & Reavis, H.K. (1994). *The tough kid tool box*. CO: Sopris West.

Lewis, D. (1988). *Helping your anxious child*. London: Vermilion.

Martino, W., & Pallotta-Chiarolli, M. (2001). *Boys' stuff: Boys talking about what matters*. Sydney: Allen and Unwin.

McEwan, E.K. (1998). *When kids say no to school: Helping children at risk of failure, refusal, or dropping out*. Harold Shaw Publisher.

McInerney, D. (2000). *Helping kids achieve their best*. Sydney: Allen & Unwin.

Milholland, C. (1999). *The girl pages: A handbook of the best resources for strong, confident, creative girls*. Hyperion.

Radencich, M.S., & Schumm, J.S. (1997). *How to help your child with homework*. Minneapolis: Free Spirit Publishing.

Rimm, S.B. (1995). *Why bright kids get poor grades and what you can do about it*. New York: Crown.

Saunders, J., & Espeland, P. (1991). *Bringing out the best: A guide for parents of young gifted children*. MI: Free Spirit.

Seligman, M.E.P. (1995). *The optimistic child: A revolutionary approach for raising resilient children*. Sydney: Random House.

Smutny, J. (2000). *Stand up for your gifted child: How to make the most of kids' strengths at school and at home*. MI: Free Spirit.

Stipek, D., & Seal, K. (2001). *Motivated minds: Raising children to love learning*. Owl Books.

Sullivan, K. (2000). *The anti-bullying handbook*. Oxford: Oxford University Press.

Tanner, S., & Ball, J. (1989). *Beating the blues: A self-help approach to overcoming depression*. Sydney: Doubleday.

Thompson, L., & Lowson, T. (1995). *Raising self-esteem in the young*. MI: Free Spirit.

Walker, S.Y., & Perry, S.K. (1991). *The survival guide for parents of gifted kids: How to understand, live with, and stick up for your gifted child*. MI: Free Spirit.

Waters, B., & Kennedy, L. (2001). *Every kid: Parenting your five to twelve year old*. Sydney: Double day.

West, D. (2001). *Negotiating with your school: A practical guide for parents*. Sydney: Choice Books.

West, P. (2002). *What is the matter with boys?* Sydney: Choice Books.

Zentall, S., Goldstein, S., & Dimatteo, R. (1999). *Seven steps to homework success: A family guide for solving common homework problems*. Florida: Specialty Press.

Further Reading for Students
This list is designed to provide a sense of the breadth of books available to students and does not necessarily represent an endorsement by the author.

Adderholdt-Elliott, M. (1987). *Perfectionism: What's bad about being too good*. MI: Free Spirit.

Benson, P.L., Galbraith, J., & Espeland, P. (1998). *What teens need to succeed: Proven, practical ways to shape your own future*. MI: Free Spirit Press.

Davis, L., Sirotowitz, S., & Parker, H.C. (1996). *Study strategies made easy*. Florida: Specialty Press.

Dodge, J. (1994). *The study skills handbook*. Scholastic Trade.

Edwards, P. (1994). *7 keys to successful study*. Melbourne: ACER Press.

Evans, M. (2002). *Exams are easy when you know how*. How to books.

Fisher, A. (2002). *Critical thinking*. Cambridge University Press.

Freeman, R., & Meed, J. (1995). *How to study effectively*. London: Collins Educational.

Frender, G. (1990). *Learning to learn: Strengthening study skills and brain power*. Incentive Publications.

Fry, R. (2000). *Ace any test*. New Jersey: Career Press.

Fry, R. (2000). *Get organized*. New Jersey: Career Press.

Gilbert, S.D. (1998). *How to do your best on tests*. Beech Tree Books.

James, E., James, C., & Barkin, C. (1998). *How to be school smart: Super study skills*. Beech Tree Books.

Jones, C.F. (1991). *Mistakes that worked*. Doubleday.

Kornhauser, A.W., Enerson, D.M. (1993). *How to study: Suggestions for high school and college students*. University of Chicago Press.

Lashley, C., & Best, W. (2001). *12 steps to study success*. London: Continuum International Publishing Group.

Lewers, R. (1998). *Study without stress*. Ballarat: Wizard Press.

Lewis, R. (1994). *How to manage your study time*. London: Collins Educational.

Locke, E.A. (1998). *Study methods and motivation: A practical guide to effective study*. Second Renaissance.

Luckie, W.R., & Smethurst, W. (1997). *Study power: Study skills to improve your learning and your grades*. Brookline Books.

McLean, I., & Redman, E. (1999). *Power tools for positive living*. VIC: HiPerform Learning.

Orr, F. (1997). *How to pass exams*. Sydney: Allen and Unwin.

Orr, F. (1999). *101 great exam tips*. Sydney: Allen and Unwin.

Palmer, P., & Froehner, M.A. (2000). *Teen esteem: A self-direction manual for young adults*. Impact Publishers.

Robb, J., & Letts, H. (2000) *Succeed in exams. Triumph in tests*. Sydney: Hodder.

Robinson, A. (1993). *What smart students know: Maximum grades, optimum learning, minimum time*. Crown Publications.

Romain, T. (1997). *How to do homework without throwing up*. MI: Free Spirit Publishing.

Romain, T., & Verdick, E. (2000). *Stress can really get on your nerves*. MI: Free Spirit Press.

Smith, J. (1999). *100 study tips that work*. Sydney: Smith Mathematics.

Tracey, E. (2002). *The student's guide to exam success*. Buckingham: Open University Press.

Wells, R.H. (1993). *Becoming an effective student: Personal power-Succeeding in school*. Texas: pro-ed.

Wells, R.H. (1986). *Developing appropriate classroom skills*. Texas: pro-ed.

Withers, G. (1999). *Tackling that test*. Melbourne: ACER Press.

INDEX

ACKNOWLEDGEMENTS

Heartfelt thanks go to my wife and children for their love and patience as I fitted this book into an already busy life. Thanks also to Tara Wynne at Curtis Brown for taking a chance on me and then proactively advocating for the book and me. The folk at Random House – Jane Southward, Roberta Ivers and Benython Oldfield in particular – have provided great support, guidance and encouragement throughout. Amanda O'Connell, who did a superb job editing the manuscript, and John Shakespeare, who did great illustrations, also have my gratitude. Thanks to my two mentors, Herb Marsh and Ray Debus, who have guided and encouraged me through my early career – and continue to do so. Much appreciation goes to Stephanie Compton for her down-to-earth feedback on early draft chapters of the book. I also thank my parents for making my education a priority in their lives. Thanks to the thousands of teachers, students and parents whose paths have crossed mine over the years – I hope you learned as much from me as I learned from you. Final recognition must go to the many researchers whose work over the past six decades has dramatically impacted on my thinking about how to motivate and engage students.